Hebrew
— FOR THE —
Rest Of Us

Hebrew
— FOR THE —
Rest Of Us

Using Hebrew Tools without Mastering Biblical Hebrew

Lee M. Fields

ZONDERVAN®

ZONDERVAN.com/
AUTHORTRACKER
follow your favorite authors

ZONDERVAN

Hebrew for the Rest of Us
Copyright © 2008 by Lee M. Fields

Requests for information should be addressed to:
Zondervan, *Grand Rapids, Michigan 49530*

ISBN 978-0-310-27709-5

Interior design by Miles V. Van Pelt

Printed in the United States of America

Table of Contents

Preface viii

Abbreviations xiv

Week 1: "Getting to Know You": Consonants and the History of Hebrew

1   It Doesn't Look Like Greek to Me - The Hebrew Alphabet 1

2   Whose Language is Dead? - The History of Hebrew 12

Week 2: "Getting to Know All About You": Vowels and How We Got the OT

3   Get the Point? - The Hebrew Vowels 17

4   Canon, Text, and Versions 32

Week 3: Roots, Clauses, and Function Words

5   Getting to the Root of the Matter - Hebrew Word Roots 49

6   "Yes, Virginia, There Are ... Clauses" 65

7   Wow! - The Conjunction Waw and Friends 76

8   Prepositions Come Before 88

Week 4: Nominals

9   What's in a Name? - Overview of Nominals 99

10   Be Sure You Read This! - The Article 106

11   A Tale of Two States - Case Functions 112

12   An Apt Description - Adjectives 133

Week 5: Verbals

13   Where the Action Is - Overview of Verbs 147

14   When the Perfect Comes - Perfect Forms 169

15   There's Nothing Wrong with ... Imperfect Forms 181

v

16   Where There's a Will, There are … Volitional Forms 191

17   To Infinitives and Beyond! - Infinitives & Participles 200

Week 6: A Method to Our Madness

18   What Do You Mean? - Hebrew Word Studies 221

19   Tools of the Trade - Books in Paper and Electronic Form 234

20   If It's Not Poetry, It's … Hebrew Prose 247

21   It May Not Rhyme, But It's Still … Hebrew Poetry 258

Appendices

1   Hebrew Songs 273

2   Word Study Guide 277

3   Action Figures 280

Acknowledgments

It is impossible to thank all who played a role in making this possible. I begin by thanking the many great teachers at Hebrew Union College-Jewish Institute of Religion and Cincinnati Christian University, of whom I am a humble beneficiary, plus those who have taught me through their writings. I thank my colleagues at Roanoke Bible College for encouraging me to pursue this project. Thanks also to my students in Biblical Language Tools, in particular Kelli Macqueen and Ashley Baker, spring semesters of 2007 and 2008, for their patience and suggestions as we worked through much of this material together. Thanks also to my colleagues and readers, Ken Greene, Kevin Larsen, and Bob Smith. I thank Verlyn Verbrugge and the staff at Zondervan for giving me this opportunity, and for all of their encouragement and expertise to bring this to reality. Thanks also to Bill Mounce, and especially to my friend Miles Van Pelt for encouragement, typesetting, and invaluable contributions. Without their patient help, this would not have been possible. I thank my wife, Julie, my daughter, Beth (during her senior year of high school), and my son, Brian, for their patience and encouragement during all the inconveniences my work caused to their busy schedules. Most of all, I thank God, on whose account this work was done. I pray that the readers will be drawn more deeply into his love.

To Julie, Brian, and Beth

נֵר־לְרַגְלִי דְבָרֶךָ וְאוֹר לִנְתִיבָתִי

Ps 119:105

Preface

There you are at your church carry-in fellowship meal. People rave about the carrot cake you always make; it's a special recipe with expensive ingredients and homemade frosting. You know that the cake turns out right only when you hand-mix the ingredients – no electric mixer. It takes a lot of time and effort to make, but this is your church family. They are worth it. It gets your attention when little Johnny walks by with two huge pieces. A few minutes later he runs out to play, leaving his plate on the table. You notice that only a couple of bites are gone from the cake, and the remains are tossed on top of the other uneaten food on his plate. What sort of thoughts run through your head?

God used many authors over about a thousand years to produce the Old Testament (OT). It makes up over 75 percent of the Bible. Yet, like little Johnny, some Christians take a few bites from the OT and leave the rest uneaten, together with a few remains from the New Testament (NT). Do you wonder what sort of thoughts run through God's head?

If the church is fed best when it feasts on all of God's Word, then why do so many act like they are on a diet? Perhaps a few Christians have an inadequate opinion of the OT, such as viewing the NT as Christian and relevant but the OT as Jewish and less useful. Probably most, who dabble in familiar passages, are intimidated by the OT. In comparison to the NT, people often feel that the historical, linguistic, and cultural gaps between the OT and the modern world require too much effort or expertise to bridge. True, it does take effort, but these bridges can be built and the results will be well worth the effort.

Rationale for mastering tools for Old Testament study.

The first reason for mastering tools is to be able to mine the OT for the spiritual riches that lie buried but are accessible to those willing and able to dig for them. I assume that studying the OT is necessary and valuable, simply because it is God's Word. It just requires a little more digging to reach the treasure. Obviously, knowing biblical Hebrew is the most fundamental tool for OT studies, but not everyone is able to devote the amount of time required to learn the language.[1] Thankfully, more than ever, there exists a greater number of original language tools to help reduce this language barrier. Learning to use these resources is like trading in a spoon for a shovel to do the digging.

Second, mastering Hebrew tools is not only valuable for studying the OT, it is also one of the most overlooked and valuable tools for studying the NT. This may surprise many, but it makes sense. All of the NT writers rely on the OT and base arguments on it. The better a reader understands the OT, the better he or she can understand the NT.

I strongly believe that students of the English Bible who are able to use some of the original language tools to study the OT will both receive more benefit and joy when studying the OT and get even more out of their study of the NT. But using these tools to their greatest advantage involves some training.

The purpose of this book.

Hebrew for the Rest of Us (HRU) is a companion to Bill Mounce's *Greek for the Rest of Us* (GRU). These books are intended to enable English Bible students to maximize the benefit gained from using the many tools that exist to help bridge the language gap.

New resources are being published all the time and technology continues to grow. How can a person or a book possibly keep up? Mounce's solution is to teach a little about how the Greek language works so that the reader can more effectively use tools both current and those yet to be developed. In *HRU* I offer a similar solution. By learning some elementary facets of biblical Hebrew, the English-only Bible student can maximize the benefit gained from these original language tools. This basic knowledge empowers an English-only student to refine study techniques on the Bible text itself and to read advanced secondary works such as dictionaries and commentaries that make direct reference to the original text.

The goal is to move toward greater independence in OT studies. Even the most advanced scholars rely on the work of others. God wants us to be

---

[1] Even here, don't sell anyone short. I once met a person who was teaching biblical Hebrew to a class of about seventy members at a large congregation. I heard that people visited from the nearby major university to see how he was recruiting so many.

interdependent. In this way we are connected to the church of every age. As we grow in knowledge and skill, we will grow in independence, but never absolutely so.

The style and scope of this book.

My hope is that this book will appeal not only to college students, but also to all people in the church who desire to study the Scriptures more deeply. Toward this end of a broad appeal, I have followed Mounce's example in *GRU* of adopting an informal, conversational tone. Also I have limited footnotes as much as possible and included examples and illustrations that hopefully will be interesting and educational, sometimes even funny (if you laugh occasionally while you read, I will be happy – as long as we are laughing at the same things!).

Bill Mounce has graciously invited me to post audio recordings of my lectures on his site, www.teknia.com. My plan is to provide these and other resources in the future. One item located there is a MSWord document of all the exercises in this book. These may be downloaded and completed on your computer. The exercises are identical to those in the book, but sometimes include tables enabling you to work in an electronic format.

What level of independence can you reasonably gain after a few weeks of study?

Here are some things you can expect. After studying the material in this book, you will:

- know the Hebrew alphabet, vowels, and how to pronounce the words

- learn some of the elementary features of Hebrew

- be able to perform word studies responsibly

- be able to use certain study techniques especially useful to the OT

- be able to understand your English Bible better, both because you will understand translation issues and because you will learn English better

- be able to read the better commentaries and Bible tools that use Hebrew.

Here are two things you should *not* expect. (1) After you finish this course, you should never tell anyone that you know Hebrew. You will not know Hebrew, unless you take a full-fledged Hebrew course. (By the way, my ulterior motive in writing *HRU* is to inspire students to study full Hebrew.) (2) You will not be able to dispute scholars on the basis of your knowledge of Hebrew, but you can ask questions and better follow the arguments of various scholars with different views, helping you to make informed choices. As Mounce says in *GRU* (p. x), it's not a little bit of knowledge that is a dangerous thing, "it is a little bit of *arrogance* that is dangerous." Knowing everything in this book will not make you an expert.

How to use this book.

This book is designed to be covered in one half of a three-hour semester course. This allows the other half to be used for Mounce's *GRU*, as I do in my course, or to use an elementary book on interpretation, such as *How to Read the Bible for All Its Worth* (3rd ed.; Grand Rapids: Zondervan, 2003) by Gordon D. Fee and Douglas Stuart. Nearly every chapter of *HRU* includes exercises. They are designed to give you practice on the principles covered in that chapter.

The final two chapters on OT narrative and poetry move the student to a new level of application for what has been learned in the previous chapters. If time runs short in a semester, these could be omitted. They might be used, then, in a course that studies either of these types of literature.

What other resources will you need to go along with this book?

The following resources are the bare minimum: an exhaustive concordance, an interlinear Bible, and a word book. I recommend the following:

Edward W. Goodrick, John R. Kohlenberger III, and James A. Swanson, *The Strongest NIV Exhaustive Concordance* (Grand Rapids: Zondervan, 2004).

This is identical to the 1999 edition entitled, *The Zondervan NIV Exhaustive Concordance.* If your personal Bible study library is designed around a version other than the NIV, you should buy an exhaustive concordance for your version. The ones by Kohlenberger and published by Zondervan are clearly the best in my opinion. Select either:

John R. Kohlenberger, III, *The Interlinear NIV Hebrew-English Old Testament* (Grand Rapids: Zondervan, 1993).

or

Jay P. Green, ed., *The Interlinear Bible: Hebrew-Greek-English* (Peabody, Mass.: Hendrickson, 2005).

Finally, for word studies, use:

William D. Mounce, ed., *Mounce's Complete Expository Dictionary of Old and New Testament Words* (Grand Rapids: Zondervan, 2006).

Why go to all this work to study so carefully?

B. F. Westcott, a famous NT scholar from the nineteenth century said, "It is as perilous to live on borrowed opinions as to live on borrowed money: the practice must end in intellectual or even in moral bankruptcy."

Christians ought to pursue better Bible study because ministry – service to others – demands it. If people want to speak about the meaning of passages and about theology only in vague generalities, if people want only to give pat answers memorized from what others have told them, they probably won't find this book of much value. But if you want to be careful and precise when you study and explain the Bible, if you want to be able to minister to others by having a reason for your beliefs, if you want to "own" your beliefs, because you've studied them yourself, then you will benefit much from learning how to use the marvelous tools available to you today. You can only be as precise in your understanding and explanation of Scripture or biblical doctrine as you are able to study Scripture closely.

The college where I teach is only about an hour from the Atlantic Ocean. A number of our students enjoy surfing. The goal is to skim across the top, not to go deep. Careful study of the Bible is the opposite. At first many Christians seem to avoid deeper Bible study because it involves too much effort. However, it is my experience in teaching groups from junior high on up that once Bible readers get a taste of deeper study, an understanding that is below the surface, they are never satisfied with "surfing" the Bible again.

Finally, we must never forget the reason we study at all: to be transformed into Christ's likeness by the renewal of our minds, until we all grow up into maturity. "Deep" study is no guarantee that mature faith will result, but shallow study guarantees that immaturity continues. Bible study is never complete until it results in worship. If, as a result of learning things presented in *Hebrew for the Rest of Us*, study and teaching of God's Word becomes more dynamic and lives become more Christ-like, my prayers will be answered.

Abbreviations

Bible Book Abbreviations

Gen	Genesis
Exod	Exodus
Lev	Leviticus
Num	Numbers
Deut	Deuteronomy
Josh	Joshua
Judg	Judges
Ruth	Ruth
1-2 Sam	1-2 Samuel
1-2 Kgs	1-2 Kings
1-2 Chr	1-2 Chronicles
Ezra	Ezra
Neh	Nehemiah
Esth	Esther
Job	Job
Ps (Pss)	Psalm(s)
Prov	Proverbs
Eccl	Ecclesiastes
Song	Song of Songs/Solomon
Isa	Isaiah
Jer	Jeremiah
Lam	Lamentations
Ezek	Ezekiel
Dan	Daniel
Hos	Hosea
Joel	Joel
Amos	Amos
Obad	Obadiah
Jonah	Jonah
Mic	Micah
Nah	Nahum
Hab	Habakkuk
Zeph	Zephaniah
Hag	Haggai
Zech	Zechariah
Mal	Malachi
Matt	Matthew
Mark	Mark
Luke	Luke
John	John
Acts	Acts
Rom	Romans
1-2 Cor	1-2 Corinthians
Gal	Galatians
Eph	Ephesians
Phil	Philippians
Col	Colossians
1-2 Tim	1-2 Timothy
1-2 Thess	1-2 Thessalonians
Titus	Titus
Phlm	Philemon
Heb	Hebrews

Jas	James
1-2 Pet	1-2 Peter
1-2-3 John	1-2-3 John
Jude	Jude
Rev	Revelation

Version Abbreviations

ESV	English Standard Version
KJV	King James Version
NASB95	New American Standard Bible (1995 revision)
NET	New English Translation
NIV	New International Version
NLT	New Living Translation
NRSV	New Revised Standard Version

Grammatical Abbreviations

1	First Person
2	Second Person
3	Third Person
A	Active
abs	absolute state
Acc	Accusative case
Adj	Adjective
Art	Article
c	common
cj	conjunction/conjunctive
cs	consecutive
cst	construct state
Coh	Cohortative
Dat	Dative case

DO	Direct object
Emph	Emphatic aspect
f	feminine
Fut	Future tense
Gen	Genitive case
Hiph	Hiphil stem
Hith	Hithpael stem
Hoph	Hophal stem
Imp	Imperfect tense
Imv	Imperative mood
Ind	Indicative mood
Inf	Infinitive
InfA	Infinitive Absolute
InfC	Infinitive Construct
IO	Indirect object
Juss	Jussive
m	masculine
MnCl	Main clause
n	neuter
Ni	Niphal Stem
Nn	Noun
Nom	Nominative case
OC	Objective case
P	Passive
p	plural
PC	Possessive case
Pf	Perfect tense/aspect
Pi	Piel Stem
PN	Predicate Nominative
pp	preposition
PPhr	Prepositional Phrase

PPrn	Personal Pronoun		Q	Qal Stem
Pr	Present tense		RC	Relative Clause
Prg	Progressive aspect		RP	Relative Pronoun
Pret	Preterite		s	singular
PrnSf	Pronominal Suffix		Sbj	Subjunctive mood
PrPtc	Present Participle		SC	Subject case
Pst	Past tense		SbCl	Subordinate Clause
PstPtc	Past Participle		Smpl	Simple aspect
Ptc	Participle		V	Verb
PtcA	Participle Active		Va	Verb active voice
PtcP	Participle Passive		Vp	Verb passive voice
Pu	Pual stem			

"Getting to Know You"
Consonants and the History of Hebrew

C H A P T E R   1

"It Doesn't Look Like Greek to Me"
The Hebrew Alphabet

Objectives

1. Be able to write the letters of the Hebrew consonants in order
2. Be able to name the letters
3. Understand the two kinds of Daghesh
4. Be able to transliterate the Hebrew letters into English letters

Introduction

If you have skimmed this book at all and found that these letters "do not look like Greek to you," that's a good thing! The Hebrew alphabet is quite different in appearance from the Greek and, even more, from the English alphabet. I have decided that the best thing to do is to jump right in to learning the letters and the vowels and to alternate chapters that supply background information. This will give you a little extra time to learn the shapes and sounds well.

If you have already learned the Greek alphabet from studying Mounce's *Greek for the Rest of Us*, you will note some similarities with Hebrew, because both the Greeks and the Israelites got their alphabet from the Phoenicians. The Greeks simply converted into vowels some of the Semitic letters that represented sounds that the Greeks didn't use and added a few extras for Greek sounds not represented in Hebrew. We in turn get the English alphabet from the Greeks through Latin. Watch for similarities in order and in the names of the Greek letters.

The Hebrew alphabet consists of 22 (some count 23) letters with a total of 28 forms. These 22 (or 23) letters constitute the consonants alone. Originally the vowels, though pronounced, were not written. We will learn the vowels in chapter three.

This chapter consists of two parts. The first is a writing guide teaching you the letters. Its purpose is to show you the proper order of strokes to write each letter. The letters are initially placed in an order to help you distinguish those that are similar in shape. After you master writing the forms, practice writing them in alphabetical order. If you want to, you can make flash cards with the letter on one side and the name of the letter on the other (see www.teknia.com for a document).

Remember three things: (1) Hebrew is read right to left and anytime we write in Hebrew, it is in Hebrew order; when we write in English it is in English order. (2) In this chapter we are discussing only the consonants. (3) *Have fun with this!* You will enjoy doodling in Hebrew and answering when your friends and family say, "What's that?"

The second part is a chart of all the forms of the Hebrew alphabet in alphabetical order. Its purpose is to provide you with the necessary information to learn the names and the order of the letters, plus a few other things, just for reference.

You may find it helpful to learn the letters in groups: the first five, then the next five, then the last twelve in three groups of four. Many people learn them in a song. Also, comparison with the order of the English alphabet will help in learning (e.g., נ מ ל כ <=> *k l m n*). The last column gives a guide to pronunciation. Since there were no audio recorders 3,000 years ago, we cannot know exactly how words were pronounced. In fact, the Bible itself indicates that there were various pronunciations at different times and places, just as words are pronounced differently in New York than in North Carolina today. So, the pronunciation guide is approximate and designed mostly to be helpful for learning.

The Names and Shapes of the Hebrew Letters

The names of the Hebrew letters are simply words that start with that sound. So, the second letter *Bet* begins with the sound *b*. As children we learn phrases like "A is for apple;" if we named our letters as the Phoenicians did, we would call the first letter *apple*. That's not really so strange, though, when you remember that we have a letter named "double-u."

Whereas we write our English letters sitting on the line, Hebrew letters sort of hang from the upper line. To learn the shapes, Hebrew letters may be categorized according to length and width. One letter does not reach the lower line; most do reach the lower line; a few extend below the bottom line; one extends above the top line. We treat narrow letters first, then wide ones, moving from simple to more complex strokes.

Directions

1. *Trace* the printed strokes starting at the top.
2. *Copy* the letters in the remaining space.
3. *Repeat* the name of the letter aloud each time you write it (a rhyming English word is in italics below the name of each letter to indicate proper vowel sounds).

Narrow Letters

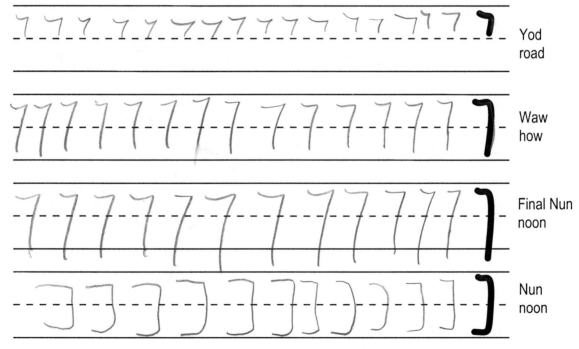

Yod
road

Waw
how

Final Nun
noon

Nun
noon

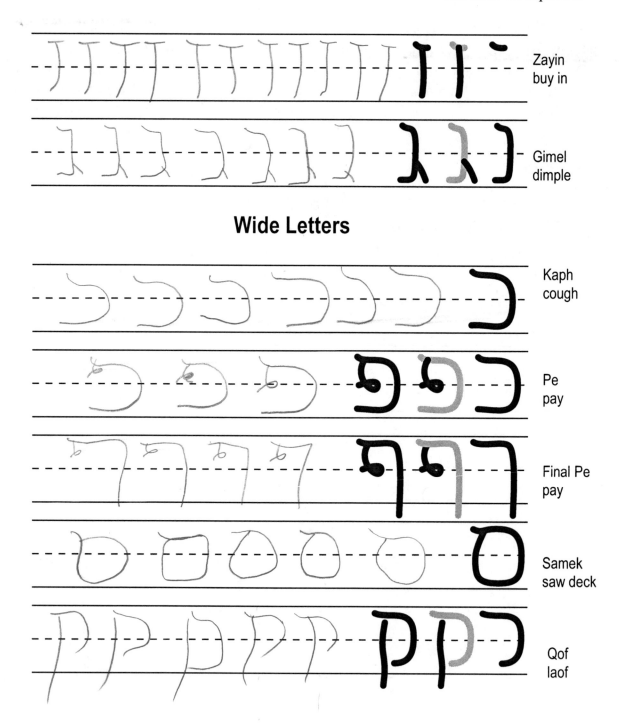

Zayin
buy in

Gimel
dimple

Wide Letters

Kaph
cough

Pe
pay

Final Pe
pay

Samek
saw deck

Qof
laof

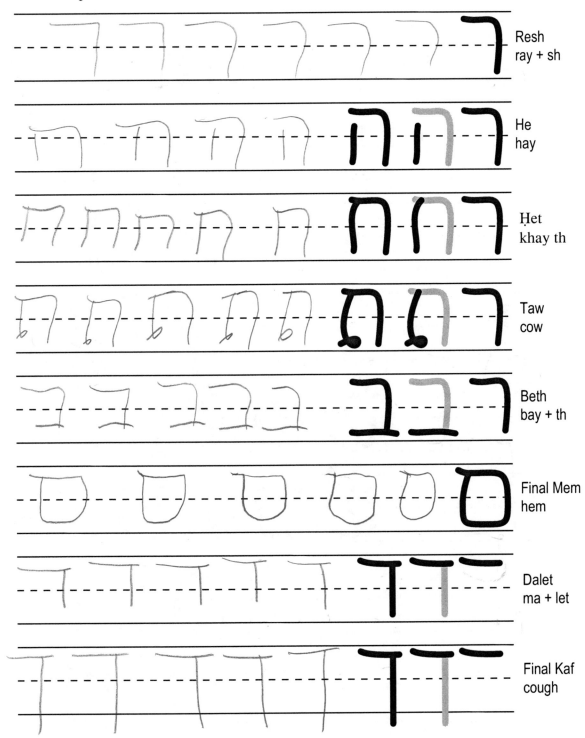

Resh
ray + sh

He
hay

Ḥet
khay th

Taw
cow

Beth
bay + th

Final Mem
hem

Dalet
ma + let

Final Kaf
cough

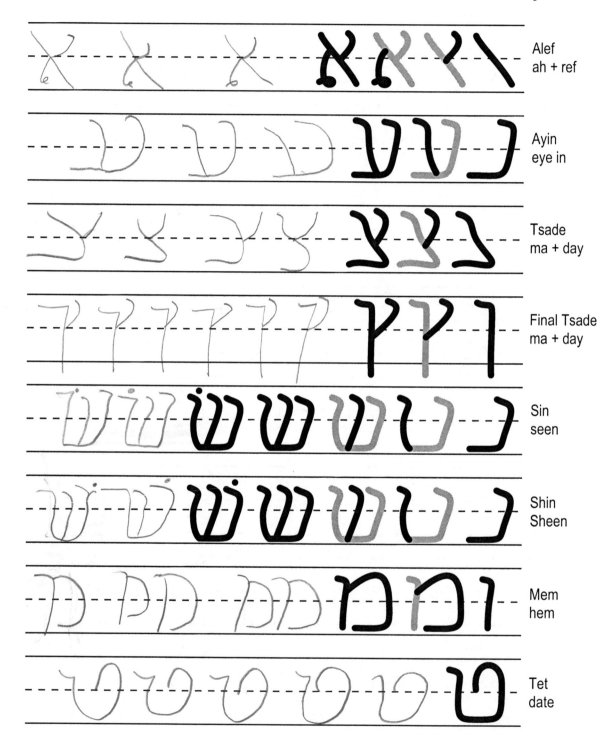

Alef
ah + ref

Ayin
eye in

Tsade
ma + day

Final Tsade
ma + day

Sin
seen

Shin
Sheen

Mem
hem

Tet
date

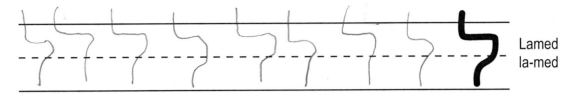

Lamed
la-med

The Hebrew Letters in Alphabetical Order, Etc.

The chart of the Hebrew alphabet is given below. In explanation, let me point out some things about each column.

1. The square forms of the letters given above are the shape used in Jesus' day. There are six letters known as *begadkephat* (**Beth**, **Gimel**, **Daleth**, **Kaph**, **Pe**, and **Taw**) letters that may be written with or without a dot (called a *Daghesh*) inside that letter resulting in a change in sound. The Daghesh is present when these letters begin a syllable and serves to mark their sounds as hard (or plosive) rather than soft.

2. There are five letters which, when found at the end of a word, have a form different than when they are located elsewhere in the word. These are known as final forms.

3. Many works use transliteration instead of the Hebrew letters. So, you will need to be able to convert Hebrew letters into transliterated symbols and vice versa. Unfortunately, there are a number of different transliteration systems. The one given here is that used by Gary D. Pratico and Miles V. Van Pelt, *Basics of Biblical Hebrew,* 2nd ed. (Grand Rapids: Zondervan, 2007).

4. The sounds of the Hebrew letters are approximated by similar sounds indicated by the sounds of the **bold** letters in the English words listed in the last column. Again, we don't know exactly how they were pronounced but scholars can come up with a fair approximation by comparison of manuscript spellings, by comparison of words in cognate languages, and by seeing how other ancient languages like Greek transliterated Hebrew words.

5. Finally, the Hebrew letters were also used for numbers (the Greeks followed them with a similar system).

Name	Square Forms	Final Forms	Trans- literation	Modern Sound	Numeric Vaule
Alef	א		ʾ	(silent)	1
Bet	בּ		b	boy	2
	ב		$\underline{b}$	very	
Gimel	גּ		g	girl	3
	ג		ḡ	girl	
Dalet	דּ		d	dog	4
	ד		$\underline{d}$	the	
He	ה		h	help	5
Waw	ו		w	way	6
Zayin	ז		z	zero	7
Ḥet	ח		ḥ	chemistry	8
Tet	ט		ṭ	tin	9
Yod	י		y	yell	10
Kaf	כּ	ך	k	kangaroo	20
	כ		$\underline{k}$	chemistry	
Lamed	ל		l	loud	30
Mem	מ	ם	m	marry	40
Nun	נ	ן	n	noun	50
Samek	ס		s	see	60
Ayin	ע		ʿ	(silent)	70
Pe	פּ	ף	p	paint	80
	פ		$\underline{p}$	photograph	
Tsade	צ	ץ	ṣ	hits	90
Qof	ק		q	kangaroo	100
Resh	ר		r	red	200
Sin	שׂ		ś	see	300
Shin	שׁ		š	shed	300
Taw	תּ		t	tin	400
	ת		$\underline{t}$	thin	

The Other Kind of Daghesh

As I explained above, the **Daghesh** serves to indicate a hard (or plosive) sound in the *begadkephat* letters and occurs only in these six letters. This particular Daghesh is called the **Daghesh Lene**. There is another Daghesh, called the **Daghesh Forte**, that indicates the doubling of a letter. So, ט without Daghesh Forte is transliterated *t*, and ט with Daghesh Forte is transliterated *tt*. Daghesh Forte can occur in any letter (including the *begadkephat* letters) except for א, ה, ח, ע, and ר. These first four letters are called guttural letters (because the sounds are made in the back of the throat), and none of the five can be doubled.

Exercises

1. On a separate sheet of paper, practice writing the letters of the alphabet in alphabetical order. (a) Write each letter five times, repeating the name of the letter each time you write it; begin with Alef, then Beth without Daghesh and Beth with Daghesh, etc., not forgetting the five final forms. (b) You might sing the "Hebrew Alef Beth" song in the appendix. Then (c) write each letter once in alphabetical order, again naming the letter as you write. Complete the alphabet five times.

2. Below are the words from Isa 66:17. For now, treat the Daghesh in all the *begadkephat* letters as Lene and all those in other letters as Forte by writing the letter twice. So, בּ = *b*, ב = b, and ט = *tt*. Below the Hebrew text, copy the Hebrew words in Hebrew. Below your copy of the Hebrew text, give a transliteration, remembering that English is transliterated left-to-right. Finally, alphabetize the words in the verse by writing the number, 1-16, above each word in the first line to indicate the order. One word is done as an example.

4

המתקדשים והמטהרים אל הגנות אחר אחד בתוך

אֵל

ʾ*l*

אכלי בשר החזיר והשקץ והעכבר יחדו יספו נאם יהוה

3. Transliterate each of the following biblical names back into Hebrew letters. Can you figure out who or what they represent? You will need to supply the vowels in English.

Transliteration	Hebrew	English Name
a. *šlmh*	שלמה	Solomon
b. *byt lḥm*	מ	
c. *rwt*		
d. *ʾbymlk*		
e. *dwd*		
f. *ʾbrm*		
g. *dnyʾl*		
h. *bnymyn*		
i. *yḥzqʾl*		

Advanced Information and Curious Facts

You may wonder how we know the order of the Hebrew alphabet. The answer comes from Hebrew poetry. There are a number of poems in the Bible that are alphabetic acrostic poems; that is, the first word of each verse begins with a successive letter of the alphabet. This is almost impossible to bring out in English. The best example is Ps 119. The reason it has 176 verses is because 176 is a multiple of 22 (by a factor of 8). Each group of eight verses begins with the same letter of the alphabet. Many English versions give the name of each letter at the beginning of each stanza.

One more interesting tidbit. Rev 13:16 says the number of the beast out of the earth is the number of a man, 666 (six hundred sixty-six). One of the ancient identifications of him was Nero. How did they come up with this? Someone realized that if you take the Latin name Nero Caesar and transliterate it into Hebrew (with an additional Hebraizing final Nun), the sum of the numeric values of the Hebrew letters is 666. Here we go:

Caesar   Neron

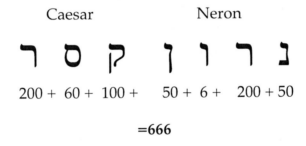

200 + 60 + 100 +   50 + 6 +   200 + 50

=666

CHAPTER 2

Whose Language is Dead?
The History of Hebrew

Introduction

A "dead" language is one that is no longer spoken in a living people group. No one would think of English as dead, but English has changed over time. Words come into use and sometimes fade out of use. For example, if I describe something to my students as "groovy" (60s and 70s), they would think I was "wack, dude" (21st century?). Sometimes words change meaning (*gay* meant something different in the 1890s than it did in the 1990s).

The history of English is organized into several periods by scholars. Old English is the name of the language from the fifth to the twelfth century. A little over a thousand years ago, the Model Prayer read like this:

> *Fæder ure þu þe eart on heofonum,*
> *Si þin nama gehalgod.*
> *To becume þin rice,*
> *gewurþe ðin willa, on eorðan swa swa on heofonum.*
> *urne gedæghwamlican hlaf syle us todæg,*
> *and forgyf us ure gyltas, swa swa we forgyfað urum gyltendum.*
> *and ne gelæd þu us on costnunge, ac alys us of yfele. soþlice.*[1]

Though many might be able to make out a few words (e.g., *Fæder ure*), few people can understand it. Yet, it is English.

---

[1] This text of the Lord's (Model) Prayer in the West Saxon literary dialect of the eleventh century is taken from www.ruf.rice.edu/~kemmer/Words04/history/paternoster.htm (accessed January 21, 2008).

Similarly, Hebrew is a living language, though there are numerous differences between ancient and modern. Compared to English, however, Hebrew has remained generally the same over 3,000 years![2]

Hebrew is a Semitic language. "Semitic" simply means a group of similar languages based on the names of the descendents of Shem as listed in Gen 10:21-31 – languages such as Ugaritic, Akkadian, Aramaic, and Arabic. In this lesson we will delineate the periods of Hebrew. You will also get a little more practice with the alphabet that you learned in the last lesson.

The Periods of Hebrew Language

Biblical Hebrew

There is a long prehistory to biblical Hebrew found in the archaeological remains of the cities where languages similar to Hebrew were spoken. As we mentioned above, Hebrew has enjoyed rather remarkable uniformity over the last 3,500 years. Scholars, however, have been able to identify some periods of development in the language.

Hebrew has been in existence at least from the time of Moses, the middle of the second millennium BC. Scholars, even conservative ones, disagree over the date of the compilation of our OT. Most conservatives think that Moses wrote the bulk of the Pentateuch during the fifteenth century BC, but that the text as we have it shows definite signs of later editing. The earliest extrabiblical Hebrew is found in inscriptions from the Iron Age (1200-540). There is great similarity between these texts and biblical Hebrew, but there is simply not much evidence.

The biblical texts themselves, assuming Mosaic authorship, were written over a period of about one thousand years. Remarkably, the language remained very uniform, such that grammars of biblical Hebrew can treat it as one unified language. Still, differences can be identified between texts composed before and those composed after the exile in the sixth century BC.

---

[2] Bruce K. Waltke and M. O'Connor, *An Introduction to Biblical Hebrew Syntax* (Winona Lake, Ind.: Eisenbrauns, 1990), 4: "A well-educated Hebrew speaker can read and understand Hebrew literature from all stages, from the oldest portions of the Hebrew Scriptures to Modern Hebrew."

Postbiblical Hebrew

After biblical Hebrew, changes do become more obvious and different periods can be described.

1. The writings of *Qumran* date from about 200 BC (the likely date of the foundation of the community) to AD 135 (the Bar Kochba rebellion). This important body of writings includes biblical texts, apocryphal texts, and sectarian writings, i.e., documents written by the community on various matters.

2. *Mishnaic Hebrew,* or Rabbinic Hebrew, is the language of the learning of Jewish teachers after the turn of the era. Mishnaic Hebrew is similar to the language of Qumran[3] and they probably overlap. But our evidence comes from the Mishnah, a document that was composed about AD 200, but preserves older material. It represents the written form of the oral Jewish law and was an attempt to apply and codify the Mosaic law in circumstances without the temple. Of the same dialect are other rabbinic works such as the Tosefta (c. 300), and the Hebrew portions of the Palestinian Talmud (c. 400) and the Babylonian Talmud (c. 500 or 600). Perhaps the commentaries known as *midrashim* (which overlap these writings in time) should be included here, but some see their language as distinctive.

3. *Medieval Hebrew* is the period after the Talmudic period (c. 500-600) to c. 1700. This literature includes an ocean of materials written in many places by many Jewish teachers and includes all types of literature.

4. *Modern Hebrew* is the term for the language since c. 1700. Its reemergence as a living language in Palestine is due to the efforts of Eliezer Ben-Yehuda beginning in the late nineteenth century. It is based on biblical Hebrew, though there are differences, of course. It was made the official language of Jews in Palestine in 1921, and in 1953 the Israeli government founded the Academy of the Hebrew Language to make dictionaries, study the language, and direct its development by creating words, regularizing spelling, etc.

---

[3] In fact, M. H. Segal, *A Grammar of Mishnaic Hebrew* (Oxford: Clarendon, 1927) 1, includes Qumran literature within the Mishnaic Hebrew and dates the period 400/300 B.C. - A.D. 400.

Exercises

1. In the following words, some have Daghesh Lene (only in *begadkephat* letters), some have Daghesh Forte (doubling letters that may be found in almost any letter, including *begadkephat* letters), some have neither. **Circle** the words that must have Daghesh Forte (for this exercise, even though it will not be right, assume that all *begadkephat* letters are Lene). **Underline** all words with no Daghesh at all

תקחו באהלו מספר לגלגלת איש ממנו אשר הדבר

2. Of the following words circle those that have final forms.

נתן בז הארץ טבור מקנה ישבי ואל על ידו

3. Mark each word from the following that has … (circle all that apply)

   a. an *s* but not *sh* sound
   משה בשר   סור   כלב   נגד

   b. a *p* or *ph* sound
   אלף קל   נפש   כל   בלע

   c. an *m* sound
   מות טור   חם   סדה   קדש

   d. a *t* or *th* (as in thin) sound
   היוד   שלח   דלת   צור   תורה

   e. a *b* or *b̲* (*v*) sound
   אדם   כלב   נח   בלע   פלג

   f. a *k* or *ch* sound
   כוס   בגד   פלג   מלך   נפל

   g. a *g* sound
   בוא   בגד   בנה   ויאמר   כון

   h. an *r* sound
   אגדה   לך   נדר   כנען   דוד

   i. *n* sound
   רוץ   בזה   שפן   שלג   נגד

Advanced Information and Curious Facts

What language did Jesus speak? This has been a matter of great debate. It is almost certain that he and the Galilean apostles were able to speak Greek. Many Jews of Palestine were bilingual, at least enough to do business with a Greek-speaking world. In John 12:20-21, some Greeks come to the disciples requesting to see Jesus. They would not have known Hebrew. The disciples and Jesus would have to know Greek to understand them. Likewise, when Jesus heals the Gerasene demoniac (Mark 5:1-20), it is probable that he spoke to the man in Greek, since it was a Greek-speaking area. Jesus also knew Hebrew, and he clearly knew Aramaic. This was probably the common language of the Jews of Judea. When he healed Jairus's daughter, Mark 5:41 quotes the Aramaic and translates: "Taking her by the hand he said to her, 'Talitha, cumi,' which means, 'Little girl, ... arise'" (ESV). Although *cumi* might be Aramaic or Hebrew, *Talitha* is clearly Aramaic. Similarly, when Jesus was on the cross, one statement was a quotation from Ps 22:1; Mark 15:34 reports, "And at the ninth hour Jesus cried with a loud voice,'*Eloi, Eloi, lema sabachthani'*" which means in Aramaic, 'My God, my God, why have you forsaken me?'"" (ESV). Omitting the vowels, the Hebrew of Ps 22:1 may be transliterated as *ʾly, ʾly, lmh ʿzḇtny*.

WEEK 2

"Getting to Know All About You"
Vowels and How We Got the OT

CHAPTER 3

Get the Point?
The Hebrew Vowels

Objectives

1. Write the Hebrew vowels
2. Pronounce Hebrew vowels
3. Transliterate Hebrew to English and English to Hebrew

Introduction

So far, by learning the Hebrew alphabet, you have only learned the consonants. Naturally the question arises, "What about vowels?" As we mentioned in chapter 1, originally Hebrew was written with consonants alone. Of course when people spoke, they pronounced the words with vowel sounds; the vowels simply were not written. The vowel sounds of a written text had to be figured out from context. Scribes later developed systems of indicating vowels without having to alter the consonants. This was done by adding small symbols above or below the consonants. These symbols, arrangements of dots and short lines, are called *vowel points*, as opposed to the consonants, which are called *letters*. Vowels are not called letters as they are in English.

At first, trying to read consonants without any vowels may sound unbelievably difficult. But, if you know the language well (as an ancient native speaker would), it is manageable. You can do this in English:

Ths wh tk Hbrw lv t stdy th ld tstmnt.

This sentence is a pretty complex example for vowelless English, but you probably figured it out without much difficulty as "Those who take Hebrew love to study the Old Testament." In Hebrew, this works out a little easier in one way, since virtually no word or even a syllable starts with a vowel. However, because of Hebrew inflections (changes in form to indicate changes in meaning), there may be more variations than in English. Most Hebrew words are built on three-letter roots that have a basic meaning, to which are added vowels and various combinations of prefixes and suffixes that make meaning more specific. To illustrate, a sentence of unpointed Hebrew might include the word דבר, the root having to do with the formation of words. Without a context, the word might be pronounced in a number of different ways, depending on the intended meaning. In Figure 3.1 I've put the three letters of the root in shaded type and the various vowel points in regular type to give only *some* of the possibilities. In the transliterations, I've shaded the English letters that correspond to the Hebrew consonants.

Figure 3.1: Be Grateful for Vowels!

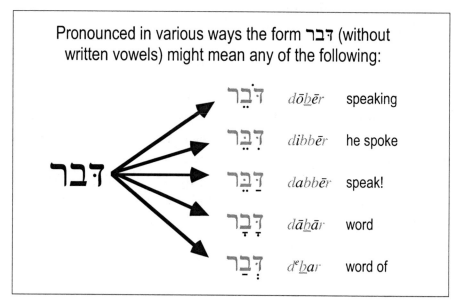

Notice:

1. Remember that Hebrew reads right to left, and English, even in transliteration, reads left to right.

2. Most vowel points are written above or below the consonant.

3. Every consonant in a word, except the last one, has a point with it. The last letter only has a vowel point with it when the word ends in a vowel. The only time when a consonant in the middle of a word will not have a vowel point with it is when the consonant is a vowel letter or when it is Alef at the end of a syllable. Alef is always a consonant and is transliterated as such, but at the end of a syllable it becomes silent. In those instances, there will be no vowel point with it and the preceding vowel will be long. For example, in the second syllable of מָצֵאתִי (צֵא) the א has no vowel point with it because it is silent. However, the transliteration is still *māṣēʾtî*, with the א represented by the symbol ʾ.

4. The consonant is read first and the vowel is read after. The first word of Figure 3.1 begins with the syllable דֹ. The little dot, or *point*, above the Dalet is a vowel (a Holem sounds like *o* as in *hole*). To pronounce the syllable, the Dalet is read first, then the vowel: *dō*. This syllable sounds just like the English word *doe* (of course there is no correspondence in meaning).

At first these "points" may seem confusing and intimidating. Do not become discouraged! You will soon become familar with them. Besides, this is not the most important material to get right to the smallest detail.

Origins and Systems

The written system of vowels found in the Hebrew Bible are the culmination of many centuries of work. We may describe the development of written vowels to have taken place in three overlapping stages. The first stage is the period of **no vowels**, extending to the tenth century B.C.

The second stage is the period of **vowel letters**, also known as *matres lectionis* ("mothers [aids] of reading"). During this period the consonants ה, ו, and י began to be added to indicate certain vowel sounds. The use of vowel letters generally increased through the biblical period, into the period of the Dead Sea Scrolls (c. 150 B.C. - A.D. 70) and into the Mishnaic period (up through about A.D. 400).

The third stage may be called the period of **vocalization**. Vowel points began to be added to the consonantal text several centuries after the composition of the last book of the OT. Jewish scholars worked in three regions developing different systems of vowel pointing known today as the Palestinian, Babylonian, and Tiberian systems. These systems were designed in such a way that vowel sounds could be indicated by adding marks to the text without altering the Hebrew consonants in any way. The system that became standard is the Tiberian system developed by the Masoretes during the period A.D. 500-950. This is the system that you will be learning.

English Vowels

A vowel is a sound made by passing air through the throat and mouth with no stoppage. The English alphabet contains vowels. Of the 26 letters, five are vowels. However, there are more vowel sounds than five and also more than five ways to write vowel sounds. We can speak of simple vowels, "vowel letters," and diphthongs.

Each simple vowel, *a, e, i, o, u*, has at least two sounds, long and short.

Figure 3.2: Simple Vowels in English

Simple Vowel	Short Sound	Long Sound
a	cat	cake
e	bed	complete
i	bit	bite
o	or	hole
u	put	brute

What I'm calling "vowel letters" refers to those consonants that combine with a vowel to form a sound. You know of w and y, but also h are English consonants that combine with vowels to form a sound (in British pronunciation, also r). Here is one example for each: bl**ew**, t**hey**, **rah**!

English also has many diphthongs. A diphthong is two vowels used for one syllable, e.g., f**ee**t and f**ea**t. Hebrew usually avoids diphthongs, though there is one important exception you will learn about below.

Hebrew Vowels and Sounds

Hebrew vowels are actually less confusing than English. Whereas English only has five vowel symbols plus three "vowel letters" (not counting the numerous diphthongs), Hebrew indicates sounds using twenty different symbols, two of which represent two different sounds. This amounts to twenty-two different vowel symbols.

Teachers of Hebrew instruct students to pronounce the vowels in different ways. You should follow what your teacher says. I will present vowels according to modern Israeli pronunciation because it is simple and won't offend the ears of modern native speakers and scholars. You will learn to pronounce five vowel sounds.[1]

Classification of Vowels

Hebrew vowels may be classified according to a number of qualities. Fig. 3.3 illustrates how I will present them. Hopefully this classification will help you learn the symbols quickly.

Figure 3.3: Classification of Vowels

Duration	Symbol	Short	Long
Full	Simple		
Full	Composite	Ø	

Duration	Symbol	Silent	Vocal
Reduced	Simple		
Reduced	Composite	Ø	

Notice:

1. The empty spaces in Fig. 3.3 are where vowels will be placed. The symbol Ø represents categories that do not exist.

---

[1] For a brief summary of the history of Hebrew vowel sounds throughout the biblical period and beyond, see Randall Buth, *Living Biblical Hebrew: Introduction Part One* (Jerusalem: Biblical Language Center, 2006) 119. I realize that I am combining a modern pronunciation of vowels with an attempted ancient pronunciation of consonants.

2. Vowels may be "full" or "reduced." According to the Masoretic system, full vowels were required to form a syllable; and so a word has as many syllables as it has full vowels. Most modern grammarians treat all vowel points except silent Shewa as syllables. You should follow your teacher.

3. Full vowels are either "simple" (i.e., points with no vowel letters) points or "combination" (i.e., points with vowel letters), and either long or short. The term *long* as opposed to *short* is thought by scholars to refer to the vowel's sound quality (how the vowel sounds) instead of its quantity (the length of time a vowel sound lasts).

4. Reduced vowels are either "simple" (i.e., Shewa alone) or "composite" (i.e., a Shewa + a short vowel). Simple Shewas are either silent (no sound) or vocal (with a very quick sound).

Before we get started on Hebrew vowels, you need to understand three things about transliteration. First, as we mentioned when discussing consonants, there is more than one system of transliteration. When you are reading a book that transliterates Hebrew, there will usually be an explanation or key at the beginning. Some systems are detailed enough to enable you to transliterate back into Hebrew without any confusion, while other systems are simplified to enable you merely to pronounce a word similarly to the Hebrew word, but transliterating from English back to the Hebrew may not always be clear. Most of the time you will have no difficulty. For Hebrew vowels, we are going to use a modification of the system of transliterations found in R. Laird Harris, Gleason L. Archer, and Bruce K. Waltke, *Theological Wordbook of the Old Testament* (Chicago: Moody, 1980) because it is complete and unambiguous.

Second, because English has only five vowels and three vowel letters, transliterating the twenty-two Hebrew vowel symbols into English means that in addition to English letters, extra marks are required, such as "long" marks (e.g., the line above ō), etc.

Third, you will need to pay particular attention to the guides to pronunciation, because the symbols used for transliterating foreign languages are different than what you may have learned when you studied English. For example, in English the symbol ē represents the vowel sound in f**ee**t; in transliteration this same symbol represents the vowel sound in c**a**ke.

We will treat full vowels and then reduced vowels. After that you will learn how to tell the difference between a pair of identical symbols that have different sounds.

Simple Full Vowels

Similar to learning the consonants, we will move from simple to more complex. I'm also going to give you the names of the vowels. As non-Hebrew students, I don't think you need to memorize them, though your teacher may require it. You do, however, need to learn what sounds they make so you can pronounce Hebrew words.

There are eight simple vowel points. In Figure 3.4 I use the consonant ב to represent any given Hebrew consonant. This allows you to see the position of the vowel with a consonant. The vowels are arranged from simple to complex in form. After the symbol I give the name of the letter, then the sound it makes by giving an English word that has the same vowel sound. The last two columns are transliteration and length (Long or Short). The ability to match the sound and transliteration with the correct vowel is important for you to pronounce the word correctly.

Figure 3.4: Eight Simple Hebrew Vowels

Symbol	Name	Sound	Trans– literation	Length
בִ	Hireq	mach<u>i</u>ne	i	S
בֵ	Tsere	th<u>ey</u>	$\bar{e}$	L
בֶ	Seghol	th<u>ey</u>	e	S
בֻ	Qibbuts	br<u>u</u>te	u	S
בֹ	Holem	h<u>o</u>le	$\bar{o}$	L
בַ	Pathach	f<u>a</u>ther	a	S
בָ	Qamets	f<u>a</u>ther	$\bar{a}$	L
בָ	Qamets Hatuf	h<u>o</u>le	o	S

Notice:

1. When Holem is followed by Shin, sometimes the dot on the right shoulder of the Shin functions as both the marker for Shin and Holem. So the word Moses, *mōšeh,* may be written either מֹשֶׁה or מֹשֶׁה.

2. Qamets and Qamets Hatuf are identical in form but distinct in sound and transliteration. In this chapter I will show you how to tell the difference between the two. Qamets is much more common, so if in doubt, guess Qamets.

Composite Full Vowels

As we mentioned above, Hebrew began to use ה, ו, and י to indicate vowel sounds. Many centuries later, the Masoretes incorporated their points into these vowel letters.

As for the sound these combinations make, the letter plus the vowel go together to form one vowel sound. In transliteration the presence of vowel letters must be indicated. This is done in two ways: (1) placing a circumflex above the English letter (e.g., *ô*) or (2) transliterating both the vowel and the vowel letter (e.g. *ōh*).

Figure 3.5: Nine Hebrew Composite Vowels

Symbol	Name	Sound	Transliteration	Length
בִּי	Hireq Yod	machine	*î*	L
בֵּי	Tsere Yod	they	*ê*	L
בֶּי	Seghol Yod	they	*ey*	L
בוֹ	Holem Waw	hole	*ô*	L
בוּ	Shureq	brute	*û*	L
בֵּה	Tsere He	they	*ēh*	L
בֶּה	Seghol He	they	*eh*	L
בָּה	Qamets He	father	*â*	L
בֹה	Holem He	hole	*ōh*	L

Notice:

1. All combination vowels are long.

2. Except for Shureq, the names for these vowels are the vowel name plus the letter name.

3. These vowel letters are pronounced after the consonant that precedes them. I think it is helpful to separate the syllables with a vertical stroke (|). So דָּבָר with simple vowels is pronounced *dā | bār* with each simple vowel point pronounced after the consonant above or before it. However, הוֹרִידוּ is pronounced *hô | rî | dû*.

Reduced Vowels, Simple and Composite

There are five reduced vowels. These are all forms of Shewa. They are illustrated in Figure 3.6.

Figure 3.6: Five Reduced Vowels

Complexity	Vowel	Name	Sound	Transliteration
Simple Shewa	בְּ	Shewa	banana	^{e}
	בְּ	Shewa	[silent]	[none]
Composite Shewa	בֲ	Hateph Pathach	banana	ă
	בֱ	Hateph Seghol	banana	ĕ
	בֳ	Hateph Qamets	banana	ŏ

Notice:

1. Vocal Shewa is transliterated with a superscripted e. Thus the word דְּבַר, with Vocal Shewa, is transliterated *d^{e}bar*.

2. Silent Shewa is not transliterated: דִּבְרֵי is transliterated *dibrê*, not *dib^{e}rê*.

3. The Vocal Shewa and all three of the Composite Shewas may be pronounced the same, namely with a very short "uh" sound as in the first syllable of *banana*. However, they must be transliterated differently.

Final Steps for Pronunciation

You need to memorize the symbols, their sounds, and their transliterations. One way to do this is to make flash cards, putting the vowel symbol on one side with its name, sound, and transliteration on the other side (see www.teknia.com).

In order to fine-tune your ability to pronounce Hebrew, you will need to know how to do five more things: (1) distinguish Dagesh Forte from Dagesh Lene, (2) distinguish Shureq (וּ) from Waw with Dagesh Forte (וּ), (3) identify syllables, (4) distinguish Silent Shewa from Vocal Shewa, and (5) distinguish Qamets from Qamets Hatuf. To do this quickly takes some practice, so be patient with yourself.

1. Distinguishing Dagesh Forte and Lene (two rules):

    a. If there is a Dagesh in any letter other than a *begadkephat*, it must be Dagesh Forte, the doubling Dagesh. So, in the word קַטֵּל, the Dagesh in the ט must be Forte and the word would be transliterated *qaṭṭēl*.

    b. If a *begadkephat* with Dagesh is immediately preceded by a full vowel, it is Forte. If it is preceded by no vowel, including Silent Shewa, it is Lene.

2. Distinguishing Shureq from Waw with Dagesh Forte (one rule): If the letter before וּ has no vowel, it is Shureq. In כָּתוּב the Taw before וּ has no vowel and so וּ must be the vowel Shureq: *kātûḇ*. In מְצֻוֶּה the Tsade before וּ has a vowel under it (Pathach) and וּ must be a doubled consonant: *mᵉṣawweh*.

3. Syllables and Accents. A word has as many syllables as it has full vowels. Hebrew words are accented only on one of the last two syllables; in this book the accent is marked only when it does not occur on the last syllable. In דָּבָר there is no accent mark, so the accent is on the last syllable. In דֶּרֶךְ there is an accent mark on the next to last syllable. Most commentaries and other Bible study tools that you will use do not mark the accented syllable. When in doubt, accent on the last syllable.

4. Distinguishing Silent Shewa from Vocal Simple Shewa (two rules):

    a. Vocal Shewa begins (or is) a syllable. Silent Shewa ends a syllable. In the word דְּבַר, the Shewa is at the beginning of a syllable (obviously, since it is at the beginning of a word) and must be vocal. Composite Shewas are always vocal. In יַעֲשֶׂה the Composite Shewa is vocal and begins the second syllable.

b. Shewa after a short vowel in an unaccented syllable is silent. In מֶרְכָּבָה, the רְ (Resh + Shewa) is preceded by a short vowel, Seghol, and there is no accent. Therefore the Shewa is silent and closes the syllable. The word מֶרְכָּבָה is a three syllable word (three full vowels) and the syllables may be divided: מֶרְ ׀ כָּ ׀ בָה.

5. Distinguishing Qamets from Qamets Hatuf (one rule): Qamets Hatuf occurs only in a closed, unaccented syllable. In הָכְמָה the כְ closes the syllable and חָכְ is both closed and unaccented. Therefore, the vowel must be Qamets Hatuf and transliterated *ḥokmâ*. In וַיָּקָם the Qamets under the Yod appears in an open, accented (note the accent mark) syllable and must be long; the Qamets under the Qof appears in a closed, unaccented syllable and must be short. The transliteration is *wayyāqom*.

Other Marks and Remarks

If you open a printed Hebrew Bible, you will notice that there are many more marks in the text than consonants and vowels. Many of these you can ignore. But some of them you will need to know about.

What You Can Ignore

Almost every word in the Hebrew Bible has some type of accent mark, sometimes even two. The accents, developed by the Masoretes, serve three purposes: (1) to mark the primary stressed syllable, (2) to divide the verse into logical phrases, and (3) to indicate musical notes. These accent marks are very complicated and beyond the scope of what we are doing here. In commentaries and other materials that discuss the text of the Hebrew Bible accent marks are rarely included, but sometimes commentators discuss them as a record of the interpretation of the rabbis.

What You Need To Pay Attention To

There is one accent mark you should pay attention to and some other marks occasionally used in the text that you might want to know about.

1. **Soph Pasuq** (meaning "end of verse") is an accent mark found at the end of each verse. It looks similar to an English colon (but two diamond shapes): הָאָרֶץ׃. The Hebrew verse divisions are *almost* identical to our English Bibles.

2. **Mappiq** looks exactly like a Dagesh. However it only appears in the letter He at the end of a word to mark the He as a true consonant instead of a vowel letter: הּ. In this case the הּ is to be pronounced and is always transliterated with *h*. This makes a difference in meaning. For example, סוּס is the word meaning a male "horse." In the word סוּסָהּ, the Mappiq indicates that the ending הּ is a suffix meaning *her* and the entire construction means "*her* horse." On the other hand, in סוּסָה, the הָ ending indicates that the noun is feminine meaning "mare" (a female horse).

3. **Maqqef** looks like and functions similarly to a hyphen in English. The main difference in appearance is that it appears at the top of the line, rather than in the middle; so וּבְכָל־הָאָרֶץ (not וּבְכָל-הָאָרֶץ). It indicates a close connection between two words.

Exercises

1. Using the information in this chapter, indicate whether each Shewa in each word is vocal or silent by circling each vocal Shewa and placing an X over each silent Shewa.

   a. מִשְׁפָּחוֹת   c. וַיֹּאמְרוּ   e. שָׁבְרָה

   b. מְקַטְּלִים   d. הָלַכְתִּי   f. וַיֵּבְךְ

2. Indicate the number of syllables in each word by drawing a line between them. For letters with Daghesh Forte (doubling Daghesh), draw a line through the middle of the letter.

   a. מְדַבְּרִים   d. בְּרֵאשִׁית   g. נַעֲשֶׂה

   b. דְּבָרַי   e. אֱלֹהִים   h. יִשְׂרָאֵל

   c. יֶלֶד   f. שָׁלוֹחַ   i. הַגִּידוּ

3. Each line below gives an English word with an underlined vowel followed by a list of Hebrew syllables (assume they are all unaccented). Circle each Hebrew syllable that rhymes with the underlined vowel in the English word (there may be more than one per row). The first one is done as an example.

a. f<u>a</u>ther	(בָּ)	(בַּ)	בוֹ	(בִּי)	בְ
b. h<u>ey</u>	בֶּ	בֶּ	בוּ	בִּי	בֵּי
c. mach<u>i</u>ne	בֹ	בָּת	בוֹ	בִּי	בָּ
d. h<u>o</u>le	בֶּ	בוּ	בַּ	בָּת	בֵּי
e. th<u>ey</u>	בֶּ	בְ	בֶּ	בֵּי	בֵּי
f. br<u>u</u>te	בֶּ	בַּ	בָּ	בוּ	בֹּ
g. h<u>o</u>le	בוֹ	בוּ	בָּ	בָּג	בֵ
h. br<u>u</u>te	בְ	בוּ	בִּי	בָּי	בֹּ
i. mach<u>i</u>ne	בִּי	בֵּ	בֹ	בֶּ	בַ
j. f<u>a</u>ther	בָּת	בַּת	בוֹ	בָּ	בֵ
k. b<u>a</u>nana	בָּ	בוּ	בְ	בַ	בֵ

4. Here are some real Hebrew words. They are names of people and places. First give an accurate transliteration and then give the name as we normally spell it. The first one is done as an example. All words not accented on the last syllable are marked with the accent .

    a. רָחָב   *rāḥāḇ*   Rahab

    b. בֵּית לֶחֶם

    c. יְרוּשָׁלַ͏ִם

d. נָעֳמִי ²

e. יְהוּדָה

f. גָּלְיָת

g. דָּוִד

h. יְהוֹשָׁפָט

i. בַּת שֶׁבַע

Advanced Information and Curious Facts: A Synagogue Torah Scroll.

In a Jewish synagogue, the Torah scroll (Hebrew text of the first five books of the Bible) is kept in an ark at the front of the synagogue, facing the congregation. The Hebrew Bible that people commonly buy includes vowel points and accent marks. An official Torah scroll, however, is written by hand in unpointed Hebrew text on meticulously prepared animal skin. Each copy has exactly the same number of "pages" and the exact same words on each page and on each line.

In the photograph below, a group assembles around an open Torah scroll. The reader does not touch the scroll, but uses a *yad* (Hebrew for "hand") to point to the words in the text he is reading. The end of the *yad* is in the shape of a hand with the index finger pointing.

Incidentally, the reader in the synagogue memorizes how to pronounce the text and may even chant it in a worship service. The one who chants the text is called a "cantor." As mentioned above, one of the functions of Masoretic accent marks is to indicate series of musical notes. Each one represents a musical series or chant. The ability to learn and perform the chanting requires a great amount of training and practice.

---

² The Qamets before the Hateph Qamets is always Qamets Hatuf (o-class). In the English form of this name, the Hebrew o-class vowel is rendered with an English a-class vowel.

Figure 3.10: Reading a Torah Scroll

Photograph contributed courtesy of the Klau Library,
Hebrew Union College-Jewish Institute of Religion, Cincinnati.

C H A P T E R   4

Canon, Text, and Versions

Objectives

1. Gain additional practice reading and writing Hebrew consonants and vowels.
2. Learn something about the Hebrew canon of the OT, the text of the OT, and modern translations.
3. Understand Kethib and Qere readings.

Canonization

Have you ever wondered why the OT has the books in it that it does? Or why the Catholic and Orthodox Bibles contain books that the Protestant Bible does not? These are questions concerning the *canon* of Scripture. The area within biblical studies called "general introduction" deals with matters pertaining to the Bible in general: canon, text, and versions.

The English word *canon* comes to us in English through Latin and Greek ultimately from the Hebrew word קָנֶה, *qāneh*. This word first meant the "reed" or "stalk of a plant." Later it came to mean the instrument made from such a thing, "measuring stick, rule, straightedge." Eventually it was used metaphorically for a "standard" of any measurement. In our case, the term canon is used for a "standard" list.

It is essential to realize that the phrase "canon of Scripture" refers to the "list of authoritative books"; it does not mean an authoritative list of books. Several books that explore this issue are listed here:

Arnold, Clint. *How We Got the Bible*. Grand Rapids: Zondervan, 2008.

Beckwith, Roger. *The Old Testament Canon of the New Testament*. Grand Rapids: Eerdmans, 1985.

Geisler, Norman L., and William E. Nix. *A General Introduction to the Bible.* Rev. ed. Chicago: Moody, 1986.

Wegner, Paul D. *The Journey from Texts to Translations.* Grand Rapids: Baker, 1999.

Arnold's work is of a popular nature containing lots of pictures. Wegner's book is a much more substantial read and also well illustrated. Beckwith and Geisler and Nix are more technical, but excellent standard works done by scholars holding to the inspiration and inerrancy of Scripture.

It is common to recognize three phases in the development of the canon: writing, collecting, and recognizing. These phases overlap in time and even in task, but it is still a helpful way to begin to understand the process. Figure 4.1: The Formation of Our Bible below gives an approximate timeline for these three processes for both testaments.[1] Following the chart I will offer a few facts and offer a possible scenario for how the process of canonization of the OT took place.

Figure 4.1: The Formation of Our Bible

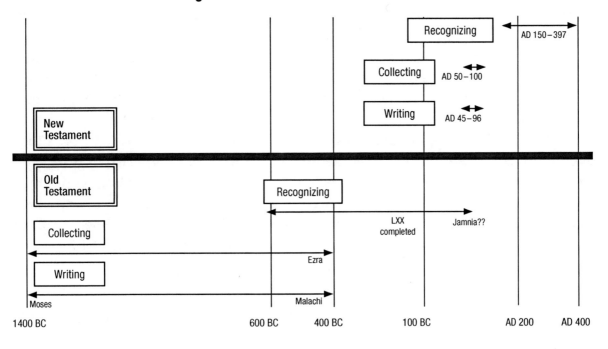

---

[1] I assume in this figure that Moses wrote the Pentateuch, without denying that there may have been later editing.

The Writing, Collecting, and Recognizing of the OT Books

There was a period when parts of the Bible were oral. The Pentateuch itself contains stories of events that occurred long before the books were written, and we have no indication that written records of them existed before Moses. We don't know how long God's words were only in oral form, but early on they were committed to writing. For example, Moses was commanded to write an account of the battle with the Amalekites as a memorial (Exod 17:14; see also Exod 34:27 and Deut 31:19).[2] This does give us an insight into the writing of the first five books: they were first composed in small parts.

Some seem to think that collecting the books was a process far removed in time from writing. The evidence suggests, however, that this may not have been the case. The OT mentions that sacred writings were stored in Israel's sanctuary from the very beginning. So the books of Moses were collected immediately upon being written (Deut 31:24-26; cf. Josh 1:8; 2 Kgs 22:8).

Moses' successor, Joshua, also placed his writings near the sanctuary (Josh 24:26). This was also the practice of the judge Samuel (1 Sam 10:25). It is not to be expected that every book in the Bible explicitly say that it was put aside in the sanctuary, but it is very possible that this was a normal pattern followed.

If it's true that books of God's revelation were stored at the sanctuary, then was everything that was ever written by Israelites included in this collection? No. In fact, we know of twenty-five books named in the OT itself that were not included in Scripture, for example, the Book of Jasher (Josh 10:13; 2 Sam 1:18).[3]

How did Israelites living during OT times know to include only the ones that eventually comprised our thirty-nine books? Deut 18:20-22 gives two tests. The first was doctrinal. Verse 20 mentions that those who speak in the name of other gods are not prophets of the Lord. This suggests that the standard for evaluating new purported revelation was the law of Moses itself. If a self-proclaimed prophet taught something that disagreed with what the Lord had revealed to Moses, he was a false prophet and was to be stoned.

---

[2]   I am aware that some scholars do not believe that Moses even lived. For more information see Raymond B. Dillard and Tremper Longman III, *An Introduction to the Old Testament*, 2nd ed. (Grand Rapids: Zondervan, 2006).

[3]   See Lee M. MacDonald, *The Biblical Canon* (Grand Rapids: Kregel, 2007), 147-48, for a complete list.

The second test was fulfillment. Deut 18:21-22 says that the way to know whether a prophet was from God was to see if what he predicted came true. We see this same standard applied centuries later as recorded in the book of Jeremiah. Chapter 28 records a scene in which Jeremiah and another prophet, Hananiah, had a showdown. Jeremiah had been proclaiming that the Babylonian captivity would last seventy years, while Hananiah was saying it would last only two years. Both were claiming to be prophets of the Lord. How would the audience know who was right? In 28:9 we see that they determined reliability based on the same Deuteronomy test. Nobody, not even Hananiah, disputed the validity of this test. Clearly it was still in place. Over the next few years the readers would learn who was right.

It seems likely, then, that books that passed both tests were recognized to be the words of God. Those that failed one test or the other were removed from the sanctuary, though not necessarily destroyed or unused. Books that were unconfirmed in their prophecies were probably kept until they could be verified one way or the other.

The Closing of the OT Canon

When and why did the Jews recognize the canon of the OT as closed (i.e., no more Scripture was being written)? We can't set a precise date, but the Jewish sources indicate that they knew very well the difference between the writings of God's spokesmen (prophets) and those of other people. Two facts indicate this. First, the Jews during the intertestamental period recognized a "period of silence" when God was no longer speaking. Second, their writings reflect a known and commonly recognized body of literature.

Our first point, then, concerns the "period of silence." This is a modern term used to describe the roughly 400 years between the writing of the last book of the OT, Malachi, and the appearance of John the Baptist. "Silence" does not mean that the Jews were not writing, just that what was being written was seen as not being direct revelation from God. We get clues that the Jews during the intertestamental period were aware of such a silence. This awareness may have been the result of the OT itself. Zech 13:3 seems to predict that a time of silence from God, a cessation of the prophetic voice, was coming in anticipation of the coming of the Messiah.

Second, there existed a recognized body of literature that was accepted as Scripture. Two books from the Apocrypha (Jewish writings written between 300

BC and 30 BC) use language referring to a set body of books. First, in the Prologue to Ecclesiasticus (written c. 130 BC) we read, "my grandfather Jesus, when he had much given himself to the reading of *the law, and the prophets, and other books of our fathers … the law itself and the prophets, and the rest of the books.*" Then in 2 Maccabees 2:13 (written c. 100 BC) we read, "The same things [as in the writings of Moses] also were reported in the writings and commentaries of Nehemiah; and how he founding a library gathered together *the acts of the kings, and the prophets, and of David,* and the epistles of the kings concerning the holy gifts."

More evidence for a set body of books comes from other sources. First, the Septuagint (abbreviated LXX), the Greek translation of the Hebrew OT prepared c. 250-130 BC, included the thirty-nine books of our OT. Copies of the LXX from five hundred years later include the books of the Apocrypha, but we do not know when they were added.

The NT also indicates a known body of books, where we see both a twofold and threefold division as abbreviated references to the OT books. In the Sermon on the Mount, Jesus indicates a twofold division when he says, "the Law and the Prophets" (Matt 5:17; 7:12; et al.). In Luke 24:44 a threefold division is indicated when the OT is referred to as "Moses and the Prophets and the Psalms." These two designations follow the Jewish canonical order (see Figure 4.3 below).

Figure 4.2: The English Arrangment of the OT Canonical Books

Law	History	Poetry	Major Prophets	Minor Prophets
Genesis	Joshua	Job	Isaiah	Hosea
Exodus	Judges	Psalms	Jeremiah	Joel
Leviticus	Ruth	Proverbs	Lamentations	Amos
Numbers	1 & 2 Samuel	Ecclesiastes	Ezekiel	Obadiah
Deuteronomy	1 & 2 Kings	Song of Songs	Daniel	Jonah
	1 & 2 Chronicles			Micah
	Ezra			Nahum
	Nehemiah			Habbakuk
	Esther			Zephaniah
				Haggai
				Zechariah
				Malachi

Figure 4.3: The Jewish Arrangment OT Canonical Books

Division	Subdivision	Hebrew Name	Translation	English Name
Law		בְּרֵאשִׁית	In the beginning	Genesis
		שְׁמוֹת	The names of	Exodus
		וַיִּקְרָא	And he called	Leviticus
		בְּמִדְבַּר	In the wilderness of	Numbers
		דְּבָרִים	Words	Deuteronomy
Prophets	**Former**	יְהוֹשֻׁעַ	Yehoshua	Joshua
		שֹׁפְטִים	Judges	Judges
		שְׁמוּאֵל	Shemuel	Samuel
		מְלָכִים	Kings	Kings
	Latter	יְשַׁעְיָהוּ	Yeshayahu	Isaiah
		יִרְמְיָהוּ	Yirmeyyahu	Jeremiah
		יְחֶזְקֵאל	Yechezkel	Ezekiel
		שְׁנַיִם עָשָׂר	The twelve	The Twelve
Writings	**Book of Truth**	תְּהִלִּים	Praises	Psalms
		אִיּוֹב	Job	Job
		מִשְׁלֵי	The proverbs of	Proverbs
	Megilloth	רוּת	Ruth	Ruth
		שִׁיר הַשִּׁירִים	The song of songs	Song of Songs
		קֹהֶלֶת	preacher	Ecclesiastes
		אֵיכָה	How?	Lamentations
		אֶסְתֵּר	Esther	Esther
		דָּנִיֵּאל	Daniel	Daniel
		עֶזְרָא	Ezra	Ezra
		נְחֶמְיָה	Nechemyah	Nehemiah
		דִּבְרֵי הַיָּמִים	The words of the days	Chronicles

Summary

The fact that the term *canon* was not used until long after the death of the apostles does not mean that the church as well as the people of Israel before her had no concept of a list of authoritative books. Moses was a known prophet of the Lord, proved as such by many miracles. Subsequent writings were checked against this standard to see if their prophecies came true.

The Text of the OT

Perhaps you have wondered why your version reads differently from others – differences not just representing updating of language, but substantively different words. For example, when reading the phrase "they have pierced" in Ps 22:16, what does the NIV footnote mean when it says, "Some Hebrew manuscripts, Septuagint and Syriac; most Hebrew manuscripts *like the lion*"? Or perhaps you had a night with nothing but time on your hands and you decided to read the Preface to your NIV (seriously, it is valuable reading). You went along pretty well until the sentence, "The translators also consulted the more important early versions – the Septuagint; Aquila, Symmachus and Theodotion; the Vulgate; the Syriac Peshitta; the Targums; and for the Psalms the *juxta Hebraica* of Jerome"— at which point you quit reading. These matters deal with the *text* of Scripture, the words of the Hebrew Bible themselves. Included here is the topic of ancient versions, because they also are witnesses to the text.

Why is this question important for Bible believing students? Because our service to others demands it. Dan Wallace is a top-notch conservative scholar of Greek and NT and has worked closely with "nonevangelical" scholars. In his contacts he has learned that most of them used to be conservatives. When confronted with challenges to the inerrancy of the Bible, the answers they received from their conservative friends were either simplistic or wrong. As a result, they concluded that there are no answers for the problems that can allow them to trust in the Bible. Evangelicals need to be able to face questions squarely and honestly, if we really have confidence that God's truth can stand up to close scrutiny. As Wallace has said in one of his lectures, "It would be better for us to have some doubts in our pursuit of truth than no doubts as we try to protect our certainties."[4]

---

[4] Taken from his Textual Criticism series taught at a church. A video is available for viewing on his website (http://www.bible.org/page.php?page_id=2439; see "Text Criticism 1").

Transmission of the Hebrew Text

The history of the OT text can be divided into five periods. Prior to AD 100, the books were composed, copied, and translated. The script changed from Paleo-Hebrew to Square Script. There were also changes in spelling and the use of vowel letters. The work of the "scribes," known from the NT, also took place. These men diligently copied and studied the Scriptures. Before 1900, we had no manuscripts from before AD 100. Since then archaeologists have made several important finds of manuscripts from this period. Chief among these are the famous Dead Sea Scrolls (abbreviated DSS), discovered in 1948.

Also during this period the Hebrew OT was translated into Greek and eventually called the Septuagint (a Latin word meaning "seventy" and abbreviated with the Roman numeral LXX), completed at least by 130 BC. Studies in DSS, LXX, and other sources have led some scholars to believe that before AD 100 there were three main text families that all descended ultimately from the original text of the books. The original texts were copied and, while the recognition phase was going on, there developed what scholars call the Proto-Masoretic Text. From the Proto-Masoretic Text came three traditions, each associated with a geographical area: Palestine, Babylon, and Egypt.

Figure 4.4: Textual Families of the OT

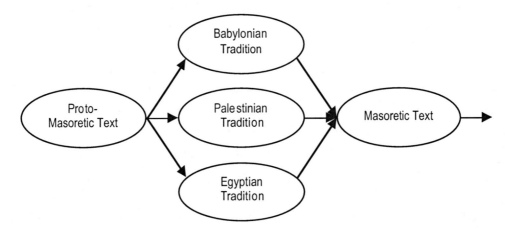

Because the DSS biblical texts, written before 100 BC, have more variants than later texts after the destruction of the temple in AD 70, scholars think that by about AD 100 the Jews of Palestine standardized the text from the various traditions.

This important development means that all of our manuscripts after this time largely follow the tradition of this standardized text. This text was copied and preserved by later scholars known as Masoretes.

During the second period, AD 100-300, the Jewish scholars known as Tannaim (תַּנָּאִים) labored.[5] They were the successors of the Scribes (סֹפְרִים, c. 500 BC to AD 100). The word *Tannaim* is an Aramaic plural noun meaning "repeaters" or "teachers," since much of the learning and teaching they did was by repetition. An important product of their work is known as the Mishnah, which records some of the Jewish oral teachings aiming to apply Mosaic law to daily life in a postbiblical and post-temple world.

The successors of the Tannaim were the Amoraim (אֲמֹורָאִים), who worked during the third period, AD 300-500. The word itself means *speaker* and then comes to mean "teacher," much like the term *Tannaim*. These men taught and preserved the oral teachings for the Jews and were responsible for its written form in what we know as the Talmud. The Talmud consists of the Mishnah plus additional teaching or commentary, known as Gemara. There are two versions of the Talmud: the Palestinian Talmud, put into writing about AD 400 in Tiberias of Galilee, and the more well-known and much more complete Babylonian Talmud, put into writing about AD 500 or AD 600. These two groups of Jewish scholars were largely responsible for copying the standardized text of the OT.

During AD 500-1000 (the fourth period) the Masoretes were at work. The word *masorah* probably means "tradition," most likely from a Hebrew root meaning "hand over." The Masoretic text (MT) is the textual tradition preserved in manuscripts copied by these people. Besides copying, the Masoretes developed the system of vowel points and accent marks that are used universally in the Hebrew OT. They also collected and recorded special notations, known as *masorah,* to the text for accuracy. They noted variants and even errors, but they would not alter the received text, not even obvious errors though they did carefully note errors in the margins.

Finally, after AD 1000 manuscripts continued to be copied. Manuscripts continued to be produced for synagogue use, but they have no relevance for textual criticism, since their content was set. It is also during this period that chapter and verse divisions were added. The concept of verses is ancient. Rabbinic discussions

---

[5] Some scholars date the existence of the Tannaim to the 3rd century B.C.

at times concerned these divisions. These were standardized by the Masoretes about AD 900. Chapter divisions were added in the fourteenth century following the system derived from Steven Langton (AD 1150-1228).

Textual Criticism

Whenever some people hear the word "criticism" in the context of Bible studies, they think that the Bible is under attack from non-believers. This is not the only use of the term "critical"; here it means a careful analysis of the text of the Bible. Because the original manuscripts of the Bible no longer exist (these are called "autographs"), because there exist hundreds of hand-written Hebrew manuscripts, and because there are differences between them, scholars who print a Hebrew Bible cannot avoid making choices from among the different readings. What we see from the history of the Hebrew OT is that textual criticism has actually been in practice at least since the time of the Qumran community, who made corrections to the consonantal text of their copies of Scripture.

Editing and correcting certainly continued among the Jews. The Talmud records debates over how to pronounce (that is, what vowels to read in the unpointed text) certain words in the text. The Masorah records various readings and textual difficulties that were known.

As we mentioned above, the Masoretes would not make any changes to their received text - not even to correct obvious errors. However, certain readings were written in the margin and marked "Qere." The word **Qere** is a command to "read" the word in the margin instead of the word in the text. The word in the text is called **Kethib**, meaning "written." So it is not a question of whether textual criticism has been practiced, but how well, and the quality of the work is largely determined by the amount and quality of information possessed by copyists, printers, and translators.

Basically there are two kinds of variants readings: intentional and unintentional. By far the most common intentional changes have to do with spelling – remember the use of vowel letters beginning about 1000 BC and gradually increasing over time. The reason for these changes was almost always not to deceive, but to clarify.

It is the unintentional variation that we may properly call an error. Sometimes when I try to copy something, I amaze myself with the amount of errors I make. This is true especially when I'm in a hurry, but it even happens when I'm trying to be careful. Ancient copyists had the same difficulty, though they were trained and did far better than I do. Unintentional errors may result in omission of text, addition of text, substitution of text, or wrong word division. These errors can have many causes.[6] There may be mistakes of the ear. If a scribe is copying by listening to someone recite, he may mishear a word, or the reader may mispronounce. Much more common are mistakes of the eye. A scribe might mistake one letter for another. Sometimes when a scribe moves his eye back from his copy to the original, his eye may skip to the text in a different place, either above or below where he was because the same word is repeated, or even because another word begins or ends similarly.

So how do scholars decide which is the correct original text? They look at the evidence from Hebrew manuscripts and ancient translations and analyze it based on general principles. Note that these are *not* strict rules.

1. *Manuscripts must be weighed, not counted.* Generally it makes sense that the text of older manuscripts should be closer to the original than the younger. Since the older manuscripts are much more rare, we can't simply count the number of manuscripts for a given reading and expect to always have the answer. If a mistake occurred in AD 800 and most of the manuscripts after that (the vast majority of all manuscripts) copied the same mistake, then the majority reading would be wrong. This principle applies to the OT text, since the vast majority of MSS are all from the same (Masoretic) tradition. Though older MSS such as the DSS are therefore very important, still one should not automatically assume that they are always better than the MT.

2. *The best reading is the one that explains all the others.* In Gen 20 we read the story of Abimelech taking Sarah into his harem. The Lord appears to him in a dream and threatens him. In v. 4, Abimelech addresses the speaker as אֲדֹנָי. All English versions translate this passage as "Lord," because the Hebrew word אָדוֹן means "master, sir, lord, Lord." The critical apparatus to the BHS, however, reports that instead of אֲדֹנָי, several manuscripts read יהוה, Lord, the actual name for God! It is much easier to explain how an original יהוה in the mouth of a Gentile might have been changed to

---

[6] For a nice list of nine types with OT and NT examples, see Wegner, *A Student's Guide to Textual Criticism of the Bible* (Downers Grove: InterVarsity, 2006), 44-50.

אֲדֹנָי than it is to explain how an original אֲדֹנָי in the mouth of a Gentile came to be changed to יְהוה. This suggests that יְהוה might in fact be original.

3. *The shorter reading is to be preferred.* The tendency of scribes was to clarify by further explanation, rather than by removing words.

4. *Most difficult reading is to be preferred.* Again, the tendency of scribes was to make a reading more understandable, rather than less so.

Inspired Text

So here's the situation: no autographs (original manuscripts) exist and the manuscripts that do exist show many differences. What do conservatives hold to be inspired? The preservation of God's Word involves two processes: inspiration and providence. Conservatives hold the autographs to be inerrant and infallible (see Figure 4.5 below). God is absolutely perfect and, though infinitely beyond humankind in his being, is perfectly able to communicate to them in a way that they can understand. Men wrote as God miraculously directed them using whatever means he chose.

The other process is providence. Nowhere are we told that copyists or translators were miraculously and infallibly guided by God. Consequently, they were open to error. Yet, God works through his people, faithful and flawed though they be, to work through the evidence that we have.

Figure 4.5: Textual Criticism and Inspiration

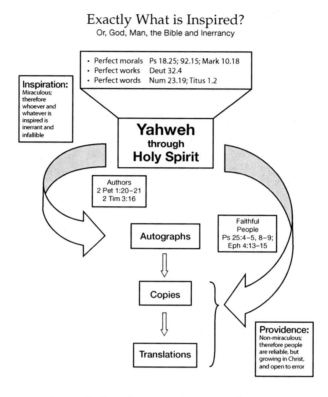

How can conservatives defend any claim to have God's very words? The situation is not as bleak as it first may appear. Two points are in order. First, the reliability of the OT text is extremely high. Only about 10 percent is disputed at all. And of that 10 percent, the vast majority of variations are matters such as spelling that have no significant affect on the meaning of the text. Second, though the study of textual criticism may affect the meaning of an individual passage, no major doctrine of Scripture rests solely on any disputed text.

Versions

Many people find it confusing when the preacher or teacher they are listening to reads from a Bible version different from the one in which they are reading. Sometimes the versions are nearly identical. On the other hand, sometimes they are so different that it is hard to believe they translated from the same Hebrew text. This is a question of the modern English *versions* of Scripture.

To illustrate the issue, compare the following versions of 1 Kgs 20:11.

Figure 4.6: Six Versions of 1 Kgs 20:11

KJV 1611	And the king of Israel answered and said, Tell him, Let not him that girdeth on his harness boast himself as he that putteth it off.
LB 1971	The king of Israel retorted, "Don't count your chickens before they hatch!"
NIV 1984	The king of Israel answered, "Tell him: 'One who puts on his armor should not boast like one who takes it off.'"
NASB 1995	Then the king of Israel answered and said, "Tell him, 'Let not him who girds on his armor boast like him who takes it off."
NLT 1996	The king of Israel sent back this answer: "A warrior still dressing for battle should not boast like a warrior who has already won."
NET 1998	The king of Israel replied, "Tell him the one who puts on his battle gear should not boast like one who is taking it off."

Here are some questions for you to consider and discuss:

1. What differences do you notice?

2. Which versions seem to be most literal?

3. Which one changes the imagery? Is that significant?

4. Which version is easier for you to understand? most interesting? most easily memorized?

5. From which versions would you prefer to do detailed Bible study? simple rapid devotional reading?

Remember: a version is rendering from one language into another and a paraphrase is rewording within the same language. To deal with this issue, we'll look at the task of translation.[7]

---

[7] For a good analysis of this issue, see Gordon P. Fee and Mark L. Strauss, *How to Choose a Bible Translation for All its Worth* (Grand Rapids: Zondervan, 2007). For a different view also held by evangelical scholars, see Wayne Gruden et al., *Translating Truth* (Wheaton, Ill: Crossway, 2005).

The Task of Translation

The process of translation is quite complicated (see Figure 4.7). It begins with the original text and ends with a target text (the translation) in the language of the intended audience. In between is the original meaning the author intended. The black arrows track the translator's task. The first arrow involves the interpretation of the original text to ascertain the author's original meaning. The second arrow involves the interpretation of the target language (and culture) with the intention that the target text will communicate to the modern reader as nearly as possible the same meaning as the author intended. In the figure, the closer the two circles, the better.

Figure 4.7: Overview of the Translation Process

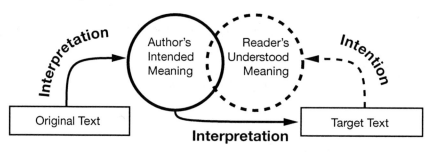

The process indicated by Figure 4.7 points out some of the issues involved in translation. The first is the quality of the text. How close is it to the original? This is the issue of textual criticism. Second, there are always differences between the original language and the target language. Translators must make choices on how they are going to deal with these differences. What are the translation principles, more formal or more functional? How can the translator bring the circle of "Reader's Understood Meaning" to coincide more closely with the "Author's Intended Meaning"? Third, since the translator must interpret the original text to determine the author's intended meaning as well as interpret the language of the target text, *every translation is an interpretation.*

This need not cause undo concern. First, our English translations are very well done; i.e., the centers of the circles in Figure 4.7 are pretty close. Second, the difference in circles is true of all human communication. Think of the many times you and a friend or spouse have had a breakdown in communication.

This is also true for readers of the Bible. We would have the same problem even if we were studying full Hebrew – or even if God were speaking to us orally! The good news is, though, that even though there is always a gap, communication still happens with excellent results. When a mom tells her three-year-old not to play in the street, the child knows what not to do. That doesn't always translate into obedience, however. How often God's people are just like children. We usually understand the Bible well enough to understand what behavior is pleasing to God, but that doesn't always translate into obedience.

Why So Many Translations?

We have an embarrassing wealth of translations of the Bible into English. What reasons are there for new translations?

- An improved Greek and Hebrew text base. As the results of textual criticism improve our original text, new translations or revisions may be called for.

- Different target audiences. Some translations cater to different English speakers: adults, children; long-time Christians, non-Christians; native and non-native English speakers.

- Different translation principles. Some translations strive to be more formal while others strive to be more functional. Formal translations (sometimes referred to as "literal" or "word-for-word") try to retain the structure (or *form*) of the original language as much as possible. Functional translations (sometimes referred to as "free" or "sense-for-sense") try to convey the meaning (or *function*) of the original text into the closest meaning of the target text.

- Increased learning about languages, ancient and modern. There has been progress just in the last few decades in understanding both Greek and Hebrew. This has an effect on the possible quality of translations.

- Changes in style and vocabulary of target language. For example, the word *conversation* now means talking between two or more people. Four hundred years ago it meant manner of life.

- Different intended use and audience. For example, is it intended for close study or for devotional use, public reading or private study, adults or children, more educated or less, the seeing and hearing or the blind and deaf?

One final question! Can we have confidence in our English Bible? Solidly, yes. Our modern English (including KJV) translations are very well done. The information in this chapter has explained why there are differences between translations: text base, target audience, translation principles, increased learning about Hebrew, changes in English, and intended use. The careful Bible student will compare versions. An awareness of the issues involved, such as we have treated here, should enhance such comparison. The bottom line is that when people pick up an English Bible, they can safely regard what they hold in their hands to be the authoritative Word of God.

Exercises

1. Briefly define the following terms:

    a. Autograph

    b. MT

    c. Version

    d. LXX

    e. Textual criticism

2. How would you explain why English translations are so different to a group of Christians who has not read anything on the topic?

WEEK 3

Roots, Clauses, and Function Words

CHAPTER 5

Getting to the Root of the Matter
Hebrew Word Roots

Objectives

1. Understand that most Hebrew words are formed from a three-letter root
2. Understand how roots are altered to form different kinds of words
3. Understand how different Hebrew lexicons are arranged
4. Learn how to use the *SNIVEC*

Tools Used: *SNIVEC*

Introduction

In chapter three we introduced the concept that most Hebrew words are built on three-letter roots that have a basic abstracted meaning. At that point we were talking about adding vowels to identify specific meanings or uses (see Figure 3.1). In this chapter, I want to show you a little more about word formation and how this affects Hebrew vocabulary as well as some aspects of modern study (the arrangement of lexicons and the performance of word studies). Before we begin, I need to introduce you to the Hebrew parts of speech and the qualities or characteristics of each.

Hebrew Parts of Speech

Below are two figures that we will use again in future chapters. The first figure lists the parts of speech in Hebrew. We can classify these into three basic categories: nominals, verbals, and function words. Within each class are various kinds of words. Note Figure 5.1: Hebrew Parts of Speech:

Figure 5.1: Hebrew Parts of Speech

Nominals	Verbals	Function Words
Nouns	Verbs	Article
Pronouns	Infinitives (Verbal Noun)	Conjunctions
Adjectives	Participles (Verbal Adjective)	Prepositions
		Adverbs

Nominals and verbals are distinctive and have their own set of grammatical qualities, which will be described in the next paragraph. Function words lack these grammatical qualities.

Figure 5.2 summarizes the grammatical qualities of verbals and nominals. If you were learning full Hebrew, you would learn to parse Hebrew words. "To parse" means to describe all the grammatical qualities of a word. We will expand the figure as our knowledge of Hebrew grammar grows. For now it's enough to explain the elements of the chart. "Nn" means "noun" and "V" means a Finite Verb. The marks in the boxes indicate the features that nouns and verbs have. In the coming chapters we will cover these grammatical qualities in more detail and instead of simple Xs, you will actually be able to label specific information.

Figure 5.2: Parsing Information for Nominals and Verbals

			← Verbal Qualities →					← Nominal Qualities →			
PoS	Word	Lex	Stem	Form	P	G	N	State	Det	Case	Suff
Nn						X	X	X	X	X	
V			X	X	X	X	X				

1. **PoS** - Part of Speech. This column is used purely for educational purposes. When I use a variation of this chart for my Hebrew students, I have students give the verse number instead of PoS. They learn to complete this chart for every type of word. You, as a student of "pre-Hebrew," will gather most of this information from Bible study tools.

2. **Word** - the word as it actually appears in the Hebrew Bible.

3. **Lex** - the lexical form is the word as it appears in a dictionary.

4. **Stem** - a characteristic of Verbs (see ch. 13).

5. **Form** - another characteristic of Verbs. I use the term *Form* to include either the Tense/Mood of the Finite Verb (chs. 14-16) or the non-finite forms, Participles and Infinitives (ch. 17).

6. **P** - stands for Person, a quality of finite verbs and, of course, Personal Pronouns.

7. **G** - stands for gender, a grammatical quality that is only generally related to sex. Note the overlap here of Nominal and Verbal Qualities headings. In Hebrew, both nouns and verbs have gender.

8. **N** - stands for number. This also is a quality shared by both nouns and verbs.

9. **State** - is the quality of nouns; they are either Absolute or Construct (ch. 11).

10. **Det** - stands for Determination or definiteness. A noun is definite when it has the article, but that is not the only time (ch. 10).

11. **Case** - is the grammatical function of nouns or noun substitutes in a clause (ch. 11).

12. **Suff** - stands for Suffix and refers to Pronouns attached to the end of other words (ch. 11).

Tri-literal Roots

Hebrew word formation is a bit different from English word formation. Most Hebrew words are built from tri-literal roots. **Tri-literal** means "three letter." The **root** is a theoretical reconstruction of the simplest part of a word that has meaning. It is what is left once all the vowels, prefixes, suffixes, and infixes are removed. So in the example we gave in Figure 3.1, the root דבר has something to do with making words. How a speaker pronounces the vowels or adds other things to the root determines whether the words are things (nouns) or actions (verbs).

Roots are theoretical in the sense that they are never found in a real text or speech. Even in unpointed texts the words must be pronounced with vowels. What we do see in a pointed text, of course, are the real words. Look at the following list of words:

Figure 5.3: Words Built from the Root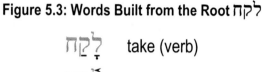

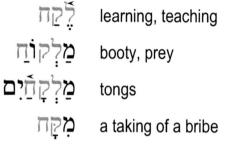

לָקַח	take (verb)
לֶקַח	learning, teaching
מַלְקוֹחַ	booty, prey
מֶלְקָחַיִם	tongs
מִקָּח	a taking of a bribe

These words all have in common the idea of taking or receiving something. They also all have in common the same three consonants: לקח, seen in grey type. Because of this, scholars assume that these three letters form a root meaning common to all these words.

I need to point out one more thing: notice that in the last example, the ל seems to have disappeared. Actually it has been replaced by a Dagesh Forte. There are a number of letters that do strange things in Hebrew. If you were learning full Hebrew, you would learn the ways some letters behave under various circumstances. Because of the tools that are now available to the English-only reader, you will still be able to find roots of words successfully. All you need to know is that sometimes letters may drop out.

Hebrew Roots and Vocabulary

One way we change the meaning of words in English is by adding prepositions. Greek forms compound verbs similarly. For example, if we are simply moving, we use the word "go." If we are ascending, we add the proposition "up"; if we are leaving, we add the preposition "out," etc. Greek can accomplish the same thing by attaching prepositions to the beginning of words. At times Hebrew uses prepositions after words to specialize meaning, but much more often uses completely different roots.

Below is a figure giving English, Greek, and Hebrew verbs of motion. The English is dictionary form is "go" (the Infinitive "to go" without the "to"); the Greek lexical form is "I go" (the Present Active Indicative first person singular); the Hebrew lexical form is "he went" (the Qal Perfect third person masculine singular; this will make sense later). I have put English and Greek prepositions in bold type to define the preposition for you.

Figure 5.4: Comparison of English, Greek and Hebrew Word Formation

English	Greek	Hebrew
go	ἔρχομαι	הָלַךְ
go **in**	εἰσέρχομαι	בוֹא
go **out**	ἐξέρχομαι	יָצָא
go **away**	ἀπέρχομαι	עָזַב
go **near**	προσέρχομαι	קָרַב

I have simplified things a bit. For example, a given Hebrew word may function in more than one category. But notice the way Hebrew uses completely different roots to indicate the different directions for movement.

Nominal and Verbal Formation [1]

Hebrew nominals and verbals can be derived from three sources (see Figure 5.5).

Sometimes verbs are derived from nouns and are called "denominatives." An example of this in English is the verb "dust" derived from the noun "dust." (By the way, with respect to the verb, what is the difference between "dusting furniture" and "dusting roses"?) Occasionally nouns are derived from verbs and are called "deverbatives."

---

[1] I use the term *nominal* to mean nouns plus anything that can substitute for a noun, such as Pronouns, Adjectives, Participles, even whole clauses. I use the term *verbal* to include not only finite verbs, but the non-finite ones, Participles and Infinitives.

Figure 5.5: Hebrew Word Derivations

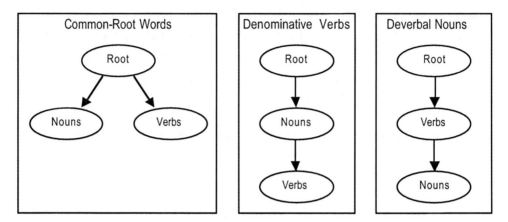

Most often nouns and verbs come from a common root. Basically, Hebrew can form new words either by changing only the vowels of a root or by also adding prefixes and suffixes to the root. We do the same thing in English, though perhaps not to the same degree. Let's begin with English, then go to Hebrew.

Take for example the word *wind*. If it's pronounced with a long-*i* so that it rhymes with *kind*, it is a verb indicating an action you might perform with a string. By adding -*ing* it becomes a Present Participle; changing the vowel to -*ou* gives *wound*, which can be either a simple past finite verb or a past participle. However, if the root *wind* is pronounced with the short-*i*, then it is a completely different word, a noun referring to the movement of air molecules (there are other meanings). By adding an -*s* the noun becomes plural; by adding -*'s* it become possessive; by adding -*s'* it is plural possessive. But then, by adding-*ed*, it becomes a verbal adjective (Past Participle) referring to someone's condition who is breathing heavily after strenuous activity.

It's kind of funny when you think about it. We make jokes this way: "How did the Polish husband figure out that his wife was trying to kill him? In her purse he found a bottle of polish remover." A spam email making the rounds every so often and called "You Think English is Easy???" collects a number of these. One particularly good one is, "The soldier decided to <u>desert</u> his <u>dessert</u> in the <u>desert</u> before he got his just <u>deserts</u>."

This is the nature of language. Hebrew does the same thing. Figure 5.6 below reproduced from chapter three illustrates the first method, simple change of vowels (ignoring the Dagesh Lene in the first consonant of each Hebrew word). The first three examples are verbals: an Active Participle (in English a Present Participle), a finite verb (English Simple Past), and an Imperative. The last two examples are nouns, both singular; translating the second one requires English to add a preposition such as *of*.

Figure 5.6: Hebrew Roots and Verb Formation

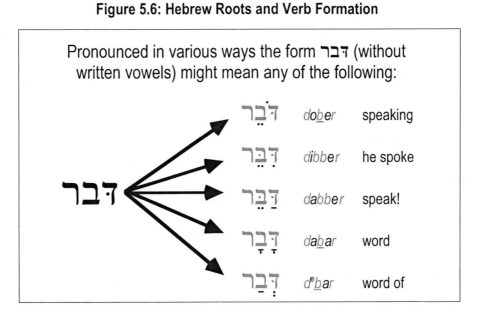

Hebrew can also add prefixes, suffixes, infixes, or various combinations. Look at the examples in Figure 5.7:

Figure 5.7: Hebrew Roots with Prefixes and Suffixes

Nouns	דְּבָרִים	words
	דְּבָרוֹ	his word
	מִדְבָּר	wilderness
	דְּבִיר	anteroom
Verbs	יְדַבֵּר	he will speak
	דִּבְּרוּ	they spoke
	דַּבְּרוּ	(you [pl.]) speak!
	מְדַבְּרִים	(those who are) speaking

As above, the gray letters are root letters. Notice that the first noun is plural, the second is singular and requires the English possessive Pronoun. Not only can a number of different words come from the same root, but sometimes there are two different roots that are identical. The third and fourth are from completely different roots with the same three letters, one with a prefix and one with an infix (an insertion in the middle of the root). Besides the root דבר having to do with words, there is another root דבר having to do with departing or destroying (G/K 1818; these "G/K" numbers identify individual Hebrew words and will be explained below), from which is formed the noun מִדְבָּר meaning "wilderness" (G/K 4497). As for the verbs, the first three are finite; the last is an active participle translated by the English present participle.

The point is that Hebrew forms its words differently than English. Still, it may form them by using similar processes (adding prepositions or prefixes), but they do different things. Hebrew words, which in an unpointed text would be identical, are distinguished in printed Hebrew Bibles by the vowel points. These points represent visually the pronunciations that the original audience would have heard in speech.

Roots and Lexical Forms

There are two terms that are often used interchangeably, *dictionary* and *lexicon*. For our purposes, it is useful to make a distinction: a lexicon is simply a dictionary between two languages. When we speak of "lexical forms," we mean the forms as they are entered in a lexicon.

For example, starting out with English, again, if you read the sentence, "He wound the bandage around his arm with the wounds," to find the verb for *wound*, we would have to look up the entry for *wind*; in English the Infinitive is the dictionary form for verbs. We would find *wounds* under the entry for *wound*; in English the dictionary form is the singular form. Now, imagine that you didn't know English well and read this sentence. If you picked up your lexicon and searched for the verb under *wound* and read the entry, "n. physical injury, emotional injury" and the next entry, "v. to injure physically or emotionally." Without knowing the dictionary form, you would become confused.

The same is true for Hebrew. You need to know that you have the right Hebrew word. Hebrew lexicons are arranged in one of two ways. The older way is to group together all of the words that come from the same root. The newer way is to list all the words alphabetically, regardless of root. For example, the noun תּוֹלֵדָה, the plural of which is translated "generations" in Genesis, comes from the root יׁלד, which as a verb means "beget." Under the older system, in order to find the noun תּוֹלֵדָה you would have to be able to identify the root and look in the י section of the lexicon, and there isn't even a Yod in the word. Under the newer system, תּוֹלֵדָה is found under the ת section of the lexicon, far away from the root יׁלד. Still, finding the lexical form can be a challenge, but there are many helpful tools today. We will discuss this in the chapter on word studies.

Other Roots

The vast majority of Hebrew words come from tri-literal roots. However, there are a small number of common words that come from bi-literal roots. Rarely quadri-literal (four-letter) roots appear. Here is a short list of examples.

Figure 5.8: Words with Bi- and Quadri-literal Roots

Nouns with Bi-literal Roots		Nouns with Quadri-literal Roots	
יָד	hand	עַקְרָב	scorpion
דָּם	blood	אַלְמָנָה[2]	widow
אָב	father		
אָח	brother		

Finding Roots

It is important for you to grasp the concept of roots, because many commentators will make reference to them and there may be times when you will want to find the root of a word. Finding them is actually quite simple. Here are three ways.

Using an Exhaustive Concordance

I am assuming that most readers of this book know what a concordance is and have used an exhaustive concordance at least a little. So, here I'm going to explain only briefly the *Strongest NIV Exhaustive Concordance (SNIVEC)*

---

[2] The ה ending marks the feminine gender and is not a root letter.

The *SNIVEC* contains three main parts:

1. The main **Concordance**, which is the bulk of the book, a listing of all the occurrences of each English word in the NIV.

2. The **Dictionaries and Indices** of original language words listed alphabetically and numerically and arranged in three sections: (a) Hebrew in regular type numerals, (b) Aramaic in regular type numerals beginning with 10,001, and (c) Greek in italic type numerals.

3. The G/K-Strong conversion **Index** arranged in two sections: (a) Strong ➔ G/K [Hebrew, Aramaic, Greek], then (b) G/K ➔ Strong [Hebrew, Aramaic, Greek].

The Dictionary section allows you to find both roots and derivatives from the roots.

Please use an *SNIVEC* to follow this example. Suppose you are reading Gen 5:1 in the NIV, "This is the written **account** of Adam's line." So you look up "account" in the Concordance section (p. 12), find the reference to Gen 5:1, and note the number identifying your Hebrew word, 9352. Next you turn to that part of the Dictionary section that lists Hebrew words and find the entry with your number (p. 1507), which reads:

> **9352** תּוֹלֵדוֹת *tôlēdôt*, n.f.pl. [39] [√3528]. account, record, genealogy, family line, records (14), account (10), listed genealogy (3) genealogical records (2), genealogy (2), account of line (1), account of the family (1), birth (1), descendants (1), family line (1), genealogical record (1), lines of descent (1), order of birth (1)

Following the G/K number, 9352, is the word in Hebrew (which you can now read), the transliteration (which you no longer need), then grammatical information (noun, feminine, plural), and frequency in brackets (the Hebrew word occurs 39 times in the OT) and then also in brackets the root symbol, √, and the G/K number for the root. That's it!

Once you have found the root, you can now look up your word in Bible reference works that are not coded to Strong's or to G/K numbering systems. Also, just within the *SNIVEC*, you can now look up G/K 3528 in the Lexicon section, p. 1416, and see that the root is יָלַד. There is no root symbol (because you've found the root), but in brackets an arrow, ➔, listing all of the words derived from the root יָלַל, or what we might call the word family. When you do word studies, you want to stick with your word. But when you want to study a word with too few occurrences to give you an accurate range of meaning, fewer than 20 or so, it *may* be helpful to study other words from the family. But even in this case, you will need to be very tentative in your conclusions and rely more on the experts. We'll discuss this more in the chapter on word studies.

Using an Interlinear Bible

The word *interlinear* means "between the lines." So a traditional interlinear OT gives an English translation between the lines of the Hebrew text. There are two main books like this in print:

> Green, Jay P., ed. *The Interlinear Bible: Hebrew-Greek-English.* 2nd ed. 1985; rpt., Peabody, Mass.: Hendrickson, 2005. (*IBHGE*)

> Kohlenberger, John R., III. *The NIV Interlinear Hebrew-English Old Testament.* 1985; rpt., Grand Rapids: Zondervan, 1993. (*NIVIHEOT*)

Both give the Hebrew text according to the Masoretic tradition first and below the text a literal translation of the Hebrew. The chief differences lie in the Hebrew text base and in formatting details.

The Hebrew text base of the *IBHGE* is (presumably, he doesn't actually state it) the Second Rabbinic Bible, which was used as the text base for the KJV. The base for the *NIVIHEOT* is the *Biblia Hebraica Stuttgartensia* (*BHS*), which is used as the text base for most modern translations.

In terms of formatting, the *NIVIHEOT* gives in parallel the NIV. The *IBHGE* includes a parallel literal translation prepared by Green (for the NT he uses the KJVII, a version that was new at the time, but never became popular). In addition, the *IBHGE* places above each Hebrew word its *Strong's Concordance* number. This is a handy feature; once you locate your Hebrew word, you immediately know the Strong's number, which gives you the lexical form and ultimately the root by means of an exhaustive concordance.

Using Electronic Sources

The *NIVIHEOT* does not give you G/K numbers, but you will still want to find that information. You can use the process described above for *SNIVEC*, or perhaps better, you can use an electronic Bible study program. There are many programs that provide this information in a reliable, usable format. Pradis, the software by Zondervan, has windows that make all that information immediately available. In addition, there are links to all the Zondervan products in electronic format. In Logos Research Systems, simply hovering the cursor over a Hebrew word causes a pop-up window to appear that provides the root plus other information.

If you have already studied Bill Mounce's *Greek for the Rest of Us*, you probably used his book, *Interlinear for the Rest of Us*, which is a reverse interlinear. A traditional interlinear Bible gives the text of the original language in the first line and below each original word the English equivalent. The result is that the English is out of order. A reverse interlinear, however, gives the English text in the first line and the original language equivalent under each English word. In this case the original language text is out of order and some system is required to indicate the order of words. As of this writing, I know of no printed reverse interlinear for the Old Testament. Logos Bible Software, however, does have a reverse interlinear for the whole Bible. It is available for ESV and NRSV. This features a text in four lines. The first line is English according to the version of choice (they are continuing to add more). The second gives the Hebrew text according to BHS. The third line is the lexical form of the word. The last line is the grammatical labeling (tagging) for each word. Here is Gen 1:1 from the Logos Research Systems:[3]

Figure 5.9: The Logos ESV English-Hebrew Reverse Interlinear

In	the	beginning,	God	created	•	the	heavens	and	•	the	earth
בְּ₁ →		רֵאשִׁית₂	אֱלֹהִים₃	בָּרָא₄	אֵת₅	הַ₆	שָׁמַיִם₇	וְ₈	אֵת₉	הַ₁₀	אֶרֶץ₁₁
ב		ראשׁית	אלהים	ברא	אות	ה	שׁמים	ו	אות	ה	ארץ
PB		NCsSFC	NPDSMN	VqAsSM3	PA	XD	NCcDMNH	CC	PA	XD	NCcSFPH

---

[3] Chip McDaniel and C. John Collins, *The ESV English-Hebrew Reverse Interlinear Old Testament*, Genesis 1:1 (Logos Research Systems, Inc., 2006) containing The Holy Bible, English Standard Version (Wheaton, Ill.: Crossway, 2001).

Notice the following:

1. The dots (•) in the English text indicate places that have no English translation for the Hebrew word below. [4]

2. The Hebrew words have subscript numbers to indicate the word order of the Hebrew text. Further, the Hebrew words are sometimes divided into parts.

3. In the second line the arrow (➜) under the first occurrence of *the* points to the Hebrew word that contains the notion of the English word, when there is no separate Hebrew equivalent.

4. The grammatical tagging in the fourth line looks complicated, but in Logos the definitions become visible in a box when the mouse is hovered over the abbreviations.

Exercises

1. Using the *SNIVEC*, find the roots to the following nouns. For each word give a definition, its G/K number, the G/K number of the root and a definition. The first one is done as an example.

Word	Definition	G/K	G/K of √	Definition of Root
a. אַדֶּרֶת	cloak	168	158	to prove powerful
b. טְרֵפָה *t reat*				
c. טְמֵאָה				
d. קָדֵשׁ *place* *Kadesh*				

---

[4] You should not worry that the translators left out something. We will learn more about this later, but for now it is enough for you to know that the Hebrew word marks the following word as the direct object and does not have any content. This Hebrew mark for the direct object is represented in English by word order, rather than by an English word.

e. תּוֹדָה

f. מֶרְכָּבָה   *m ey r ko b* (ᵃ)

2. Proper names in the OT are often combinations of words, frequently words referring to God. The *SNIVEC* defines the names for you. Verify their definitions: (1) copy the name in Hebrew, (2) write the G/K number and (3) below it its definition from the *SNIVEC* lexicon, (4) list the G/K numbers of the components of the name, and (5) below each of these write the definitions. The first one is done for you as an example.

   a. Abram

Hebrew	G/K # of Name + Definition	G/K Num of components + Definitions
אַבְרָם	92/exalted father	3+8123/father + to be high

   b. Abimelech

Hebrew	G/K # of Name + Definition	G/K Num of components + Definitions

   c. Melchizedek

Hebrew	G/K # of Name + Definition	G/K Num of components + Definitions

   d. Zedekiah

Hebrew	G/K # of Name + Definition	G/K Num of components + Definitions

   e. Joel

Hebrew	G/K # of Name + Definition	G/K Num of components + Definitions

   f. Elijah

      Hebrew   **G/K # of Name + Definition**   **G/K Num of components + Definitions**

   g. Isaiah

      Hebrew   **G/K # of Name + Definition**   **G/K Num of components + Definitions**

   h. Hoshaiah

      Hebrew   **G/K # of Name + Definition**   **G/K Num of components + Definitions**

3. Hebrew often uses wordplay, similar to puns we make in English. Of course, these are completely lost in translation. Many English Bibles, however, do draw attention to these in footnotes. Using the tools and methods explained above (try different ones), identify the two similar words that the author is playing on by (1) copying the words in Hebrew as they appear in the Hebrew Bible, (2) giving the G/K and Strong's numbers, and (3) writing the G/K numbers for the roots. Then explain the wordplay. You may check your work by seeing if your Bible has a footnote explaining the play. The first one is done as an example. For confirmation, see the notes in the NET Bible (available on line at http://www.bible.org/netbible)

   a. Explain the wordplay of the bold words in Jer 1:11-12 using a traditional interlinear and the *SNIVEC*.

      11 The word of the Lord came to me: "What do you see, Jeremiah?"

          "I see the branch of an **almond tree**," I replied.

      12 The Lord said to me, "You have seen correctly, for I am **watching** to see that my word is fulfilled."

NIV	Hebrew	G/K	Root G/K	Strong's
Almond tree	שָׁקֵד	9196	9195	8247
Watching	שֹׁקֵד	9193	(9193)	8245

Explanation: The almond tree is a symbol that God is watching Israel. There is no connection in meaning, just sound.

b. Explain the wordplay of the bold words in Gen 11:9 using any method.

9   That is why it was called **Babel** -because there the Lord **confused** the language of the whole world.

NIV	Hebrew	G/K	Root G/K	Strong's
Babel				
Confused				

Explanation:

c. Explain the wordplay in Gen 2:25-3:1a. You may find an interlinear or reverse interlinear helpful.

25 The man and his wife were both **naked**, and they felt no shame. 3:1 Now the serpent was more **crafty** than any of the wild animals the Lord God had made. (NIV)

ESV	Hebrew	G/K	Root G/K	Strong's
naked				
crafty				

Explanation:

CHAPTER 6

"Yes, Virginia, There Are . . . Clauses"

Objectives

1. Understand various types of clauses and how they differ from phrases
2. Identify different types of clauses in Hebrew
3. Flow chart subject, verb, indirect object, and direct object
4. Be motivated to make flowcharts

Introduction

Clauses are not difficult to understand. We use them all the time without need of explaining them. But when we study Scripture, we want to look at the text closely in order to understand and explain the meaning. Identifying clauses is an important part of this process. Explaining them can be tricky, though, when our memory of grammar gets a little foggy. Usually the main idea a writer wants to get across appears in a main clause. If our attention is misplaced in a secondary idea, we run the risk of misunderstanding exactly what the author intended.

In this chapter we will brush the dust off those parts of our brains that once learned clauses in English. Then we will move to the less familiar territory of Hebrew clauses. At this point we are just looking at the big picture of clauses. We will get to the finer points within the clauses in later chapters.

Finally, we will learn a system of flowcharting. Flowcharting is a simplified form of sentence diagramming. If you were one of the few who learned and loved diagramming sentences, I hope you will find this modified form still interesting and perhaps even more useful. If you were one of the many who hated diagramming sentences (I confess that I was), clear away your prejudices and give this a try. I use this all the time in studying Scripture. Sometimes meaning becomes more clear; sometimes other options of interpretation become apparent. In either case, the text comes alive.

Clauses

We need to start with some terminology. A clause is made up of a subject and a predicate (it contains a verb or finite verbal idea; more on this in the next chapter). The subject or the verb may be present or implied, but both are required. A phrase is a word or word group that does not contain a predicate, i.e., it has no finite verb.

A sentence is made up of one or more clauses. There are two basic types of clauses: independent clauses and dependent or subordinate clauses. Just as the names imply, an independent clause can stand alone; a dependent clause "depends on," or hangs from, another clause.

An *independent clause* can be a complete sentence all by itself. Since a dependent clause by definition requires a main clause, it does not by itself form a complete sentence. When an independent has a dependent clause attached to it, this independent clause is called a main clause. The only difference between a *main clause* and an independent clause is that a main clause has one or more subordinating clauses modifying it, whereas an independent clause has no subordinate clause.

A *dependent clause* is introduced by a relative pronoun (who, which, that, etc.) or by a subordinating conjunction (words such as after, although, because, if, except, etc.). A relative pronoun introduces a relative clause and functions like an adjective. Dependent clauses introduced by subordinating conjunctions are adverbial; that is, they modify verbs. This simple concept is important to grasp, in order to understand the functions of clauses.

Study the examples below. I have numbered the sentences "S1," etc. Subjects are in bold type; the verbs or verb phrases are underlined; subordinating conjunctions are in italics.

S1. **Bill** <u>loves</u> Hebrew.

S2. *Though* **Bill** <u>loves</u> Hebrew, **he** also <u>likes</u> food.

S3. **Bill** <u>prefers</u> pizza, but **Jill** seafood.

S4. **Bill** <u>will eat</u> seafood, but <u>hates</u> raw oysters.

S5. **Oysters** <u>make</u> Bill sick.

S6. **Bill** <u>made</u> a strange facial expression, *when* he <u>ate</u> raw oysters, *because* **Jill** <u>dared</u> him.

S7. **Jill**, *who* <u>should have been</u> sorry, <u>laughed</u>, *because* **Bill** <u>made</u> a funny face.

S8. **Bill** and **Jill** <u>are</u> still friends.

S1 is an independent clause. A sentence with only one independent clause is called a simple sentence.

S2 has two verbs and subjects. Therefore there are two clauses. The first clause is introduced by a subordinating conjunction, "though," and is dependent. If someone said to you, "Though Bill loves pizza," and stopped, you would be waiting for something to complete the thought. The second clause is the main clause. A main clause plus a dependent clause forms a complex sentence.

S3 also has two clauses, but they are joined by a coordinating conjunction, "but." Both clauses are independent; this is a compound sentence. You will notice that the verb in the second clause is implied.

S4 is another compound sentence, but in the second clause the subject is implied.

S5 has two direct objects (DOs) joined by and, "Bill" and "sick." Both words refer to the same entity. Notice that "and" is not a subordinating conjunction. It is a coordinating conjunction joining elements of equal weight in the sentence.

S6 has three clauses. The main clause comes first. The first subordinate clause depends on the main clause, giving the time when Bill made the face. The second subordinate clause depends on the first subordinate clause (based on context), giving the reason that Bill ate the raw oysters.

S7 again has one main clause and two subordinate clauses. The main subject is Jill, but the comma marks an interruption in the clause. "Who" introduces a relative clause, which functions like an adjective, describing the noun, Jill. Within the relative clause "who" is the subject of the verb phrase "should have been." After a second comma the main clause resumes, and its verb is "laughed." The last clause is introduced by a subordinating conjunction "because" and is adverbial, giving the reason why Jill laughed.

S8 has two subjects and one verb. "Bill and Jill" form a compound subject. In this case, the "and" joins two nouns that both function as subjects of the verb.

Notice that the verb is a form of "to be." The subjects ("Bill and Jill") and the noun "friends" all refer to the same people. Bill and Jill are not doing something to the friends, they are the friends. So the word "friends" is not a DO; it is called a predicate noun in English.

Now that you have the general idea of how clauses function in English, you are ready to be introduced to Hebrew clauses.

Hebrew Verb and Noun Clauses

Hebrew clauses may be analyzed internally and externally. By externally, I mean how a given clause relates to surrounding clauses. By internally, I mean the nature of the verb within the clause itself. In this chapter we will look at clauses internally. There are two types of clauses based on the verb: verb clauses and noun clauses. The identity of the clause is determined by whether the verb is a form of "to be" or not "to be" (with apologies to Shakespeare) in any tense.

If the verb is anything other than a simple "to be," the clause is a verbal clause. Sentences S1–S7 above are verbal clauses; in all of these a verb other than "to be" is either present or implied (S3). This is something so familiar, I don't need to give any biblical examples right now. As in English, the verb may be omitted, especially in poetry, but these are still considered to be verbal clauses, because some verb must be understood from the context. We will treat Hebrew verbal clauses in the unit on the verb.

If, however, the verb is a form of the verb "to be," the clause is a noun clause (or verbless clause). The Hebrew verb for "to be" is הָיָה, but it has a range of meanings. When it means anything other than "to be," the clause is considered to be verbal. Its most common meaning, though, is simply "to be." A peculiarity of Hebrew is that it regularly omits the verb הָיָה ("to be"), unless there is some particular reason for including it, such as to specify time. English will almost always include it in translation. For example, if S7 were in Hebrew, the verb "are" would be omitted.

When Hebrew does omit הָיָה, translators must make a decision about the time frame (past, present, or future) based on context. I give an example of each time frame below with an English interlinear using marks to show where a verb must be understood and then the NIV with the verb in italics. Notice that in each case there is no Hebrew verb "to be" and context determines the time frame.

Past Time (Genesis 1:2)

תְהוֹם   פְּנֵי   עַל-   •   וְחֹשֶׁךְ

| the deep | the face of | over | x | and darkness |

and darkness *was* over the surface of the deep

Present Time (Leviticus 19:2)

אֱלֹהֵיכֶם   יְהוָה   אֲנִי   •   קָדוֹשׁ   כִּי

| your God | the Lord | I | x | holy | for |

for I the Lord your God *am* holy

Future Time (Ruth 1:16)

עַמִּי   •   עַמֵּךְ

| my people | x | your people |

Your people *will be* my people

Flowcharting

Bible students may use various systems for flowcharting. I hope you will find the following presentation helpful. In this chapter I will give an overview of the process. Then in subsequent chapters we will add various features to it.

The task of flowcharting has three steps: (1) identify clauses and phrases, (2) indent clauses and phrases to show relationships, and (3) label the functions of clauses and phrases. In this chapter you will learn step 1: telling the difference between a clause and a phrase. A phrase will modify some element of the clause of which it is a part. At this point I want to make sure that you can identify the clause components of a sentence and isolate them.

In flowcharting each clause and phrase gets its own line. There are four possible components of the clause line: subject (S), verb (V), indirect object (IO), and direct object (DO). As we mentioned before, the subject and verb are essential, whether they be expressed or implied (by context or the verb form itself). The indirect and direct object are optional. Anything that is not one of these four elements is either a conjunction or a modifier.

The only other things you need to know before getting started are (1) what is an indirect object (IO) and (2) how we treat subordinate clauses differently. First, the IO. Simply put, if a sentence has one, the IO is who or that which receives the direct object (DO). English indicates the IO in one of two ways, word order or in a prepositional phrase with the preposition "to." If the clause order is S – V – IO – DO, the preposition "to" is not used. If the clause order is S – V – DO – IO, English uses a prepositional phrase with "to." In the following examples, again bold words are subjects and underlined words are verbs; in addition I've used an arrow (➜) to mark the DO, a double arrow (=>) to mark the predicate noun or adjective, and italic type to mark the IO.

S9. **Bill** <u>gave</u> *Jill* ➜ the money.

S10. **Bill** <u>gave</u> ➜ the money *to Jill.*

In both cases the DO is "the money" and in both cases Jill receives the money. So Jill is the IO. Second, while main clauses are kept to the far left in the column, subordinate clauses are indented with their subordinating conjunction. Otherwise they are treated in the same way as main clauses.

When we identify clauses and phrases, we want to keep subjects, verbs, and any direct or indirect objects on the same line. Any other component is a modifier. Modifiers are indented below the element that they modify.

Helpful Techniques

There are a number of ways to make flowcharting easier. First, you can save time in typing by downloading text from an electronic Bible or from the internet. Second, there are several ways of maneuvering words. You can print out the text on paper and use scissors and tape to group clauses and phrases then physically move them around to the desired positions and tape them to a piece of paper. Far superior to this is to use a computer program that allows you to do diagramming (or flowcharting). I still like using MSWord charts. In a MSWord chart, not only can you have a product you can print out, you can also easily maneuver text. You can even use color coding. Here are the guidelines to using a MSWord chart. I recommend that you follow along trying to reproduce my figures as you read.

1. Set up the page to landscape view (in my example below I'm still in portrait view) with margins as you like them. Format Tabs to .25 inches.

2. Create a chart with two rows and three columns; the first column 2 inches, the second column .25 inches and the third column the rest.

3. Format the first row as a "Heading Rows Repeat" and label the three columns "Function," "Vs" (for verse), and "Flowchart." You may format them any way you like. For details on using MSWord charts, see their Help files. The hint my students found most helpful was learning that pressing "Tab" moves the cursor to the next box (at the end of the table pressing "Tab" will add a new row), and Ctrl–Tab inserts a Tab space within the cell.

4. Copy the desired Bible text into the flowchart box and move the verse numbers into the "Vs" column, just for sake of appearance. For shorter passages you may keep all the text in one cell. For longer passages you may wish to have a separate row for each sentence or for each verse.

In the examples below, I have prepared figures using sentences S1 through S8 from above; I used the sentence numbers in the "Vs" column. The "Function" column will be left blank for now. In the upcoming chapters you will learn how to complete this task. As you begin, you should have something that looks like this:

Figure 6.1: MSWord Chart to Begin Flowchart

Function	**Vs**	**Flow Chart**
	S1	Bill loves Hebrew.

Next, identify S – V – IO – DO and give those elements of the clause a separate line. In Figure 6.2 I used fonts and an arrow as above to mark these features. This is optional but I use it here for illustration; you should use what you find most helpful. I also separated these elements with tabs (remember: "Ctrl–Tab"). This is another way of marking the S – V – IO – DO. There is only one verb, so there is only one clause, so we keep in far left in the column. There is no IO.

Figure 6.2: MSWord Chart Identifying Clauses and Phrases

Function	**Vs**	**Flow Chart**
	S1	**Bill** <u>loves</u> → Hebrew.

At this point we are done flowcharting the sentence. Study how I treat the rest of the sentences. The exercises will give you some practice from the Bible. Here are the other sentences. See if you can reproduce them on your computer.

Figure 6.3: Example Flowcharts

Function	Vs	Flow Chart
	S1	**Bill** <u>loves</u> ➜ Hebrew.
	S2	*Though* **Bill** <u>loves</u> ➜ Hebrew, **he** also <u>likes</u> ➜ food.
	S3	**Bill** <u>prefers</u> ➜ pizza, but **Jill** ➜ sea food.
	S4	Bill <u>will eat</u> ➜ seafood, but <u>hates</u> ➜ raw oysters.
	S5	Oysters <u>make</u> ➜ Bill ⇔ sick.
	S6	Bill <u>made</u> ➜ a strange facial expression, *when* **he** ➜ <u>ate</u> ➜ raw oysters, *because* **Jill** <u>dared</u> ➜ him.
	S7	who <u>should have been</u> sorry, **Jill,** . . . <u>laughed</u> *because* **Bill** <u>made</u> ➜ a funny face
	S8	**Bill** and **Jill** <u>are</u> still ➜ friends

What Good is Flowcharting?

There are some limitations to flowcharting. It does not solve all exegetical problems, but it can help clarify the issues. Context is always the most important factor. The student of Scripture must learn to deal with other finer hermeneutical points as well. Flowcharts are least helpful (or necessary) for the simplest sentences and usually for narrative (stories). For example, no one would need to make a flowchart of S1. Even S2 through S8 are all very simple. But let me give you four reasons why flowcharts are helpful.

1. Flowcharting forces you to pay attention to relationships between clauses and phrases.

2. Sometimes flowcharting reveals options that you may not have considered. For example, in the Hebrew word order of Hab 2.4 and in the Greek quoted by Paul, the text reads: "The just by faith will live." The main clause is simple enough, but what does the prepositional phrase modify, the noun (subject) or the verb?

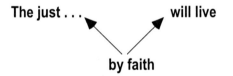

If it modifies the noun, then it means people, who are righteous by means of their faith, will live. It is similar to saying, "If people are declared just by faith, then they will live." But if it modifies the verb, then it means that those who are righteous (already) will live by means of a life of faith. The thought here is, "Those who are truly just will live lives by the principle of faith, lives characterized by faith." The student of Habakkuk and Romans needs to determine which meaning is intended based upon the context.

3. Another value is the ability to compare versions. Considering the various possible interpretations possible from all the translations boggles the mind and illustrates the difficulty of the text.

4. The greatest benefit, however, is for expository preaching and teaching. Once you have completed your flowchart and labeling, you can derive sermonic questions from the "answers" you have discovered and get points

from the text. The thesis statement of a sermon or devotion might be derived from the main clause and its context. Subpoints might come from the subordinate clauses. Take Deut 32:46, for example. A flowchart might look like this (I have omitted the "Function" column for sake of space):

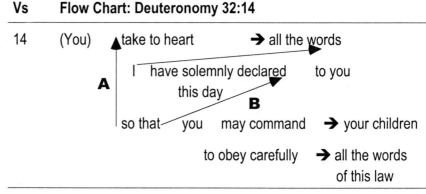

Vs   Flow Chart: Deuteronomy 32:14

The main clause is a command (the implied subject is you, which I have placed in parentheses) by Moses to the people to take to heart (I'm treating "take to heart" all together as a verb phrase) his teaching. This command answers the question, "What are we supposed to do?" The second clause explains "all the words" to mean the law that he had just recited to the people. It answers the question, "What words are we to take to heart?" The third clause is introduced by the subordinating conjunction "so that" and gives the purpose. It modifies a verb in a previous clause. It might modify either of the two preceding clauses. If it modifies the main clause (option A), it answers the question "Why should we take these words to heart?" If it modifies the relative clause (option B), it answers the question "Why am I declaring these things to you?" Sermonizing would develop the application of these points. A teacher or preacher looking for a quick outline could do worse.

Exercises

Make a flowchart for each of the passages below. You may prepare your own charts or download them from teknia.com. Be sure to keep all clause elements on the same line, indent subordinate clauses, and place all modifiers either above or below the line (don't worry about indenting them for now). The first one is done as an example. If you wish, you may mark S, V, IO and DO in some way.

1. Gen 1:1 – "In the beginning God created the heavens and the earth."

Function	Vs	Flow Chart: Genesis 1:1		
	1	In the beginning		
God			<u>created</u>	➔ the heavens
				and
				➔ the earth

2. 2 Sam 7:9b – "Now I will make your name great."

3. Amos 1:5a – "I will break down the gate of Damascus;"

4. Mal 2:5b – "and I gave them to him;"

5. Amos 4:6a – "I gave you empty stomachs in every city"

6. 1 Sam 18:27a – "David and his men … killed two hundred Philistines."

CHAPTER 7

Wow!
The Conjunction Waw and Friends

Goals

1. Learn conjunctions and their functions
2. Label the functions of conjunctions in flowcharts

Tools Used: Interlinear Bible (electronic or paper)

Introduction

We mentioned in the previous chapter that Hebrew clauses may be classified internally, i.e., by the type of verb in the clause, or they may be classified externally. By "externally" I mean how the clause in question relates to surrounding clauses. Languages that tend to link subordinating clauses to main clauses are called *syntactic* languages. English and Greek are syntactic languages. It is common in these languages to string together series of clauses using subordination. Paul is famous (or infamous among Greek students) for very long Greek sentences with all sorts of subordination.

Languages that link clauses together by coordination instead of subordination are called *paratactic*. Hebrew is paratactic. It does have subordinate conjunctions to introduce subordinate clauses, but more commonly Hebrew joins together clauses by a coordinating conjunction. The most common word in the Hebrew Bible is the coordinating conjunction Waw. It occurs over 50,000 times in the OT! Interestingly, even though it's considered a coordinating conjunction, the Waw can also mark structures that are subordinate. So even though Hebrew is paratactic, Hebrew uses various coordinating arrangements to communicate subordinate ideas. These will be covered in the coming chapters. You simply need to identify the three structures of Hebrew main clauses and the main functions of one of those structures.

In this chapter we will look first at English conjunctions and how they function. Then we will look at Disjunctive Clauses in Hebrew and the functions of Waw in these situations. Finally, we will look at labeling the functions of these clauses in flowcharts.

English Conjunctions and Functions

Conjunctions are words that join clauses, words, or phrases. As we've seen, there are two types. A coordinating conjunction joins clauses, words, or phrases of equal "weight" (see examples S3, S4, and S7 from the last chapter). Subordinating conjunctions introduce clauses that depend on another word or clause. The clause on which it depends may be either main or subordinate.

What you ultimately need to do is describe the function of clauses. To do this, you must familiarize yourself with conjunctions and what they mean. To aid you I have prepared three figures below. The first one identifies the more common English coordinating conjunctions; the second identifies the more common subordinating conjunctions. These figures list the conjunctions in alphabetical order and give their possible functions. Coordinating conjunctions are also in bold type. Words that may be used either as conjunctions or prepositions are followed by an asterisk (*). Some conjunctions may also function as adverbs; these are not marked. When you encounter a conjunction, simply find it on the list and write the function in the first column of your chart parallel to the conjunction. If there is more than one alternative, you will have to determine what the author meant based on context. That is part of the fun!

Figure 7.1: Coordinating Conjunctions and Functions

Word	Functions	Word	Function
and	Continuation, Addition	however	Contrast
but	Contrast	yet	Contrast
for*	Cause, Explanation, Example	or	Explanatory, Alternative (inclusive or exclusive)

Figure 7.2: Subordinating Conjunctions and Functions

Word	Function	Word	Function
after*	Time - prior	except	Restrictive
although	Contrast, Concession	for example	Example
as	Comparison, Manner	hence	Result
as ... as	Measure/degree, Comparison	however	Contrast
as ... so	Comparison	if	Condition
as a result	Result	in order that	Purpose/result
as if	Manner	inasmuch as	Cause
as long as	Extent, Cause	just as	Comparison
as soon as	Time	just as ...so	Comparison
as though	Manner	lest	Condition (negative)
because	Cause	not only...but also	Addition
before*	Time - subsequent	now	Cause
besides	Continuative	provided (that)	Condition
both ... and	Addition	since	Time (inauguration, cause)
consequently	Result	so	Cause, Result
even as	Comparison	so also	Comparison
even if	Concession	so ... as	Comparison
even though	Concession	so that	Purpose/result

You might be wondering whether the function labels will mean anything to you. Hopefully you will understand most of the labels. Some of them, though, may not seem obvious. In order to clarify the less obvious labels, I have provided a third figure. It is a reverse index of the first two figures. This figure combines both coordinating and subordinating conjunctions into one figure, then alphabetizes the items according to function, listing the conjunctions afterward. I provide a brief explanation for each function.

Figure 7.3: Function Explanations for Conjunctions

Function	Explanation
Addition	Attaching of things or actions not in sequence; common in lists. **Words**: and; both … and; not only … but also
Alternative	(Exclusive) Alternative exclusive means A or B, but not both A and B. **Words**: whether … or
Alternative	(Inclusive) Alternative inclusive means A and/or B. Or in English can function either way. Context must decide. **Words**: or
Cause	The clause so introduced is the cause of the action/state of another clause. **Words**: as long as; because; inasmuch as; now; since; so; whereas; why; for*
Comparison	Marks an item as similar to a previous item. **Words**: as; as … as; as … so; even as; just as; just as …so; so … as; so also; than
Concession	Introduces a clause recognized as compatible with the main clause, when at first glance it might appear that they are incompatible. **Words**: although; even if; even though; though; unless; while; yet
Condition	Introduces a situation necessary for the fulfillment of another clause. **Words**: if; provided (that); unless
Continuation	Marks a clause as sequential (in time) or consequential (logically). **Words**: and; besides; [untranslated]
Contrast	Marks a clause in opposition to another clause. **Words**: although; but; however; whereas; yet
Example	Marks an illustration of a previous thought **Words**: for example; for*
Explanation	Introduces a clause that explains a previous clause. **Words**: for*; or
Extent	Marks the limit of something. **Words**: as long as; till; until*
Inference	Not to be confused with the Adverb of time, the conjunction then marks the main clause, whose fulfillment depends on the fulfillment of a conditional clause. **Words**: then

Manner	Marks the method or attitude in which an action was done. **Words**: as; as if; as though
Measure/degree	Marks or compares the quantity of something. **Words**: as ... as; than; that
Place	Indicates the location of an action. **Words**: where(ever)
Purpose/result	Introduces a clause indicating the intent of the agent of an action. (Compare Result) **Words**: in order that; so that; that
Restrictive	Marks an item as excluded from the main clause **Words**: except
Result	Introduces a clause indicating the likely outcome of an action. (Compare Purpose) **Words**: as a result; consequently; hence; so; then, lest (negative);
Time	Marks the time of an action. **Words**: as soon as; when(ever)
Time (inauguration)	Marks the time of the beginning of the action in the main clause. **Words**: since
Time (prior)	Marks a clause whose action occurs prior to the action of the clause it modifies. Words: after*
Time (simultaneous)	Marks a clause whose action occurs at the same time as the action of the clause it modifies. **Words**: while
Time (subsequent)	Marks a clause whose action occurs after the action of the clause it modifies. **Words**: before*
Time (termination)	Marks the time of the end of an action in the main clause, without indicating a resulting change in state. **Words**: until*

First, do not memorize any of these figures (whew!). Second, skim over the list of conjunctions one or two times so that you can recognize them as conjunctions and know whether they are coordinating or subordinating. Third, when you are labeling the functions to your flowchart, consult the figures to put in the correct label and to understand the meaning of the label. These figures are suggestive. If none of the categories above seem to fit a word, consult a good English dictionary.

Feel free to add your own categories. After using the figures a while, you will find less need to consult them.

Waw: King of Conjunctions

In the last chapter we mentioned that clauses may be classified externally by the way they are joined together. There are two basic ways that clauses are joined: with a conjunction or without a conjunction. A conjunctive structure exists when two words, phrases, or clauses are joined by a conjunction. An asyndetic structure (the noun you are more likely to read is *asyndeton*) exists when two words, phrases, or clauses simply sit next to each other without a conjunction. (By the way, the word *asyndeton*, of Greek derivation, means "without conjunction"; the word *conjunction* is derived from Latin). Asyndeton is less common than conjunction. It is found mostly in poetry or reported speech. In these cases the writer expects the reader to understand the logical connection between clauses.

Position and the Range of Meaning for Waw

With only a few exceptions, anytime a Hebrew word begins with a Waw, that Waw is the conjunction. Waw is classified as a coordinating conjunction. But it may also introduce a subordinate clause. Waw is such a common and important feature of Hebrew that you will need to spend some time learning about it.

The conjunction Waw never stands alone, but is always prefixed to a word, even before any other prefixes that might be attached. For example, דָּבָר means "word" or "a word"; וְדָבָר means "and a word"; וְהַדָּבָר means "and the word" (הַ is the article; see ch. 10).

Range of Meaning for Waw

Waw is very flexible. The *SNIVEC* translates the Waw conjunction well over 50 different ways! Because of this flexibility it is difficult to classify its uses. Here is a chart listing *some* of its functions. To get an idea of the English words that might be used to express these functions, I give in the final column a list of English glosses. See also Figure 7.3 above. By far the most common uses are addition and continuation.

Figure 7.4: Functions of Waw

	Functions	English Glosses
Coordinating	Addition	and, also
	Alternative	or
	Continuation	and, then, [untranslated]
	Contrast	but
	Emphatic	indeed, even
	Explanation	namely
Subordinating	Cause	because
	Result	so that, so

You probably won't use Figure 7.4 very often. Its purpose is to show that Waw may introduce coordinating or subordinating clauses. More importantly, Waw is a structure marker. Its meaning is determined by structure and context. When a clause begins with ו + Finite Verb, it is a conjunctive clause. When a clause begins ו + non–verb (e.g., noun, pronoun, participle, etc.) the clause is disjunctive. We will look at these more closely in ch. 20 on Prose.

Other Conjunctions

The Waw conjunction is certainly the most common conjunction in Hebrew. There are other conjunctions, but none of them are prefixed; they are independent words or word clusters. The rest are subordinating conjunctions. Since you are learning pre–Hebrew, you don't really need to study the others. However, it might be helpful to see some examples. Here are three common conjunctions and their most common functions. For English words with the same function, compare Figure 7.3 above.

אוֹ   Coordinating conjunction joining nominals

    1. **Alternative.** Gen 44:19: "Do you have a father *or* (אוֹ) a brother?" (NIV)

כִּי   Either coordinating (1, 2) or subordinating (3–8); it may also be used as an adverb (9). Among the possible functions are the following:

1. **Explanation.** Gen 3:4–5: "You will not surely die…. *For* (כִּי) God knows that when you eat of it, your eyes will be opened …." (NIV)

2. **Contrast** (after a negative statement). Gen 17:14: "You shall *not* call her name Sarai, *but* (כִּי) Sarah shall be her name."

3. **Time** – simultaneous. Gen 4:12: "*When* (כִּי) you work the ground, it will no longer yield its crops for you." (NIV)

4. **Cause.** Gen 3:20: "Adam named his wife Eve, *because* (כִּי) she would become the mother of all living." (NIV)

5. **Condition** – of a real condition (i.e., a situation that may potentially happen). Gen 4:24: "*If* (כִּי) Cain is avenged seven times, then Lamech seventy–seven times." (NIV)

6. **Concession.** Joshua 17:18: "For you shall drive out the Canaanites, *though* (כִּי) they have chariots of iron, and *though* (כִּי) they are strong." (ESV)

7. **Result.** Gen 20:9: "How have I wronged you that (כִּי) you have brought such great guilt upon me and upon my kingdom?"

8. **Nominalizing** – this function causes a clause to be treated like a noun. Gen 3:4–5: "You will not surely die…. For God knows *that* (כִּי) when you eat of it, your eyes will be opened …." (NIV) [1]

9. **Emphasis** – this is really an adverbial function rather than a conjunctive function. Gen 22:17: "I will surely (כִּי) bless you." (NIV)

אִם Among the possible functions are the following:

1. **Condition** – of a real condition. Gen 13.9: "*If* (אִם) you go to the left, I'll go to the right; *if* (אִם) you go the right, I'll go to the left." (NIV)

2. **Concession.** Job 9:15: "*Though* (אִם) I were innocent, I could not answer him." (NIV)

---

[1] To illustrate the "nominalizing" function, notice that if you replace the whole clause "*that* when you eat of it" with a simple noun such as "the man," the sentence still makes sense ("God knows the man"). The entire כִּי clause is functioning as though it were a noun.

3. **Alternative** – this is a coordinating function used in questions to mark the second question; sometimes left untranslated. Gen 17:17: "Will a son be born to a man a hundred years old? Will (אִם untranslated) Sarah bear a child at the age of ninety?" (NIV)

כִּי אִם This word cluster can work in two ways. First, each conjunction can work independently to introduce two clauses having any of the meanings listed above. Second, the two conjunctions can work together as one compound.

1. As **two separate conjunctions**, each introducing separate clauses. Exodus 9:2–3: "*For if* (כִּי אִם) you refuse to let them go and (וְ) still hold them, behold, the hand of the Lord will fall with a very severe plague ....*" (ESV)

   Notice that the *For* (כִּי) introduces the main clause, which is found in v. 3, "behold, the hand of the Lord will fall with a very sever plague." The *if* (אִם) introduces the two conditional clauses in v. 2, which incidentally are connected by Waw conjunction.

2. **Contrast** (compound conjunction indicating a stronger contrast than כִּי). Gen 15:4: "This man will not be your heir, but (כִּי אִם) a son coming from your own body will be your heir."

Comparing Versions

At this point you are able to do some pretty sophisticated Bible study. You can compare versions and use a software interlinear for help. Because Hebrew uses the conjunction Waw so often, and because its most common meaning is addition with the translation "and," translators into English face another challenge: style. Always translating the Waw with "and" is poor style in English. To break up the monotony, translators will use different devices. Sometime they will leave it untranslated; sometimes they will use a different conjunction. Since different conjunctions have different ranges of meaning, a reader of English paying close attention to the connecting words may infer a meaning from the English that is not intended in Hebrew.

For example, in Exod 3:16–17, the Lord tells Moses to speak to the elders of Israel the Lord's message. In that message is a series of clauses, which I summarize below.

KJV	I have surely visited	… and seen	… And I have said, I will bring you up
NIV	I have watched over	… and have seen	… and I have promised to bring you up
ESV	I have observed	… and	… and I promised that I will bring you up
NASB95	I am indeed concerned	… and	… So I said, I will bring you up

There are several differences you notice and we will come to these in time. Right now I want you to focus on the beginning of the third clause, which is the beginning of v. 17. Of the eight conjunctions, *and* is used seven times. The *and* used to introduce the third clause suggests the function of addition. The NASB95 translates the last one with *so*. When you check Figure 7.2, you see that *so* may function as either cause or result. Checking the context, "result" is the more likely meaning of the NASB95. The NASB95 makes explicit that the result of the Lord's concern was to say that he would bring them up. Checking an interlinear reveals that v. 17 in Hebrew begins with a ו conjunction. Figure 7.4 reveals that this meaning is within the range of Waw. You have learned that NASB95 might well give the sense.

If you were reading a version other than NASB95, you might not have been aware of the possibility of a cause–result relationship between God's concern (v. 16) and his taking action (v. 17). Since the other versions disagree with the NASB95 on this point, you might be wondering how to check up on this interpretation. Of course you may read commentaries, but in the coming chapters you will learn more to help you make a decision. This is when Bible study can be rich!

Conjunctions and Flowcharting

In the last chapter I mentioned that I treat coordinating conjunctions differently from subordinating conjunctions. I do this because subordinating conjunctions define the adverbial function of their clauses. However, when coordinating conjunctions link clauses, they do not indicate the function of the clause; they describe the link between the clauses. Now you are ready to label the functions of both coordinating conjunctions and subordinate clauses. Here are some examples from the NIV.

Function	Vs	Flow Chart: Genesis 12:1			
	1	(You)	leave	➔ your country,	
				➔ your people,	
addition				*and*	
				➔ your father's household	
addition			*and*		
		(You)	go . . .		

The first *and* connects nouns in a list of direct objects (DO), so it is indented .25 inches under the noun phrase it follows. I determined that it functions as "addition" and wrote "addition" in the Function column parallel to its occurrence. The second *and* joins two main clauses, so it is indented .25 inches above the clause that it introduces. Again I thought it functioned as adding a command, so I wrote "addition" in the Function column.

Function	Vs	Flow Chart: Leviticus 19:2			
	2	(You)	be	holy,	
cause			*because* I	am	holy

This is a complex sentence with two clauses. The subordinating conjunction *because* introduces a subordinate clause indicating cause. The clause is indented approximately one inch with a space between columns. In the Function column I wrote "cause"; I also indented the entry because the clause is indented. This is not necessary. If you find this helpful to the eye, do it. These flowcharts are intended to be helpful. Feel free to modify my technique as you like.

Exercises

Complete flowcharts for the following passages. Label the functions of each coordinating conjunction or subordinate clause. Be sure to answer any questions after each flowchart.

1. Gen 8:21 – "Never again will I curse the ground because of man, even though every inclination of his heart is evil from childhood." (NIV)

"I will never again curse the ground because of man, for the intention of man's heart is evil from his youth." (ESV)

   a. Where the NIV reads "even though," the ESV reads "for." Briefly explain the meaning of each translation. Use the labels for Hebrew prepositions on pages 82–84.

   NIV:

   ESV:

   b. Use an interlinear to identify the Hebrew conjunction in question. Write it down: _____.

2. Judg 21:25 – "In those days Israel had no king; everyone did as he saw fit." (NIV)

3. 2 Kgs 17:7 – "All this took place because the Israelites had sinned against the Lord their God." (NIV)

   a. Use a software interlinear to identify the Hebrew word for "because." Write it down: _____.

4. 1 Sam 16:7 – "Do not consider his appearance or his height, for I have rejected him." (NIV)

   a. Use an interlinear to identify the Hebrew word for "or." Write it down: _____.

   b. Use an interlinear to identify the Hebrew word for "for." Write it down: _____.

CHAPTER 8

Prepositions Come Before

Goals

1. Be able to identify a prepositional phrase both in English and in Hebrew
2. Understand that Hebrew has prepositions that may be independent words or prefixed to other words
3. Be able to identify the functions of prepositions
4. Know how to flowchart prepositional phrases and adverbs

Tools Used: Grammatically tagged computer interlinear or paper interlinear & Davidson

Introduction

Which word are you most likely to look up in a dictionary: "occlusion" or "of"? The answer is, of course, the one whose meaning with which you are least familiar, "occlusion." But, which do you suppose has the longest, most complicated entry in your dictionary? It may surprise you that it is the little word that has the big definition. The reason for this is because prepositions have such a wide range of meaning. The same is true in Hebrew. Translating them can be difficult and depends on a number of different factors. Not only that, but the range of meaning of a given English preposition is normally very different from the range of meaning of a given Hebrew preposition.

In this chapter, I want to show you a little more about word formation and how this affects Hebrew vocabulary as well as modern study (the arrangement of lexicons and the performance of word studies).

Prepositions

Remember that a clause is made up of a subject and a predicate (something that contains a verb or finite verbal idea) and a phrase is a word or word group that does not contain a predicate, i.e., no finite verb (and therefore no grammatical subject). There are basically three types of phrases: infinitival phrases, participial phrases, and prepositional phrases. In this chapter, we cover only the last of these.

The word preposition (abbreviated "pp") means "placed (-position) before (pre-)"; i.e., a pp is placed before its object (usually a noun or pronoun). A pp plus its object constitutes a prepositional phrase (abbreviated PPhr) The symbol "(T)" refers to an optional article. This is illustrated in Figure 8.1.

Figure 8.1: Structure of Prepositional Phrases

Preposition	Object of Preposition
pp +	(T) + N
on	top
with	him
according to	the author

There are a few things to notice:

1. The article may be present between the pp and the object of the pp but is not required.

2. The object of the pp is in the objective case. English nouns are not inflected for case, but pronouns are. "He" is a pronoun in the subjective case; the objective case is "him." The pp is followed by the objective case, "him," rather than in the subjective case, "he."

3. Sometimes a word group, such as "according to," functions as a pp.

The function of a pp is to show the relationship between two words: the object of the preposition and another word outside of the PPhr. The other word may be either noun or verb. You need to conceive of the PPhr as an unbreakable unit. The role of the interpreter is twofold. You need to identify the word that the

PPhr modifies and you need to identify the function of the preposition; in other words, describe how the two words are related.

Below is a list of the most common English prepositions and the functions they can have. Words that may also function as conjunctions are marked with an asterisk (*). Note that the preposition "of" is so flexible that it is treated separately!

Figure 8.2: English Prepositions and Functions

Word	Function	Word	Function
about	Measure/degree	**in accordance with**	Cause
above	Place	**in front of**	Place
according to	Cause	**in regard to**	Reference/Respect
across	Place	**in spite of**	Concession
after*	Time	**inside**	Place
against	Dis/advantage, Place	**instead of**	Alternative/Substitution
among	Association	**into**	Place
around	Place[1]	**like**	Comparison
at	Place, Time	**near**	Place
because of	Cause	**of**	Composition, Contents[2]
before*	Place, Time	**off**	Place
behind	Place	**on**	Place
below	Place	**on account of**	Cause
beneath	Place	**only***	Restriction
beside	Place	**out of**	Cause, Composition[3]
between	Place	**over**	Place
by	Agency/means, Place	**since***	Time

---

[1] Also Reference/Respect.

[2] Also Example (that is), Objective (object of verbal idea implied by preceding noun), Source, Possession (thing possessed), Possessor, Quality, Reference/Respect , Relationship (about), Separation (from), Subjective (subject of verbal idea implied by preceding noun), Whole.

[3] Also Source.

Word	Function	Word	Function
by means of	Agency/means, Instrument	**through**	Agency/means[4]
contrary to	Dis/advantage	**to**	Destination[5]
down	Place	**toward**	Destination
during	Time	**under**	Place
except	Restriction	**until***	Extent, Time
for the sake of	Cause	**up**	Place
for*	Dis/advantage, Price	**upon**	Place
from	Source, Separation	**with**	Association, Instrument
in	Place/sphere		

The only way to work with prepositional phrases is to become familiar with prepositions. You should read over the list of prepositions until you can identify them in a text. Some prepositions may be used as conjunctions. You can tell the difference by looking to see what comes after the word. If it is a phrase (without a verb), it is a preposition. If it is a clause (with a verb), it is a conjunction.

The Structure of Hebrew Prepositions

The order of the words in a Hebrew pp is the same as in English: pp - Article (optional) - object of the pp. However, there are two ways they appear, either as prefixes or as independent words. Prepositions that are prefixed are called inseparable prepositions, because they never appear as independent words. Prepositions that are independent words are called separable prepositions.

Only three pps are inseparable, meaning that they attach to their objects as prefixes.

בְּ "in, with, by"

כְּ "like, as, according to"

לְ "to, for"

---

4 Also Destination.

5 Also Purpose, Reference / Respect.

Figure 8.3: Attaching Inseparable Prepositions to Nouns

Noun	Preposition	Prep Phrase	Translation
מֶ֫לֶךְ	בְּ	בְּמֶ֫לֶךְ	with a king
מֶ֫לֶךְ	כְּ	כְּמֶ֫לֶךְ	like a king
מֶ֫לֶךְ	לְ	לְמֶ֫לֶךְ	for a king

Most prepositions are "separable"; i.e., they stand alone. They may or may not be joined by a Maqqef (see example three below) with no change in meaning. Here are some examples:

לִפְנֵי מֶ֫לֶךְ	before a king
עַל בַּ֫יִת	on a house
אֶל־בַּ֫יִת	to a house

One preposition can be either inseperable or seperable, again with no difference in meaning:

מִן מֶ֫לֶךְ	from a king
מִמֶּ֫לֶךְ	from a king

In the first example, מִן may be followed by Maqqef. In the second example, notice that the Nun of the preposition has been assimilated into the first root letter of the noun and is represented by the Dagesh Forte. There is no difference in the meaning of the preposition מִן with either spelling.

Any of the pps can have a PrnSf attached. The way these attachments are made is beyond what we are doing here. Books and computers that give you parsing information will identify these for you.

Some Functions of a Few Hebrew Prepositions

Of the top eight most frequent words in the Hebrew Bible, prepositions occupy five spots, a total of nearly 55,000 occurrences between them! This doesn't include the sign of the direct object, which has a structure like pps, but basically has only one function. Here are the top five prepositions and a few of their main uses.

לְ

1. **Marker of Indirect Object (IO).** 1 Kgs 4:29 [Hebrew 5:9]: "God gave [untranslated לְ] Solomon wisdom and great insight" (NIV). Notice that what was given was wisdom and great insight. These are the direct objects. Solomon received them and is therefore the indirect object.

2. **Place** (אֶל [see below] is much more common than simple לְ, though לְ in compounds is commonly used for place or direction). 1 Sam 9:12: "He has just come *to* (לְ) our town today" (NIV).

3. **Dis/advantage.** Gen 47:4: "for there is no pasture *for* (לְ) your servant's flocks…" (ESV).

4. **Reference/Respect.** Exod 1:10: "Come, we must deal shrewdly *with* (לְ) them…" (NIV, ESV).

5. **Time.** Gen 21:2: "Sarah became pregnant and bore a son to Abraham *in* (לְ) his old age, *at* (לְ) the very time God had promised him" (NIV).

6. **Possession.** Gen 40:5: "… the cupbearer and the baker *of* (לְ) the king of Egypt…" (NIV).

7. **Purpose.** Gen 50:20: "God intended it *for* (לְ) good…" (NIV). Exod 13:21: "By day the Lord went ahead of them in a pillar of cloud *to* (לְ) guide them on their way and by night in a pillar of fire *to* (לְ) give them light, so that they could travel by day or night" (NIV). In the first example, the pp לְ is attached to a nominal (technically, this is an adjective being used as a noun) and in the second example the לְ marks an infinitive, just as *to* commonly does in English. Most often these expressions with the infinitive in both Hebrew and English indicate purpose. We will see more on this in ch. 17.

בְּ

1. **Place.** Gen 9:2: "They [the animals] are given *into* (בְּ) your hand" (NIV). Lev 11:33: "everything *in* (בְּ) it will be unclean" (NIV). Josh 3:11: "See, the ark of the covenant of the LORD of all the earth will go *into* (בְּ) the Jordan ahead of you" (NIV).

2. **Time.** [140 times]: "*in* (בְּ) the morning." Gen 12:4: "Abram was seventy-five years old *when* (בְּ) he set out from Haran" (NIV). In the first example, the pp בְּ is used with a noun that has to do with time. In the second example, the בְּ is attached to an infinitive. We will see more on this in ch. 17.

3. **Accompaniment.** 1 Kgs 10:2: "Arriving at Jerusalem *with* (בְּ) a very great caravan..." (NIV).

4. **Dis/advantage.** Exod 1:10: "and, if war breaks out, [they] will ... fight *against* (בְּ) us..." (NIV).

5. **Instrument.** Judg 15:16: "*With* (בְּ) a donkey's jawbone I have made a donkey out of them" (NIV).

6. **Agency/Means.** Gen 9:6: "Whoever sheds the blood of man, *by* (בְּ) man shall his blood be shed..." (NIV).

7. **Cause.** 2 Kgs 24:3: "Surely these things happened to Judah according to the Lord's command, in order to remove them from his presence *because of* (בְּ) the sins of Manasseh..." (NIV).

מִן

1. **Separation.** Ps 51:2: "Wash me thoroughly *from* (מִן) my iniquity and cleanse me *from* (מִן) my sin" (ESV). Ps 6:8 [Hebrew 6:9]: "Depart *from* (מִן) me, all you workers of evil" (ESV).

2. **Source.** Ps 68:31 [Hebrew 68:32]: "Envoys will come *from* (מִן) Egypt" (NIV).

3. **Cause.** Gen 16:10: "I will multiply they seed exceedingly, that it shall not be numbered *for* (מִן) multitude" (KJV). The word *for* here clearly means "because of."

4. **Comparison.** Josh 19:19: "Because the portion of the people of Judah was *too large for* (מִן) them, the people of Simeon obtained an inheritance in the midst of their inheritance" (ESV). Ps 84:10 [Hebrew 84:11]: "*Better* (טוֹב) is one day in your courts *than* (מִן) a thousand elsewhere" (NIV). Ps 84:11 illustrates a very common way that Hebrew expresses comparison. An adjective followed by a מִן pp.

5. **Whole (a.k.a., Partitive)**. Gen 6:2: "… and they took wives *of* (מִ) all which they chose" (KJV). The "whole" is represented by the object of the pp, *all*. The "part" is represented by the word "wives."

עַל

1. **Place**. 1 Kgs 4:29 [Hebrew 5:9]: "God gave Solomon … a breadth of insight as measureless as the sand *on* (עַל) the shore" (NIV). Josh 10:5: "The [kings] … encamped *before* (עַל) Gibeon and made war against it" (KJV). More modern translations take this example as Disadvantage. See below.

2. **Dis/advantage**. Josh 10:5: "[They; i.e., the kings] … encamped *against* (עַל) Gibeon and made war *against* (עַל) it" (ESV). Compare: "[They; i.e., the kings] … took up positions *against* (עַל) Gibeon and attacked it." (NIV)

3. **Cause**. Gen 20:3: "You are as good as dead *because of* (עַל) the woman you have taken; she is a married woman" (NIV).

אֶל

1. **Destination**. Gen 2:19: "And [God] brought them *to* (אֶל) the man…" (NIV).

2. **Place**. Gen 24:42: "I came today *to* (אֶל) the spring and said, …" (NIV).

3. **Indirect Object**. 2 Kgs 5:23: "He gave them *to* (אֶל) two of his servants, and they carried them ahead of Gehazi" (NIV). [many places]: "[A] said *to* [B]…." אֶל is commonly found after verbs of speaking indicating the person spoken to. The quotation of the words spoken actually functions as the DO of the verb, which the addressee receives.

4. **Dis/advatnage**. Gen 4:9: "Cain rose up *against* (אֶל) his brother Abel and killed him" (ESV).

Prepositions Changing the Meaning of Verbs

Some prepositions actually combine with a verb to change the meaning. When they do that, they may be understood as introducing a DO. English does this as well. For example, if you tell me, "I *worked* today," I imagine you going to a job.

But if you say, "I *worked out* today," I know that you exercised. In such situations, I like to keep the verb and preposition together as the verb phrase; *work* and *work out* simply do not mean the same.

In Hebrew similar things happen. שָׁמַע is a verb meaning "to hear," and may take a DO. For example, in Gen 3:8, "The man and the woman *heard* (שָׁמַע) the sound of the Lord God as he was walking in the garden" (NIV). On the other hand, when this verb is followed by the pp בְּ, as in שָׁמַע בְּ, the expression means "to obey," and the pp בְּ marks the DO. For example, in Gen 26:5, "because Abraham *obeyed* (שָׁמַע בְּ) my voice" (ESV), "my voice" is the object of the pp בְּ and is the DO of the verb "obeyed" (שָׁמַע בְּ).

Flowcharting Prepositional Phrases and Adverbs

There are two things to learn in this section. We have already studied how to flowchart coordinate and subordinate clauses, but in the last two chapters, we ignored prepositional phrases. We are now ready to put these into place. Prepositional phrases may modify either nouns or verbs and should be indented .25 inches above or below the word they modify.

We've worked on Gen 1:1. Now we can complete it. "In the beginning God created the heavens and the earth" (NIV).

Function	Vs	Flow Chart: Genesis 1:1		
Time	1		In the beginning	
Event		God	created	→ the heavens
				and
				→ the earth.

This is a simple sentence; i.e., one predicate with no coordinate or subordinate clauses. Notice that "in the beginning" is a pp of time, because *beginning* in this context refers to time. The interpreter must decide which element of the clause it modifies: subject, verb, or DO. Though all three are possible grammatically (remember that a PPhr may modify either a verb or a noun!), the one that makes the best sense is the verb. Therefore I indented the pp about one quarter inch to the right of the verb; I left it above the main clause, because doing that retains English word order. Notice also that I've now added the Functions in the first column. I indented "Time," because the pp is indented. To the far left I assigned the function "Event" for the independent clause. You will learn those in ch. 13.

Exercises

1. **Identifying prepositional phrases.** Circle the pp, underline the object of the pp, and write the function of each PPhr in the examples below using Figure 8.2 above; some passages may have more than one PPhr. In the "Word Modified" column, copy the word that the PPhr modifies, noting whether it is a nominal or verbal. The first one is done as an example.

Word Modified	Function	Passage
rejoice	Cause	a. "I will rejoice because of the Lord" (Hab 3:18; NET).
		b. "Go to the land I will show you" (Gen 12:1; NIV).
		c. "Serve him with wholehearted devotion" (1 Chr 28:9; NIV).
		d. The day of the Lord is near for all nations" (Obad 15; NIV).
		e. "The Lord, the God of heaven has given me all the kingdoms of the earth" (Ezra 1:2; NIV).
		f. "Yet I will wait patiently for the day of calamity to come on the nation invading us" (Hab 3:16; NIV).
		g. "If you remain silent at this time, relief and deliverance for the Jews will arise from another place" (Esth 4:14; NIV).
		h. "I will return to Jerusalem with mercy, and there my house will be rebuilt" (Zech 1:16; NIV).
		i. "And I have promised to bring you up out of your misery in Egypt into the land of the Canaanites ..." (Exod 3:17; NIV).
		j. "It [wisdom] is hidden from the eyes of every living thing, concealed even from the birds of the air" (Job 28:21; NIV).

2. **Identifying Hebrew Prepositions and functions.** (1) Write the Hebrew preposition represented by the bold typed prepositions in the following verses. Use an interlinear Bible to identify the Hebrew. If you have a grammatically tagged computer Bible, it will give you that information. If you have a printed interlinear Bible, you will need to use Davidson to identify the preposition. (2) Using the information on pp 93-95, label the function of the preposition. The first one is done as an example.

Hebrew pp	Function	Passage
בּ	time	a. "If you remain silent **at** this time, relief and deliverance for the Jews will arise **from** another place" (Esth 4:14; NIV).
		b. "... I will return **to** Jerusalem **with** mercy, and there my house will be rebuilt" (Zech 1:16; NIV).
		c. "And I have promised to bring you up **out of** your misery in Egypt **into** the land of the Canaanites ..." (Exod 3:17; NIV).
		d. "It [wisdom] is hidden **from** the eyes of every living thing, concealed even **from** the birds of the air" (Job 28:21; NIV).

WEEK 4

Nominals

CHAPTER 9

What's in a Name?
Overview of Nominals

Objectives

1. Understand the nature of nominals

2. Understand Hebrew nouns and how they compare to English nouns

3. Use information found in analytical lexicons and exhaustive concordances

Tools Used: Grammatically tagged computer interlinear or paper interlinear & Davidson

Introduction

Back in ch. 7 we put Hebrew words into three basic classes: nominals, verbals, and function words. Note Figure 9.1:

Figure 9.1: Hebrew Parts of Speech

Nominals	Verbals	Function Words
Nouns	Verbs	Article
Pronouns	Infinitives (Verbal Noun)	Conjunctions
Adjectives	Participles (Verbal Adjective)	Prepositions
		Adverbs

The last unit covered conjunctions and prepositions. In this week's study we will look at nominals and the article. In this chapter we will study nouns; ch. 10

features the article and the concept of definiteness, or as we will call it, determination; ch. 11 covers nouns and pronouns; finally, ch. 12 covers adjectives.

Nominals and Nouns

A "nominal" is any word that functions as a noun. What besides a noun can function as a noun? Well, pronouns, adjectives, participles, infinitives, prepositional phrases, or even a number. Eventually we will understand that even clauses can function as nouns. For now, however, we will limit our discussion to the basic parts of speech.

A noun is the name of a person, place, or thing. In fact, the Latin word for *noun* is *nomen* (compare with the word *nominal* above), and the Greek word is *onoma*, both of which are nouns meaning "name." Names of persons and places are "proper nouns." We capitalize these in English; e.g., Sam, Evelyn; Chicago, New York. Names of things are common nouns. English used to capitalize these, but no longer does. The "thing" may be either concrete (something you can experience with your senses, such as a flower or the sun), or it may be abstract (something you can only think of, such as beauty or friendship). Note also that the thing may refer to a person, but the emphasis will be on what type of "thing" the person is: policeman, teacher, preacher.

Hebrew nouns have five basic qualities: gender, number, state, case, and definiteness. In this chapter we treat gender and number, in the next chapter state and case, and in chapter 11 definiteness.

Here I reproduce the figure from ch. 5.

Figure 9.2: Parsing Information for Nominals and Verbals

			← Verbal Qualities →					← Nominal Qualities →			
PoS	Word	Lex	Stem	Form	P	G	N	State	Det	Case	Suff
Nn						X	X	X	X	X	
V			X	X	X	X	X				

In ch. 5 we gave an overview of the meaning of the items in this figure. Let's look at these nominal qualities in more detail.

Gender

Gender is a categorization of the various forms of nouns. Various languages have three genders labeled masculine, feminine, and neuter (which means "neither" [masculine nor feminine]). The term *common* is used for words that can be any gender without distinction.

The English system of gender is not very well defined. English pronouns carefully preserve gender, but most native English nouns do not, though some words, mostly foreign, may retain a gender-distinctive ending.

Figure 9.3: Gender in English Nouns

Gender	Pronoun	Nouns
Masculine (m)	he	boy, stallion, waiter
Feminine (f)	she	girl, mare, waitress
Common (c)	we	horse, server
Neuter (n)	it	house

Some words maintain gender loosely. For example, *car* can be neuter ("That's my car; I just waxed *it*.") or feminine (That's my car; boy, can *she* fly!"). *Hurricane* used to be feminine, but, because of recent gender sensitivity, now has a common gender (sometimes masculine, sometimes feminine).

Unlike English, Hebrew has a very careful system of gender. A Hebrew noun is either masculine or feminine; there is no neuter (unlike English and Greek). A noun never changes gender, though there are a few nouns with common gender.

It is essential to realize that grammatical gender is a separate quality from physical gender. It is true that words referring to males are normally masculine (e.g., אִישׁ, meaning "man") and words referring to females (e.g., אִשָּׁה, meaning "woman") are normally feminine, but that is not always the case. For example, the word רוּחַ is feminine in gender. It means "wind, spirit, Spirit (as in 'of the Lord')." In spite of the fact that רוּחַ is feminine, in none of these cases is the entity female.

Number

Number is the grammatical quality of singularity or plurality. English nouns have two numbers: singular and plural, normally indicated by adding *-s* or *-es*.

Figure 9.3: Number in English

singular	= one	noun + **no** ending	horse
plural	= two or more	noun + **s** ending	horse**s**

Words that come from foreign languages may retain their original plural form or they may eventually conform to English. For example, *index* is a Latin word that English adopted. The Latin plural is *indices* and English kept that. In recent years, however, English has conformed *index* into the regular pattern and *indexes* is now an accepted term. Then English has its irregular plurals. The plural of *goose* is *geese*, but the plural of *moose* is not *meese*. The plural of *ox* is *oxen*, but the plural of *box* is not *boxen*.

Hebrew nouns have three numbers: singular, dual, and plural. The dual forms would refer to two items as opposed to three or more items indicated by the plural. By the time of Biblical Hebrew, however, dual forms were restricted to things that come in natural pairs, such as eyes or ears. The plural forms, then, can refer to two or more.

Figure 9.4: Number in Hebrew

singular	(s)	= one
dual	(d)	= two
plural	(p)	= two or more

Hebrew uses the grammatical quality of number in a couple of different ways. As in English, the Hebrew singular is commonly used for what we might call a "numeric singular," i.e., one individual. Also, as in English, some nouns are collectives; i.e., a grammatically singular noun for a plural number. An example common to both English and Hebrew is *sheep*, צֹאן, which may be either a "numeric" singular or collective plural. The plural number may be used in several ways in Hebrew.

1. **Numeric Plural.** The plural number is used numerically like English, simply to mean more than one. This is by far the most common use, but there are two other uses that are important.

2. **Honorific Plural.** The plural in Hebrew can be used to indicate majesty or some kind of intensive idea. Numerous examples exist, especially terms for God, but also terms for humans. For example, in Isaiah 1:3, "the trough of its *master*," the word for "its master," בְּעָלָיו, is a grammatical plural, "its masters," but refers to one master. The most prominent example is treated in Advanced Information at the end of this chapter.

3. **Abstract Plural.** Sometimes nouns are pluralized to convert them to an abstract idea. For example, נַעַר means "boy, lad, youth"; נְעָרִים can be a numeric plural, but is also used to mean the abstract idea of "youthfulness." In Jer 3:4, the Lord says to his rebellious people, "Have you not called to me, 'My Father, my friend from my youth …?'" (NIV). Using the electronic or book tools that we have studied reveals that the word translated "youth" is a masculine plural noun. If it were a numeric plural, then the meaning would be, "My Father, a friend from among my boys." Clearly the Lord is not one of Israel's young boys!

Now for the big question: how can you tell which function of the plural is being used? Most of the time context is clear. But some passages are difficult and you as a pre-Hebrew student are not able to tell. You will have to leave this to the professionals. However, simple awareness of the concept makes it easier to comprehend discussions in commentaries.

The Absolute State

Besides number and gender, Hebrew nouns appear in either of two "states," absolute or construct. Briefly, *construct* nouns are those that are constructed to or bound to a following noun; we will deal with this issue when we study noun cases in ch. 11. The absolute state is simple because this is similar to an English noun. Nouns are called *absolute* because they can stand alone; they are not bound to a following noun.

The lexical form of a noun is the singular absolute form. This means that whenever you look up a noun in *SNIVEC*, the form that appears is the lexical form. On rare occasions, the lexical form will be plural. This occurs because there are a few nouns that do not occur in the singular. So grammarians must decide whether to make the lexical form singular, even though it doesn't exist, or leave it plural.

Summary

1. Hebrew nouns have five qualities: gender, number, state, case and determination.

2. Hebrew nouns are either masculine (m), feminine (f), or common (c).

3. Hebrew nouns are either singular (s), plural (p), or dual (d).

   a. Singular nouns may be numeric singulars or collectives.

   b. Plural nouns are usually numeric plurals. But two other important uses are the honorific plural and the abstract plural.

4. The lexical form of a noun is the singular, absolute form.

Exercises

For each bold type word in the following passages (1) write the Gender (m or f) and Number (s, d, or p) of the noun or pronoun. Use a grammatically tagged computer Bible or a paper interlinear plus Benjamin Davidson or John Owens to find out the information. (2) Indicate the use of the number as reflected in the versions: if singular, write "numeric" or "collective"; if plural, write "numeric," "honorific," or "abstract." The first one is done as an example.

GN	Use in Number		Passage
ms	collective	a.	"Let us make **man** (אָדָם) in our image ..." Gen 1:26 (NIV).
	NIV and NET	b.	"In the image of God he created **him** (אֹתוֹ);" Gen 1:27 (NIV; this is the sign of the DO with a PrnSf; the NET reads **them**).
	NIV and NET	c.	"See ... the **oppression** (וַעֲשׁוּקִים) among her people" Amos 3:9 (NIV; cf. NET **oppressive deeds**)
		d.	"behold ... the **oppressed** (וַעֲשׁוּקִים) in the midst thereof" Amos 3:9 (KJV, ESV).

GN	Use in Number		Passage
	NIV and KJV	e.	"Therefore hear, O nations; observe, O **witnesses** (עֵדָה), what will happen to them" Jer 6:18 (NIV; cf. KJV **congregation**).
		f.	"I have been with **you** (עִמְּךָ) wherever you have gone ..." 2 Sam 7:9 (NIV).
	KJV and ESV	g.	"The **upright** (מֵישָׁרִים) love thee" Song 1:4 (KJV, cf.ESV).

Advanced Information and Curious Facts:
Does the word for God teach the Trinity?

The common word for *God* in the OT is אֱלֹהִים. It is clear that the ending on this noun is masculine plural (mp). Many Christians from the second century onward have argued that the plural form proves the doctrine of the Trinity.

Number, however, is a *grammatical* quality. We must still interpret its *function*. When אֱלֹהִים is used in passages referring to the one creator God, Jews and Christians are agreed that, since Scripture clearly teaches against polytheism, this is not a numeric plural. Nor is it an abstract. This is an example of an honorific plural, or the so-called "plural of majesty." This is even more clear when the verbs used with אֱלֹהִים are verbs used with a singular subject. This conclusion rules out the possibility that the form אֱלֹהִים teaches the Trinity simply because it is grammatically plural.

Arguments for the Trinity must be made on bases other than the fact that אֱלֹהִים is a grammatical plural form. Responsible Bible students and teachers never take a shortcut by using inappropriate evidence to get to a desired conclusion, even if the conclusion is correct.

CHAPTER 10

Be Sure You Read This!
The Article

Objectives

1. Understand that English and Hebrew use articles differently
2. Understand the form of the Hebrew article
3. Understand some facts about how the Hebrew article is used
4. Distinguish between the Hebrew article and the marker for a question

Introduction

I love old movies. One of my favorites is *The Bachelor and the Bobby-Soxer*. There is a running gag in the movie where one person (A) initiates a dialog with another (B), prompting predictable questions:

A1: "You remind me of a man."

B1: "What man?"

A2: "The man with the power."

B2: "What power?"

A3: "The power of Hoo-doo."

B3: "Who do?"

A4: "You do!"

B4: "Do what?"

A5: "Remind me of a man."

B5: "What man?" …

Maybe it loses something in this book, but in the movie, it's funny. In any case, this little routine illustrates one of the main functions of articles. At the beginning, A1, a character is introduced. Since his identify is not specified, he is called "*a* man"; it could be any man. But in A2 the speaker refers back to the "a man" of A1 and specifies which man. So he is referred to as "*the* man."

If a noun is indefinite, then there is no reference to a specific individual. Instead the "thing" is viewed as any member of a class. If a noun is definite, it refers to a specific entity. The term "definiteness" is used interchangeably with the term "determination." I will use "determination" because it is quicker than saying "having the article or not" and less awkward than "definiteness." In the parsing chart that we have seen, this is indicated in the "Det" column.

Figure 10.1: Parsing Information for Nominals and Verbals

			← Verbal Qualities →					← Nominal Qualities →			
POS	Word	Lex	Stem	Form	P	G	N	State	Det	Case	Suff
Nn						X	X	X	X	X	
V			X	X	X	X	X				

What we will demonstrate is that though there is overlap between the Hebrew and English definite article, the Hebrew article has additional functions.

Finally, it may seem strange that I've included the Hebrew marker for a question in this chapter (see "Objections"). The reason for this is because Hebrew uses the consonant ה (prefixed) for both, and this requires a little explanation.

The English Articles

English has both a definite article, *the*, and an indefinite article, *a(n)*. To express the idea of definiteness, English adds the definite article; the English article has additional functions as well. To mark indefiniteness, English may use the indefinite article for singular nouns or no article for plural nouns. Here are a few examples to illustrate.

1. I'd like to ride a bicycle.

   No particular bicycle is in view; the focus is on the action of riding.

2. I'd like to ride the bicycle.

   One particular bicycle is in view and the focus is on the individual bicycle rather than on the riding.

3. The bicycle is a cheap method of transportation.

   This is a generic use of "the;" no particular bicycle is in view, but bicycles as a class is distinguished from other types of transportation. The sentence would have meant the same thing if it had started out "a bicycle ...."

4. I like to ride bicycles.

   Notice that the plural noun bicycles *has no indefinite article, but is still indefinite.*

Determination

Hebrew (and Greek) differs from English in that it has no indefinite article; Hebrew nominals either have the article or they do not. Therefore there is no need to call it a "definite article," though some grammarians do; it is simply the article. When a Hebrew word does not have the article, it may be translated with or without the English indefinite article. So the Hebrew noun דָּבָר may be translated into English as "word" or "a word."

All nouns are either determined or undetermined. Some types of words are always determined even without an article. For example, all proper nouns are determined, because a name functions to identify an individual. All pronouns are determined, because they refer back to a specific noun.

Common nouns may be determined or undetermined. There are two basic ways to make a *common* noun determined: by prefixing the article, or by joining the noun to a following noun that is determined (this includes attaching it to a pronominal suffix; see ch. 11 on the construct state). First we will look at the basic forms of the article.

The Forms of the Article

The article is always prefixed to a word and *never* stands alone. The basic form of the article is · הַ, that is, the consonant ה plus the vowel Patach and Dagesh Forte in the following letter. Study two examples.

קוֹל + הַ· → הַקּוֹל

voice + the → the voice

דָּבָר + הַ· → הַדָּבָר

word + the → the word

In the first chapter we learned about certain letters that will not take a Dagesh Forte. When a noun begins with such a letter, Hebrew makes adjustments in the attachment of the article. Below is one possible example.

עַם + הַ· → הָעָם

voice + the → the people

Notice that there is no Dagesh Forte in the עַ. To compensate for this loss, the Patach under the article has lengthened to Qamets. What about nominals (N) with both the article (T) *and* an inseparable preposition (pp) and the conjunction (cj) Waw? Any other prefixes attached to a noun with the article come before the article. Hebrew has the same word order as English: PP + Art + N. When you put בְּ + הַ· together, the ה drops out and the consonant of the pp takes over the spot previously occupied by the ה. If there is a cj Waw, it comes before the pp.

Figure 10.1: Hebrew Nouns: Some Assembly Required

	← Hebrew	English →	
שָׂדֶה	שָׂדֶה	N	(a) field
וְשָׂדֶה	שָׂדֶה + וְ	cj + N	and (a) field
בְּשָׂדֶה	שָׂדֶה + בְּ	pp + N	in (a) field
וּבְשָׂדֶה	שָׂדֶה + בְּ + וְ	cj + pp + N	and in (a) field
הַשָּׂדֶה	שָׂדֶה + הַ·	T + N	the field
וְהַשָּׂדֶה	שָׂדֶה + הַ· + וְ	cj + T + N	and the field
בַּשָּׂדֶה	שָׂדֶה + הַ· + בְּ	pp + T + N	in the field
וּבַשָּׂדֶה	שָׂדֶה + הַ· + בְּ + וְ	cj + pp + T + N	and in the field

Interrogative ה: The Question Marker

In English we form questions in a couple of different ways. First, we commonly reverse the word order of subject and verb or use an interrogative pronoun at the beginning of the question. Second, when speaking, we will usually raise the pitch of our voice at the end of a sentence, or, when writing, we will conclude the sentence with a question mark.

There is no doubt that Hebrew had voice inflection, but this is lost in writing. Spoken and written Hebrew, however, did have a prefixed ה to mark a question. Whereas the article is ה normally spelled with Patach plus Dagesh Forte, the interrogative particle is ה normally spelled with Hateph Patach: הֲ. This particle is attached at the beginning of the question. It is never attached directly to an article, and only rarely does the conjunction Waw precede the interrogative ה. Look at the following examples:

Gen 4:7	אָנֹכִי	•	אָחִי	הֲשֹׁמֵר
	I?	(am)	my brother	[the] keeper of

NIV   Am I my brother's keeper?

Expl.   The הֲ at the beginning is not the article, but the interrogative ה attached to the nominal.

Gen 18:14	דָּבָר	מֵיהוָה	הֲיִפָּלֵא
	a thing?	from the Lord	Is [it] difficult

NIV   Is anything too hard for the Lord?

Expl.   Here the הֲ is attached to a finite verb.

Both the article and interrogative particle are spelled in a variety of ways. As a pre-Hebrew student, you will need to rely on additional resources to know the difference between them. To flowchart a question, I leave the sentence in its original order, even though that may mean that the subject will not come first.

Exercises

Indicate which of the following words have the article, the Interrogative ה, or neither by writing an X in the appropriate column. Use either a computer Bible with grammatical information of the Hebrew OT, or John Owens, *Analytical Key to the Old Testament*, or Benjamin Davidson, *The Analytical Hebrew and Chaldee Lexicon*. The first one is done as an example.

		Word	Art	Int ה	Neither
1.	Gen 1:1	הָאָרֶץ	X		
2.	Gen 12:2	בְּרָכָה			
3.	Gen 14:24	הָלְכוּ			
4.	Gen 15:1	הַרְבֵּה			
5.	Gen 1:25	הָאֲדָמָה			
6.	Gen 4:7	הֲלוֹא			
7.	Exod 3:8	וּדְבַשׁ			
8.	Gen 1:1	אֱלֹהִים			
9.	Gen 17:8	לֵאלֹהִים			
10.	Exod 22:9	לֵאֱלֹהִים			
11.	Ps 121:4	שׁוֹמֵר			

CHAPTER 11

A Tale of Two States
Case Functions

Objectives

1. Understand English and Hebrew pronouns
2. Understand English and Hebrew case systems
3. Understand determination and the construct chain
4. Understand the uses of the "particles of existence"

Tools Used: Grammatically tagged computer Hebrew OT or paper interlinear plus Davidson or Owens

Introduction

A well-known chorus is taken from Ps 118:24, "This is the day the Lord has made; let us rejoice and be glad in it" (NIV). Often we sing this when we are feeling happy, especially when the weather outside is delightful. After all, the verse says, "let us be glad in *it*." The word *it* is a personal pronoun. Obviously, since it is neuter (meaning neither masculine nor feminine), it must refer back to a thing, namely, *day*. The day that the psalmist is talking about is when the Lord does the great work of making the rejected stone now to be the chief cornerstone.

You will remember, though, that in Hebrew there are only two genders, masculine and feminine. The word translated "it" by the English versions actually represents a masculine Hebrew pronoun. That means it must refer to an antecedent that is a masculine noun. Now the word "day" in Hebrew is masculine, but that is not the only option. The nearest antecedent is "the Lord." A legitimate way of translating the second line of the verse is, "let us rejoice and be glad in *him*!" One can make a case either way. The Lord is the agent bringing about the great work on that day. If we take the pronoun as referring to the Lord, then the cause and focus of our rejoicing and gladness is actually the Lord himself. In either case, "day" is the anticipated day of salvation. In the NT, this is equated with the coming of the Son. We can sing this song no matter the "weather" of our lives, knowing that salvation is from the Lord.

In this chapter, the main task is to understand Hebrew case usage. The term *case* simply refers to the role of a noun in a sentence. Pronouns serve as a good way to introduce noun cases, so that is where we will begin, covering both Hebrew and English pronouns plus English cases. Next we will turn to the Hebrew cases themselves. We will treat these in two parts, the second part being the most exegetically significant. Finally, there are two little words used commonly in Hebrew, known as particles of existence and nonexistence, that English translations normally render idiomatically.

Personal Pronouns and English Cases

A pronoun (Prn) is a word that stands in place of (*pro–*) a noun. The noun for which it stands is called the antecedent. English has several kinds of pronouns; Hebrew has five kinds. They are summarized in the figure below.

Figure 11.1: Types of Pronouns in English and Hebrew

Pronoun Type	English Examples	Hebrew Equivalents	Description
Personal	I, he, we	אֲנַחְנוּ ,הוּא ,אֲנִי	Pronouns with the grammatical person
Reflexive Personal	Myself, himself, ourselves	None	The object of the verb and refers to the same entity as the subject of the verb
Interrogative	Who? What?	מִי, מַה	Asks questions
Demonstrative	This, those	זֶה, אֵלֶּה	Points to objects near or far
Relative	Who, which, that	אֲשֶׁר	Introduces a relative clause
Indefinite	Whoever, whichever, someone, few	מְעַט, אֲשֶׁר	Refers to any member of a class

Personal pronouns have the grammatical quality of person and are the most important. While English nouns are not often inflected (i.e., they do not often add endings, etc.) for case, personal pronouns (PPrn) are. So they serve as a good introduction into a discussion of cases.

Grammatical Qualities of English and Hebrew Pronouns

English Prns indicate person, gender (in third person only), number, and case. Person refers to identities of speaker (first person), addressee (second person), and topic of conversation (third person). Number may be singular or plural. Case refers to the function that a noun has in a sentence. Languages indicate case either by word order (as English does) or by adding endings to the word (as Greek and Latin do). Hebrew actually used to have case endings before the Bible was put into writing, but they were dropped and only remnants of them appear.

English has four cases: *subjective*, *possessive*, *objective*, and *vocative*. The vocative can be treated quickly. It is simply the case of address as in, "Julie, you are beautiful." The verb is *are*; the subject is *you*; *Julie* is not part of the clause and is therefore set off by a comma; further, the words *Julie* and *you* refer to the same person. Now we'll go to the three main cases.

The chart below illustrates case forms using personal Prns. Notice that in the third person singular, English Prns have gender. Just for fun I give the Prns for Elizabethan English (the English of the KJV) in parentheses.

Figure 11.2: English Personal Pronouns

	First Person		Second Person		Third Person	
	sg	**pl**	**sg**	**pl**	**sg**	**pl**
Subjective	I	we	you (thou)	you (ye)	he, she, it	they
Possessive	my	our	your (thy, thine)	your (your, yours)	his, her, its	their
Objective	me	us	you (thee)	you (you)	him, her, it	them

Personal pronouns (PPrn) in Hebrew and English share the same qualities: person, gender (for second and third persons in Hebrew, only third person in English), number, and case. Whereas English PPrns are all independent words,

Hebrew PPrns come in two sets: **independent pronouns** and suffixed Prns, known as **pronominal suffixes** (PrnSf). The independent PPrns are, as their name implies, independent words and correspond to the English subject pronouns. PrnSfs are used for the English possessive and objective pronouns. Now we may expand our Parsing chart to include PPrns:

Figure 11.3: Parsing Chart

			← Verbal Qualities →					← Nominal Qualities →			
PoS	Word	Lex	Stem	Form	P	G	N	State	Det	Case	Suff
Nn						X	X	X	X	X	
V			X	X	X	X		X			
PPrn								Abs	D	X	
PrnSf								Abs	D	x	PGN

Just as with substantives, you will notice that PPrns have all the qualities of nouns. Because they are Prns, they are always in the absolute state (Abs) and are always determined (Det), there is no need to label these on the chart. Because they are *personal* Prns, they have the quality of person (P). Really, though, this is due to their meaning rather than inflection. Since PrnSfs are never independent, their person, gender, and number (PGN) are in the Suff column in the same line as the word they are attached to.

Now let's look at four sentences.

S1. Jill loves the man's son.

S2. *She* loves the man's son.

S3. Jill loves *his* son.

S4. Jill loves *him.*

All four sentences have an active verb. S1 has no pronoun. S2, S3, and S4 have pronouns (in italics) substituted for each of the nouns in turn. The subject is the agent of an active verb. When the Prn is substituted for Jill in S2, the subject form is used; you wouldn't say "Her loved the man's son." The man is the possessor. In S2 this is indicated on a noun with the ending -'s; in S3, the possessive Prn *his* is used. In S4 the object case Prn substitutes for the direct object (DO) of the sentences. Again, you wouldn't say "Jill loves he."

Now that we understand English cases to be simply the functions of nouns in sentences, we are ready to look more closely at Hebrew cases.

The First Three Noun Cases

Hebrew cases may be described similarly to English cases, but different names are used. The *vocative* (Voc) case is the same as in English. The *nominative* (Nom) case corresponds to the subject case, the *genitive* (Gen) case corresponds to the possessive case, and the *accusative* (Acc) case corresponds to the objective case. Hebrew uses these cases for functions, which English renders with prepositions. For the Gen and Acc cases, I have included some key words to illustrate the functions. The Gen case is the most complicated, so we will treat it last.

Nominative

1. **Subject Nom** – The substantive is the subject of an action or state. This is by far the most common use. In Hebrew noun clauses, the PPrn is simply the subject and the clause is disjunctive. Though English requires the same word in the subject case, in Hebrew verbal clauses PPrns are not needed. When they are present, they either indicate emphasis or mark a disjunctive clause.

   2 Sam 12:7: "*You* (אַתָּה) are the man!" (NIV).
   1 Kgs 18:37: "and that *you* (וְאַתָּה) are turning their hearts back again" (NIV).

2. **Predicate Nom** – The substantive refers to the same entity as the subject; most often this occurs in noun clauses, but certain other verbs may be present also have this function.

   2 Sam 12:7: "You are *the man* (הָאִישׁ)!" (NIV).
   You and *the man* both refer to David.

3. **Nom Absolute** – The substantive is isolated from a phrase and is referred to by a pronoun called a "resumptive pronoun." The clause after the Nom Absolute is a complete clause. This use is not considered good grammar in English, so it requires a little explanation. Look at the following interlinear.

Gen 9:18	אֲבִי כְנַעַן	•	הוּא	וְחָם
	Canaan the	(was)	he	now
	father of			Ham

NIV (Ham was the father of Canaan.)

Expl. The author draws the reader's attention to a significant feature about Ham.

This is not to be confused with "fronting," in which something other than a verb occurs first in the clause, but there is no resumptive pronoun.

2 Sam 7:15	מִמֶּנּוּ	יָסוּר	לֹא	וְחַסְדִּי
	from	it shall	not	but my
	him	turn aside		love

NIV But my love will not depart from him.

Expl. This is a disjunctive clause (a non–verb is first; see ch. 20), but there is no resumptive Prn.

4. **Nom in Simple Apposition** – Apposition occurs when two nouns are next to each other, refer to the same entity, and function the same way in the sentence. *Apposition can occur with any case*, including objects of prepositions. Since their function "piggybacks" on that of the first noun, multiple examples are not needed; one example should suffice.

2 Sam 16:8: "The Lord has handed the kingdom over to your son Absalom." (NIV).

Son is the object of the pp *to. Son* and *Absalom* both refer to the same person and *Absalom* functions in the same way that *son* does, namely, the object of the pp *to*. If you remove either word, the sentence has basically the same meaning.

Accusative

We mentioned that Hebrew usually marks case functions by word order. Hebrew does have a feature that marks the Acc case. When a determined noun is in the Acc case, Hebrew may precede the word with the particle אֵת. This word may be joined to the Acc noun by Maqqef, אֶת־ (with the short vowel) and may have pronominal suffixes attached, in which case the vowel is long *o*: אֹתִי or אוֹתִי (meaning "me"). The particle אֵת is not used for every determined Acc noun, and there does not appear to be any pattern as to when it is used. This particle is not translated into English, except by word order to mark the direct object. We have already seen this in Gen 1:1: "In the beginning God created *the heavens* (אֵת הַשָּׁמַיִם) and *the earth* (וְאֵת הָאָרֶץ)" (NIV).

For the examples below, none of the Acc nouns are in prepositional phrases in Hebrew, even though almost all of them are in English.

1. **Acc of DO** – The most common function with no "key words."

   2 Kgs 17:10: "They set up *sacred stones*" (NIV).

2. **Acc of Place** (*at*)

   Gen 18:1: "while he was sitting *at the entrance* (פֶּתַח־) to his tent" (NIV).

3. **Acc of Direction** (*to*)

   Josh 13:5: "and all Lebanon *to the east* (מִזְרַח הַשֶּׁמֶשׁ)" (NIV; literally, "the rising of the sun").

4. **Acc of Time** (*at, during*)

   Gen 14:15: *"During the night* (לַיְלָה) Abram divided his men ..."* (NIV).

5. **Acc of Manner** (*–ly* or other adverbial expression)

   Jer 7:5: *"day after day* (יוֹם), again and again I sent you my servants the prophets"* (NIV; KJV renders "daily").

6. **Acc of Product** (*into*)

   Exod 32:4: "He ... made it *a* molten *calf* (עֵגֶל) ..." (KJV). Compare NIV: "made it *into* an idol cast in the shape of a *calf.*"

7. **Acc of Material** (*from*)

   Gen 2:7: "the Lord God formed the man *from the dust* (עָפָר) of the ground" (NIV).

8. **Acc of Instrument** (*with, using*)

   Josh 7:25: "And all Israel stoned him *with stones* (אֶבֶן) (ESV). Compare the NIV simply, "Then all Israel stoned him."

Vocative

The vocative is the case of direct address. The substantive is used in conjunction with a second person verb.

> 1 Kgs 20:4: "As you say, *my Lord* (אֲדֹנִי), *O king* (הַמֶּלֶךְ), I am yours, and all that I have" (ESV). Compare NIV: "Just as you say, *my Lord the king* …."

Both "my Lord" and "O king" are in the Voc. Notice that the ESV took the article attached to *king* as marking the vocative (in fact, "O king" is a Voc in simple apposition).

The Construct Chain and the Genitive Case

In ch. 8 on prepositions, you learned that Hebrew has no word for the English word *of*; instead Hebrew uses a grammatical construction. That construction is the "construct chain." Some people might suggest that the Gen case means simply *of*. That is mostly true, but in fact the Gen case has a broader range of meaning than the English *of*. In any case, the interpreter of the English Bible must seek to figure out what *of* means any time it appears in the Bible.

All Hebrew nouns are in one of two states: *absolute* (abs), in which the noun is not bound to another form, and *construct* (cst), in which the noun is bound to another following form. The two words so bound are said to be in a *construct chain*. *As a rule, the construct chain cannot be interrupted by anything.* The "glue" that binds the words together is that they are pronounced as a unit. In writing, the first word loses its primary accent, often resulting in changes to the vowels. If you were learning full Hebrew, you would learn how to read these changes. As a pre–Hebrew student, you will have to rely on the work of others.

Here is how construct chains work. The chains can have several links, but to begin with we will consider only two-link chains. In a two-word construct chain the first word, the head noun (N^h), is in the construct state. The second word, the tail noun (N^t), is in the absolute state and is always in the Gen case. (Note: not all absolute nouns are tails of a cst noun; we are only talking about construct chains here.) The following diagram illustrates this graphically; remember that Hebrew reads right to left and all English letters, even in diagrams, read left to right.

Figure 11.4: State and Case

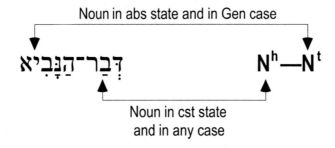

Noun in abs state and in Gen case

דְּבַר־הַנָּבִיא   Nʰ—Nᵗ

Noun in cst state
and in any case

Notice the following important points:

1. The Nʰ, דְּבַר has the lexical form דָּבָר, meaning "word"; the cst form means "word *of.* Because of the shift in accent, the vowels have changed. Not all nouns alter vowels when they are in the cst, but most do.

2. The Nᵗ has the article and means "the prophet." The article may only be attached to the Nᵗ. Whenever the Nᵗ is determined, either because of the word being intrinsically determined or because of the article, each member of the chain is also determined; if the Nᵗ is not determined, each member of the chain is undetermined. So, דְּבַר־הַנָּבִיא means "*the* word of *the* prophet"; דְּבַר־נָבִיא would mean "*(a)* word of *(a)* prophet."[1]

3. The example shows the words joined by Maqqef. This is optional and its presence or absence has no affect on the meaning.

4. *If there are three or more links in the chain, the middle items are all in the Gen case, just like the Nᵗ.* This may be graphically illustrated this way: Nʰ–N^Gen–Nᵗ. The interpreter needs to determine based on word meaning and context the meaning of the Gen relationship, represented by the "–," between each pair.

5. *A PrnSf attached to a noun functions as a Nᵗ that is determined.* For example, דְּבָרוֹ would mean "*the* word of – him," or "his word."

---

[1] To say "*the* word of *a* prophet," a construct chain could not be used. Instead Hebrew would use a לְ preposition: הַדָּבָר לְנָבִיא, in which the לְ functions to mark possession.

Figure 11.5: Terms and Nouns Bound Together

Quality	Head Noun	Tail Noun
Order:	first	last
State:	construct (cst)	absolute (abs)
Case:	any	genitive
Translation:	lexical meaning + "of"	lexical meaning
Article:	no article	article optional

The Functions of the Genitive Case

The Gen case denotes a relationship between two nouns, often translated by the English word "of." The word "of" denotes a wide variety of nuances. I have found it helpful to think of that relationship as a movement either toward or away from the N^t. The case uses are a function of word meaning and context. In Figure 11.6 below, remember to think about meaning from the perspective of the tail noun. The determination of the function depends on the meaning of the words in the chain and on context. Note that explained examples follow the figure.

Figure 11.6: Genitive Functions of the Construct State

Class	$N^h \rightarrow N^t$	Description
Possession	Gen of Possessor	N^t possesses N^h
Direction	Gen of Destination	N^t is the destination
Production	Gen of Product	N^t is the thing produced
Agency	Subjective Gen	N^t is the one doing the implied action
Action	Gen of Purpose/	N^t is actual result or intended purpose of N^h
	Result	N^t is actual result or intended
Adjectival	Attributive Gen	N^t functions as Adj describing N^h
	Gen of Apposition	$N^t = N^h$ (= Explicative Gen)
Partitive	Gen of Material	N^t is material of which N^h is made
	Gen of Measure	N^t is thing measured by quantity N^h
Authority	Gen of Thing Ruled	N^t is governed by N^h

Class	N^h ← N^t	Description
Possession	Gen of One Possessed	N^t is possessed by N^h
Direction	Gen of Source	N^t is the place of origin
Production	Gen of Producer	N^t makes the N^h
Agency	Objective Gen	N^t is the one affected by the implied action
	Gen of Means	N^t is the instrument used to effect implied action
Action	Gen of Action	N^t is the implied action done by N^h
Adjectival	Attributed Gen	N^t is described by Adj
Partitive	Partitive Gen	N^t is the whole of which N^h is a part
	Gen of Degree	N^t is plural form of N^h
Authority	Gen of Ruler	N^t governs N^h

Here are some examples. Note the many nuances of the word "of" in English.

1. **Gen of Possession**

   a. **Possessor**

      Josh 2:1: "So they went and entered *the house of a prostitute* (בֵּית־אִשָּׁה זוֹנָה) named Rahab" (NIV).

   b. **Thing Possessed**

      Exod 21:34: "*The owner of the pit* (בַּעַל הַבּוֹר) must pay for the loss" (NIV).

2. **Gen of Direction**

   a. **Destination**

      Gen 3:1: "Did God really say, 'You must not eat from any *tree in the garden* (עֵץ הַגָּן)?'" (NIV; cf. KJV: "*tree of the garden*").

      1 Kgs 12:28: "It is too much for you *to go up to Jerusalem* (מֵעֲלוֹת יְרוּשָׁלַ͏ִם)" (NIV; ignoring the prefixed מִן pp, literally, "*the going up of Jerusalem*").

b. **Source**

Job 33:17: "to turn *a man from wrongdoing* (אָדָם מַעֲשֶׂה)" (NIV; literally, "*a man of deed*").

Many times: "*the man of God* (אִישׁ אֱלֹהִים)." This might be understood in several ways, but since it is most often a technical term for a prophet, it probably means a man sent from God.

3. **Gen of Production**

a. **Product**

Isa 45:9: "Woe to him who quarrels with *his Maker* (יֹצְרוֹ)" (NIV; literally, "*the maker* of *him*").

b. **Producer**

Isa 64:8 [Hebrew 64:7]: "and we are all *the work of* your *hand* (וּמַעֲשֵׂה יָדְךָ)" (NIV).

4. **Gen of Agency**

a. **Subjective**

Isa 53:3: "he was despised and *rejected by men* (וַחֲדַל אִישִׁים)" (NIV; cf. KJV "*rejected of men*").

b. **Objective**

Josh 1:1: "the Lord said to Joshua son of Nun, *Moses' aide* (מְשָׁרֵת מֹשֶׁה)" (NIV; literally "*the aide of Moses*").

c. **Means** (this category is simply impersonal agent and is a subcategory of the Subjective Gen)

Isa 14.19: "with *those pierced by the sword* (מְטֹעֲנֵי חָרֶב)" (NIV).

5. **Gen of Action**

a. **Purpose/Result**

Isa 53:5: "*the punishment that brought* us *peace* (מוּסַר שְׁלוֹמֵנוּ) was upon him" (NIV; cf. KJV: "*the chastisement of* our *peace* was upon him").

b. **Cause** (focus is on an action implied by a noun rather than on the agent or means)

Song 2:5: "for I am *faint with love* (חוֹלַת אַהֲבָה)" (NIV; literally, "sick of love").

Isa 54:4: "you will ... remember no more *the reproach of* your *widowhood* (בֹּשֶׁת עֲלוּמַיִךְ)" (NIV; i.e., the reproach caused by your being a widow).

6. **Adjectival Gen**

   a. **Attributive**

      1 Sam 2:8: "and *a seat of honor* (וְכִסֵּא כָבוֹד)" (NIV; i.e., an honored position).

      Judg 9:51: "*a strong tower* (וּמִגְדַּל־עֹז)" (NIV; literally, "*a tower of strength*").

   b. **Attributed**

      Deut 28:20: "until you ... perish quickly on account of *the evil of* your *deeds* (רֹעַ מַעַלְלֶיךָ)" (ESV).

   c. **Apposition** (unlike simple apposition in which the two nouns are in the same case, the Gen N^t may modify a N^h that is in another case)

      Josh 1:15: "Then you shall return to *the land of* your *possession* (אֶרֶץ יְרֻשַּׁתְכֶם)" and shall possess it" (ESV; meaning, the land which is your possession. Compare NIV, "and occupy your *own* land").

7. **Partitive Gen**

   a. **Wholative**[2] (a.k.a., Partitive)

      Gen 4:4: "Abel brought fat portions from some of *the firstborn of* his *flock* (בְּכֹרוֹת צֹאנוֹ)" (NIV; i.e., "the flock" is the whole; "the firstborn" are the part).

   b. **Material**

      1 Kgs 12:28: "the king made two *golden calves* (עֶגְלֵי זָהָב)" (NIV; literally "*calves of gold*").

---

[2] For the term "wholative," I follow the example of Daniel Wallace, *Greek Grammar beyond the Basics* (Grand Rapids: Zondervan, 1996) 84-6. The Gen noun is the whole of which the N^h is a part.

   c. **Measure** (i.e., of material measured)

Exod 38:27: "The 100 *talents of silver* (כִּכַּר הַכֶּסֶף) were used to cast the bases" (NIV; the "talent" was a unit of weight).

   d. **Degree/Emphasis** (subcategory of Wholative)

Exod 29:37: "*the holy of holies* (קֹדֶשׁ קָדָשִׁים)*"* (NIV).

8. **Gen of Authority**

   a. **Thing Ruled**

Josh 24:9: "*the king of Moab* (מֶלֶךְ מוֹאָב)*"* (NIV).

   b. **Ruler**

Josh 13:12: "that is the whole *kingdom of Og* (מַמְלְכוּת עוֹג) in Bashan" (NIV).

Special Note: "mountain of my holiness" or "my holy mountain"?

The attributive Gen is a common way that Hebrew uses nouns to form adjectival ideas. For example, הַר קֹדֶשׁ, literally, "mountain of holiness," really means "holy mountain." It is easy to understand how adding the 1cs PrnSf, "my," to a cst noun changes הַר, "mountain of" to הָרִי, "the mountain of me" or "my mountain." But, how does Hebrew say, "my holy mountain"? The problem is that you can't break the construct chain הַר קֹדֶשׁ to form הָרִי קֹדֶשׁ. The PrnSf is attached to the end of the chain: הַר קָדְשִׁי. Literally this would be "the mountain of the holiness of me." But the meaning is "my holy mountain." Context decides what the Prn modifies.

Determining Noun Characteristics

If you were learning full Hebrew, you would learn how to identify gender, number, and state by reading Hebrew. What about as a pre–Hebrew student? Looking up a Hebrew word in the *SNIVEC* will show you the lexical form and the gender, but it will not tell you the number and state in a given context. You must use one of the resources already mentioned. You may use an interlinear to see if the word *of* appears between the translation of two Hebrew words. The simplest way is to use a computer Bible with a tagged Hebrew text. Case and function is something you will have to figure out based on context. We have given numerous functions earlier in this chapter.

Prepositions and Case

In the previous chapter we noted that English prepositions take their objects in the objective case. In Hebrew we might say that as well, but it is "tidier" to say that prepositions are in construct with their objects. In saying this, though, there is no need to ask how the Gen case is functioning; the pp governs the case function. Instead you look at the function of the preposition, as we saw in the last chapter.

Here is how it would look if you were to fill out a parsing chart for the expressions in the following sentences:

S1. *A servant of a king* (עֶבֶד מֶלֶךְ [no article]) ran to tell him.

S2. He heard *the word of the prophet* (דְּבַר־הַנָּבִיא [with an article]).

S3. The fame of *the wisdom of Solomon* (חָכְמַת שְׁלֹמֹה [with a proper noun]) spread throughout the world.

S4. They beat *his head* (רֹאשׁוֹ) [with PrnSf; literally, "*the head of him*"].

S5. *With pain* (בְּעֶצֶב) you shall give birth to children.

Figure 11.7: Parsing Examples

| | | | ← Verbal Qualities → | | | | | ← Nominal Qualities → | | | |
PoS	Word	Lex	Stem	Form	P	G	N	State	Det	Case	Suff
Nn	עֶבֶד	עֶבֶד				m	s	cst	U	Nom	
Nn	מֶלֶךְ	מֶלֶךְ				m	s	abs	U	Gen	
Nn	דְּבַר־	דָּבָר				m	s	cst	D	Acc	
Nn	הַנָּבִיא	נָבִיא				m	s	abs	D	Gen	
Nn	חָכְמַת	חָכְמָה				f	s	cst	D	Gen	
Nn	שְׁלֹמֹה	שְׁלֹמֹה				m	s	abs	D	Gen	
Nn	רֹאשׁוֹ	רֹאשׁ				m	s	cst	D	Acc	3ms
pp	בְּעֶצֶב	בְּ						cst			
Nn	בְּעֶצֶב	עֶצֶב				m	s	abs	U	Gen	
pp	לִי	לְ						cst			1cs

Notice the following:

1. In the "Det" column, "D" stands for determined and "U" for undetermined.

2. The case of N^h is determined by its function in the sentence; the case of the N^t is always Gen, including a PrnSf.

3. The PrnSf doesn't get its own line, since it is not independent.

4. The pp gets its own line, but has no other features. For this reason, it might be ignored in parsing or simply added as "בְּ" in the "Lex" column.

Particles of Existence

Hebrew has an interesting way of saying that something "exists" or "does not exist." These are the particles יֵשׁ and אַיִן. Literally they mean "existence" and "nonexistence," respectively. They may be used in the absolute or construct state. As a pre-Hebrew student, there is not much you need to do with these, but if you come across one in an interlinear Bible, you will need to have some idea of what they are. Here are some examples.

	הָעִיר	בְּתוֹךְ	צַדִּיקִם	חֲמִשִּׁים	יֵשׁ	•	אוּלַי
Gen 18:24	the city	in	righteous men	fifty	the exis-tence of	(there is)	perhaps

NIV What if *there are* fifty righteous people in the city?

Expl. יֵשׁ is in the cst state.

	הָאֲדָמָה	אֶת	לַעֲבֹד	אַיִן	•	וְאָדָם
Gen 2:5	the ground	–	to work	non existence	(was)	and man

NIV and *there was no* man to work the ground.

Expl. אַיִן is in the abs state.

	טָהֳרָה	אֵינֶנָּה	אֲשֶׁר	הַבְּהֵמָה	וּמִן
Gen 7:8	purity	the non existence of it	that	the beast	and from

ESV   and of animals that *are not* clean

Expl.   אֵין is in the cst state with a PrnSf referring back to the beast. Another translation might be, "and from the beasts which have no purity."

Flowcharting Cases

When I introduced flowcharting to you, I gave the general principle that the only things on the clause line are subject, verb, indirect object, and direct object. Now that you have spent time working through all these case uses, how should you treat them in flowcharts? The answer is: however you find most helpful. There are no problems with the Nom case and the Acc of DO; they are simply on the main line as we have seen. The question arises over the adverbial uses of the Hebrew Acc case and over the Gen case, which are translated by English prepositional phrases. As a general rule, I keep possessives in the clause line. They are so routine, that giving each one a separate line is more of a distraction. To the other prepositional phrases I do give a separate line and label the function.

Here are three examples. Again I have used different styles to point out different parts of speech.

Function	Vs	Flow Chart		
Event	7	**The Lord God**	<u>formed</u> ➔	the man.
Material			from the dust	
Source			of the ground	
Explanation		"From the dust" is an Acc of material in Hebrew; it modifies the verb. "Of the ground" is in Hebrew a PP using מִן.		

Function	Vs	Flow Chart		
Time	15		During the night	
Event		**Abram**	<u>divided</u> ➔	his men
Purpose			to attack ➔	them
Addition		and		
Event		he	<u>routed</u> ➔	them
Means			pursuing ➔	them
Extent			as far as Hobah,	
Location			north of Damascus	

Explanation	Here are two clauses. In the first, "During the night" is an Acc of time; "to attack" is purpose phrase with an infinitive (see ch. 17).

Function	Vs	Flow Chart		
Command	20	(You)	<u>tie</u>	➔ them
Purpose			as symbols	
Place			on your hands	
Addition		and		
Command		(You)	<u>bind</u>	➔ them
Place			on your foreheads	

Explanation	The PPs "on your hands" and "on your foreheads" include possessive PPrns; I left them on the same line as the nouns they modify.

Exercises

1. Gen 10:11: "From that land he went *to Assyria* (אַשּׁוּר) ..." (NIV); the KJV reads "Out of that land went forth *Asshur*."

   a. Identify how each of these two versions interpreted the case function of "Assyria" by naming the case.

   NIV:

   KJV:

   b. What difference is there in the understanding (check context to see who is the subject of the verb in the NIV)?

   c. Take brief notes from a commentary or two to see how they treat this modifier (always cite your source):

2. Ps 3:5: "I cried out to the Lord *with my voice* (קוֹלִי) (KJV). Compare the NIV rendering, "To the Lord I cry *aloud*. What is the case and function interpreted by each version?

   a. NIV:

   b. KJV:

3. Ps 44:23: "we are considered *as sheep to be slaughtered* (כְּצֹאן טִבְחָה)" (NIV; literally, "as sheep of slaughter"). What case and use of both nouns? Use an interlinear to identify the lexical form of "sheep." What is the prefix?

   a. sheep: case: function:

   b. slaughter: case: function:

4. Gen 37:3: "and he had made him *a long robe with sleeves* (כְּתֹנֶת פַּסִּים) (NRSV). The versions read quite differently here. You might check the NET Bible note for a brief summary. What function of the Gen case is NRSV?

5. Ps 45 title [Hebrew 45:1]: *"A Song of loves* (שִׁיר יְדִידֹת)" (KJV). Compare the NIV, "A *wedding* song"; ESV, "A *love* song." How did each translation understand the function of the Gen case noun?

   a. KJV:

   b. NIV & ESV:

6. Prov 11:30: *"The fruit of the righteous* (פְּרִי־צַדִּיק) is *a tree of life* (עֵץ חַיִּים)" (NIV). What are the functions of each Gen case noun? Compare the NET translation: "The fruit of the righteous is like a tree producing life"; if you are interested, see the NET note.

   a. the righteous:

   b. life:

7. Prov 3:1: *"My son* (בְּנִי), do not forget *my teaching* (תּוֹרָתִי)" (NIV). Remember that a PrnSf is in the Gen case and means the same as "of me." The first "my" is possessor. Although you might be tempted to interpret the second "my" as possessor also, that is probably not the best answer. What is a good alternative? Think of how you would use a Gen case function to describe the "position" of the teaching between the teacher and the student.

   my teaching:

8. Ps 23:1: "The LORD is *my shepherd* (רֹעִי), I will not be in want" (NIV). Again, the "my" is not possessor; it is quite inappropriate to view the psalmist as the "possessor" of God. Be more precise.

   a. *my* shepherd:

   b. What devotional insight does this give you?

9. 2 Sam 7:13: "I will establish *the throne of* his *kingdom* forever (כִּסֵּא מַמְלַכְתּוֹ)" (NIV). The NLT translation reads: "And I will secure his *royal* throne forever." The NIV rendering does not specify a Gen function for "kingdom." Using Figure 11.6 as a guide, what do you think is the relation of the throne to the kingdom? How did the NLT understand the Gen?

   a. NIV:

   b. NLT:

10. Gen 4:2: "Now Abel was *a keeper of sheep* (רֹעֵה צֹאן), and Cain *a worker of the ground* (עֹבֵד אֲדָמָה)" (ESV). Compare the NIV, "Now Abel kept flocks and Cain worked the soil."

   How did the NIV understand both Genitves?

Advanced Information and Curious Facts

Hebrew Noun Endings

Hebrew uses endings to indicate the gender, number, and state of nouns. In case you are curious, here is a summary of the endings.

Figure 11.8: Hebrew Noun Endings

	Absolute State		Construct State	
	Masculine	*Feminine*	*Masculine*	*Feminine*
Singular	סוּס	תּוֹרָה	סוּס	תּוֹרַת
Dual	סוּסַׂיִם	תּוֹרָתַיִם	סוּסֵי	תּוֹרָתֵי
Plural	סוּסִים	תּוֹרוֹת	סוּסֵי	תּוֹרוֹת

Since you are not learning full Hebrew, you do not need to memorize these endings (and the variations). The masculine singular (ms) is usually unmarked; i.e., it has no ending.

Immanuel

One of the frequently heard names for the Messiah is taken from Isa 7:14 and 8:8, "Immanuel." Matthew 1:23 quotes Isa 7:14, and then gives the meaning of the name, "God with us." Now that you know about Hebrew prepositions, and that they can take PrnSfs, you can understand the Hebrew behind it. In Hebrew *Immanuel* is actually two words: עִמָּנוּ אֵל. אֵל is the word for "God." עִמָּנוּ is the pp עִם, "with," plus the 3cp PrnSf, "us." It is a verbless clause meaning "God is with us."

CHAPTER 12

An Apt Description
Adjectives

Objectives

1. Understand English and Hebrew adjectives

2. Understand relative clauses

3. Learn how to flowchart adjectives and relative clauses.

Introduction

A church I used to attend had an annual event at Christmas time: "the hanging of the greens." The running joke was that one of the prominent families, whose last name was Green, was always afraid to come!

Of course, what was meant was that we would get together to hang the green wreaths and green holly and green boughs for Christmas decorations. It is still interesting, though, how words work. The reason the joke works is because in the phrase "the hanging of the greens," the word *greens* fills a noun slot (a place where we expect to hear a noun). The name *Green* is a proper noun; the color green, though, is an adjective describing the decorations. The expression gets shortened to *greens* and behold: an adjective is transformed into a noun.

After the last chapter, this chapter on adjectives will seem like a vacation. Adjectives do about the same things in English (and in all languages) as in Hebrew. First we will look at how adjectives work in both English and Hebrew. Then we will look at relative clauses, because they function just like adjectives. Finally, we will look at flowcharting adjectives and relative clauses.

By the way, in case you were worried, the Greens always came and everyone enjoyed the event.

Adjectives

An *adjective* (Adj) is a word that modifies or describes a substantive. In talking about Adjs, there are two factors: how they function and how they are structured (the arrangement of words).

Adjectives function in three ways: attributively, predicatively, or substantivally. In the first two, the noun is present; in the third, the noun is absent, but understood. In the *attributive* use, the Adj describes a noun, and in the *predicative* use, the Adj ascribes a quality to a noun. In the *substantival* use, the Adj is substituted for a noun. In the following examples, the Adj is in bold type and the Nn it modifies (if any) is underlined.

S1. **Hot** coffee costs a lot.

S2. The **hot** cups are burning my hands.

S3. The cups are **hot**.

S4. **One** dollar still buys a cup of coffee.

S5. If I had a **one** in my wallet, I would buy a cup of coffee.

S6. I have some **ones** in my wallet.

S7. I'll buy some coffee during the time **out**.

S8. How many times **out** are left?

S9. By the way, I actually heard a **sports** announcer on TV say "times out"!

Notice the following:

1. S1, S2 and S4 have attributive Adjs. The Adj is right next to the noun. In English the adjective normally precedes the noun.

2. S3 has a predicative Adj. Notice that a verb, *are,* separates the noun from its adjective. The noun and the Adj with an equative verb both refer to the same thing. Compare the predicate Nom case use from the last chapter.

3. English does not pluralize attributive and predicative Adjs. Whether the noun is singular (S1) or plural (S2 and S3), the Adj does not change; i.e., it is not inflected.

4. In S5 and S6 there is no noun present; dollar bill(s) is understood. The Adj is substantival. When Adjs substitute for nouns, then they are inflected just like nouns.

5. S7 and S8 also have attributive Adjs. In certain expressions the Adj comes after.

6. S9 is an interesting example of a noun, sports, being used as an Adj. Hebrew does this also.

Hebrew Adjs are similar to English Adjs. They have the same three functions, but there are some differences in grammatical construction. Three factors come into play in Hebrew constructions: the article (T), the Adj, and the noun (Nn). Further, the Adj and the N both have three qualities: gender, number, and definiteness. Here are the principles involved:

1. *Every Adj agrees with its Nn in gender and number.* We have already seen that gender in English is not significant, but it is significant in Hebrew. Additionally, Adjs are inflected for gender.

2. *Every attributive Adj agrees in definiteness.* This is one of the important ways that the Hebrew article is used differently from English. The article with an Adj is there to indicate the relationship to the noun rather than having any other meaning.

3. *Almost every predicative Adj disagrees with its Nn in definiteness.* Predicate Adjs occur mostly in noun clauses. When the Nn is determined and the Adj is not, English needs to insert the verb *to be* between them.

Notice that Adjs have the same kind of parsing information as nouns.

Figure 12.1: Parsing Information for Nominals and Verbals

					← Verbal Qualities →			← Nominal Qualities →			
PoS	Word	Lex	Stem	Form	P	G	N	State	Det	Case	Suff
Nn						X	X	X	X	X	
Adj						X	X	X	X	X	

All of this leads to there being four possible positions (constructions) of adjectives, nouns, and articles. These positions mark the functions:

Figure 12.2: Positions and Agreement of Adjectives

Construction	Noun	Definite Noun	Article with Adj	Function	Example	Pattern
Attributive	Y	Y	Y	Attributive	הַמֶּ֫לֶךְ הַטּוֹב מֶ֫לֶךְ הַטּוֹב the good king	T-Nn-T-Adj Nn-T-Adj
Predicate	Y	Y	N	Predicative	טוֹב הַמֶּ֫לֶךְ הַמֶּ֫לֶךְ טוֹב the king (is) good	Adj-T-Nn T-Nn-Adj
Ambiguous	Y	N	N	Attributive or Predicative	מֶ֫לֶךְ טוֹב טוֹב מֶ֫לֶךְ a good king *or* a king (is) good	Nn-Adj Adj-N
Isolated	N	–	Y/N	Substantival	טוֹב הַטּוֹב a good (man) the good (man)	T-Adj Adj

Notice the following:

1. In the attributive Nn-T-Adj construction, the noun must still be definite here, even if there is no article.

2. For the two predicative constructions, whatever is first is the focus. So, the Adj-T-Nn order places the predicate first. This order answers the question, "What is the subject?" So טוֹב הַמֶּ֫לֶךְ answers the question, "What is the

king?" The T-Nn-Adj order places the predicate last, הַמֶּלֶךְ הַטּוֹב answers the question, "Who is good?"

3. In the ambiguous positions, only context can determine whether the Adj is attributive or predicative. Only rarely is the context unclear.

4. The isolated position occurs most commonly with the article. In these cases the Adj agrees in gender and number with the supposed antecedent.

Translating substantival adjectives is interesting because of the difference of English number. For example, a well known chorus, "Blessed Be the Name of the Lord," uses Prov 18:10 as the refrain. Here is an interlinear version comparing versions:

Prov 18:10	וְנִשְׂגָּב	צַדִּיק	יָרוּץ	בּוֹ	יְהוָה	שֵׁם	עֹז	מִגְדַּל
	and he is saved	the righteous	(he) runs	into it	the Lord	(is) the name of	strength	tower of

NIV   The name of the Lord is a strong tower; the righteous run to it and are safe.

KJV   The name of the Lord is a strong tower: the righteous runneth into it, and is safe.

ESV   The name of the Lord is a strong tower; the righteous man runs into it and is safe.

In the second clause, the subject, "the righteous" is singular. The KJV preserves this by using the singular verbs "runneth" and "is." The ESV preserves the singular number and the masculine gender by adding the word *man*. The NIV could have preserved the singular verb, "runs," but thought that the isolated position "righteous," with a generic meaning, should be understood to include plural people.

A key difference between nouns and Adjs is that whereas nouns have one and only one gender, adjectives must be able to take the endings of either gender. As a pre-Hebrew student, you are not learning the endings, but a couple of examples will help you understand. We will use the Adj טוֹב, meaning "good," and the nouns אִישׁ, "man," and מִשְׁפָּחָה, "family." In the following chart, the endings are gray. The designations "m" and "f" stand for "masculine" and "feminine"; "s" and "p" stand for "singular" and "plural"; and "D" and "U" stand for "determined" and "undetermined."

Figure 12.3: Grammatical Agreement of Adjectives with Nouns

Hebrew	English	GN	Det
אִישׁ טוֹב	(a) good man	ms	U
אֲנָשִׁים טוֹבִים	good men	mp	U
הָאִישׁ הַטּוֹב	the good man	ms	D
הָאֲנָשִׁים הַטּוֹבִים	the good men	mp	D
מִשְׁפָּחָה טוֹבָה	(a) good family	fp	U
מִשְׁפָּחוֹת טוֹבוֹת	good families	fp	U
הַמִּשְׁפָּחָה הַטּוֹבָה	the good family	fs	D
הַמִּשְׁפָּחוֹת הַטּוֹבוֹת	the good families	fp	D

The Adjs agree in gender, number, and determination with their respective nouns. I purposely chose words that would have endings to make that clear. Sometimes the endings are not identical, but the gender and number still are. For example, דֶּרֶךְ is a feminine noun, even though it doesn't end in הָ . Nevertheless, "a good way" in Hebrew is דֶּרֶךְ טוֹבָה.

Adjectives Modifying Nouns in a Construct Chain

Since a construct chain is treated as a unit, it normally cannot be interrupted. If an Adj modifies one element of the chain, it is located after the chain and follows the rules given above. The adjective may modify either element of the chain. Study the following examples of attributive Adjs:

Figure 12.4: Grammatical Agreement of Adjectives with Nouns

Hebrew	English
בֶּן־הַנְּבִיאֵי הַטּוֹב	"the good son of the prophets" **Explanation:** "son" and "good" are both singular
בַּת־הַנְּבִיאִים הַטּוֹבִים	"the daughter of the good prophets" **Explanation:** Both "prophets" and "good" are plural and masculine; בַּת is singular and feminine.

בֶּן־הַנָּבִיא הַטּוֹב   "the good son of the prophet" *or*
"the son of the good prophet"
Explanation: Because both nouns and the Adj agree in gender, number, and definiteness, the Hebrew is ambiguous. The English must make a choice. Normally context makes clear which meaning is intended.

What can you do as a pre-Hebrew student?

When comparing versions, if you find differences in number, you can use the tools we have already mentioned repeatedly to get grammatical information.

Adjectives and Comparison

The simple adjective is called the positive. The comparative indicates the member of a group of items that has a certain quality to a greater degree. The superlative indicates the member that has a certain quality to the greatest degree. The figure below gives a few examples.

Figure 12.5: English Degrees of Comparison

Positive	Comparative	Superlative
big	bigger	biggest
fast	faster	fastest
good	better	best

Hebrew expresses degrees differently from English. The comparative may be expressed, as we saw in ch. 8 on prepositions (pp), by the pp מִן following an adjective. We learned in ch. 11 that Hebrew may also express a superlative with an expression that English renders with *of*, as in "king *of* kings," meaning "the greatest king." The superlative may be expressed by a simple adjective, by the phrase "from all / any of" (מִן־כָּל). It may also be expressed by the repetition of adjectives, "*Holy, holy, holy* is the Lord of hosts" (Isa 6:3).

Making Relatives Your Friends

Sometimes the people we find most difficult to get along with are those we are closest to. Who fights more often or more vigorously than brothers? And the closer in age, the more they pick at each other. Ah! But if an outsider comes between them, they gang up together like the closest of friends. This is what I want to do with relative clauses – make them your friends!

Let's begin with terms. Remember that a clause is an expression with a verb in it (as opposed to a phrase, which has no verb). A relative pronoun (RP) introduces a relative clause (RC) and relates it to a word in another clause. A RP does double duty. First, it has a grammatical function within the RC. Second, it has an antecedent outside the RC. A RC is a subordinate clause. A RC consists of a RP + the clause that follows it. Examples of RPs are: who, what, which, whose, that, whatever.

> **Important**: Do not confuse *who, what, which,* and *whose* with the interrogative pronouns that introduce questions! Or the relative *that* with the demonstrative pronoun *that*, or with the conjunction *that* that indicates purpose or result.

Sometimes the RP is omitted, as in "I *have* a car I *want* to sell." There are two clauses (both verbs are italicized). The second one describes the car. The sentence could be rewritten, "I have a car, *which* I want to sell."

In the chapter on clauses I told you that we would treat RCs here. The reason is because RCs have the same three functions as Adjs. The whole RC may function attributively, predicatively, or substantivally. When it functions substantivally, just like any noun, the RC can be the subject or object of a verb, or object of a preposition. In all three functions, a RC serves to describe.

What we need is a plan for dealing with RCs. In the concluding section, you will see how to deal with them in flowcharts. Here is a strategy for dealing with them in sentence form.

1. Circle the RP and draw an open bracket.

2. Find the end of the RC and draw a closing bracket. Sometimes this step involves some interpretation.

3. See if you can draw an arrow from RP to a noun *outside* of the RC.

   a. If you can, the RC is acting like an adjective and is describing that noun.

   b. If you cannot, the RC is acting like a noun and you need to describe it as subject or object of a verb or preposition.

   c. If it is the object of a preposition, circle the preposition and underline the complete prepositional phrase.

Here is an example illustrating each step.

Step   **Passage: Gen 11:5 (NIV)**

1   And the Lord came down to see the city and the tower,

    [(which) the children of man had built.

    Explanation: I notice the RP "which" (it doesn't introduce a question), circle it, and draw an open bracket. The RP functions as the DO of the RC verb, "had built."

2   And the Lord came down to see the city and the tower,

    [(which) the children of man had built.]

    Explanation: The RC ends at the end of the sentence, so that is where I put the closing bracket.

3   And the Lord came down to see the city and the tower,

    [(which) the children of man had built.]

    Explanation: The RP refers back to *tower*. Since I can draw an arrow to a word outside the RC, and since there is no verb "to be" between the RC and the antecedent, the RC is functioning adjectivally.

Here is another example, in which the RC has no antecedent and functions substantivally.

Step   **Passage: Gen 11:5 (NIV)**

1   And he said, "Divine for me by a spirit and bring up for me

    [(whomever) I shall name to you."]

Explanation: I notice the RP "whomever" (objective case), circle it, and draw brackets. The RP functions as the DO of the RC verb, "shall name." However, there is no antecedent outside the RC. Therefore the entire RC is functioning as a noun in the main clause, and is the DO of the verb "bring up."

To check our identification of a substantival use of the RC, substitute any noun for the RC to see if it makes sense. We might try, "Bob" or "lunch," yielding, "… and bring up Bob"; "… and bring up lunch." This checks out; the RC is functioning as a substantive.

Hebrew RCs work just the way English ones do, except they are simpler: there is only one RP, אֲשֶׁר. It may be translated by any of the English RPs, depending on the context. Oftentimes there is within the RC a resumptive pronoun or adverb that clarifies the referent of the אֲשֶׁר, and may be omitted just as in English. Study these two examples of interlinears.

The first example is Gen 7:19, which reads, "They rose greatly on the earth, and all the high mountains under the entire heavens were covered" (ESV). In Hebrew, "under the entire heavens" is a RC modifying "mountains":

	הַשָּׁמָיִם	כָּל	תַּחַת	•	אֲשֶׁר	הַגְּבֹהִים	הֶהָרִים
Gen 7:19	the heavens	all of	under	(were)	which	(the) high	the mountains

Expl. The RC begins with אֲשֶׁר and ends with the verse. Within the RC, the RP אֲשֶׁר functions as the subject Nom of a noun clause in which the predicate is a PP, "under all of the heavens." The RP has an antecedent, namely, "mountains." The RC is functioning attributively, describing the mountains.

In the next example from Gen 42:38, the RC has a resumptive pronoun. The NIV reads, 'But Jacob said, "My son will not go down there with you; his brother is dead and he is the only one left. If harm comes to him on the journey you are taking, you will bring my gray head down to the grave in sorrow."' In Hebrew, "you are taking" is a RC modifying the feminine noun דֶּרֶךְ.

	בָהּ	תֵּלְכוּ	אֲשֶׁר	דֶּרֶךְ
Gen 42:38	in her	you are walking	which	the way

NIV   the journey you are taking

ESV   the journey that you are to make

Expl.   The ESV preserves the RP; the NIV doesn't, just for stylistic reasons. The key thing to notice is the final PP בָהּ. The PrnSf is 3fs agreeing with the gender and number of the antecedent דֶּרֶךְ.

Flowcharting Adjectives and Relative Clauses

Flowcharting Adjs is going to depend on how you want to do it. Basically, I treat them the same way I treat possessive pronouns: since they have one main function (namely, describing), I usually keep them in the same line as the noun they modify. If there are lists of Adjs modifying one noun, I might indent them under the word they modify. The idea is to do whatever you find most helpful to make the grammar clear and avoid unnecessary work. Flowcharting RCs follows the example of all subordinate clauses: indent about one inch and draw a line to what the RC modifies. Note: in the function column, there is a blank line for the functions of the main clauses. You will learn how to label them in ch. 13.

Function	Vs	Flow Chart: Gen 29:2 (NIV)
(_____) Place	2	The stone . . . was large over the mouth of the well
Explanation		"Large" is a predicate Adj; it sits on the same line as the subject and rest of the predicate. In Hebrew, the phrase is גְּדוֹלָה (large) וְהָאֶבֶן (and the stone). The noun has the article, making it the subject, and the Adj does not, marking it as predicative.

Function	Vs	Flow Chart: Gen 27:34 (NIV)

Time
 (_____)
 Manner
 Description
 Addition
 Description
	34	When Esau heard his father's words,
		 he burst out
		      with a . . . cry
		      loud
		      and
		      bitter

Explanation	The Hebrew has a noun followed by two Adjs joined by the conjunction Waw. It is simpler to keep them in line; I indented them for illustrative purposes, because there was more than one. The function label for attributive Adjs is "Description"; they are indented under "cry," because that is what they modify.

Function	**Vs**	**Flow Chart** Josh 24:32 (NIV)

Sequence	32	And
(_____)		Joseph's bones, . . . <u>were buried</u>
Place		↑ at Shechem
Description		⌐ which the Israelites <u>had brought up</u>
Source		from Egypt

Explanation	The RC is subordinate and indented 1 inch. The ellipses (...) mark where the RC originally stood. The arrow points to the antecedent. Both the PPs are adverbial and are therefore indented under the verb each modifies.

Exercises

1. Identifying Relative Clauses. For the verses below, treat the RCs as we did in this chapter. If there is no antecedent, label the case function of the RC. The first one is done as an example. Watch out! Not all of these have RPs! If there is no RC at all, write "No RC" below the sentence. The first one is done as an example.

   a. **Gen 2:19b**   (He) brought them to the man to see [(what) he would call them.]
   RC = DO of "see"

   b. **Gen 28:22a**   and this stone, which I have set up for a pillar, shall be God's house.

   c. **Gen 28:22b**   And of all that you give me I will give a full tenth to you."

   d. **Gen 25:1**   Abraham took another wife, whose name was Keturah.

e. **Gen 21:17b** "What troubles you, Hagar?"

f. **Gen 15:7** And he said to him, "I am the Lord who brought you out from Ur of the Chaldeans to give you this land to possess."

g. **Gen 2:12** And the gold of that land is good; bdellium and onyx stone are there.

h. **Gen 46:6** They also took their livestock, which they had gained in the land of Canaan, and came into Egypt, Jacob and all of his offspring with him.

2. Flowcharting. Complete flowcharts for the following passages. You may use a computer following the directions given in ch. 8 or download the forms from www.teknia.com. Label each line except main clauses.

   a. 2 Sam 7:13 (NIV)

   b. Ruth 1:16 (NIV)

   c. Deut 6:6-7 (NIV)

   d. Zeph 3:12-13 (NIV)

Advanced Information and Curious Facts: The Shema.

Deuteronomy 6:4 is the famous "Shema" passage (named after the first Hebrew word in the verse). It is a verbless clause (see ch. 6). I give the text in interlinear format without supplying a verb and I have rendered God's name, traditionally rendered Lord, as Yahweh, to avoid confusion with the noun Lord. Below the interlinear I give two versions, NIV and KJV.

Deut 6:4	אֶחָד	יְהוָה	אֱלֹהֵינוּ	יְהוָה	יִשְׂרָאֵל	שְׁמַע
	one	Yahweh	our God	Yahweh	O Israel	Hear

NIV Hear, O Israel: The Lord our God, the Lord is one.

KJV Hear, O Israel: The Lord our God is one Lord.

The problems are 1) whether to translate the last four Hebrew words as one clause or two, and, 2) if one clause, where the verb should be placed. If it is two clauses, then it should be rendered, "Yahweh *is* our God; Yahweh *is* one." This makes sense, but the Greek translations of both the LXX and the NT (see Mark 12:29, for example) render this as one clause, as indicated by the fact that the Greek includes the verb *is* only at the end of the sentence.

Both the NIV and KJV follow the Greek in rendering this as one clause, but there is a difference about the placement of the verb. The KJV has taken the first phrase, in particular, "Yahweh," as the Subject Nominative and second Yahweh as a Predicate Nominative. At first read, this appears to make sense. But remember that both the LXX and NT render the name Yahweh with the Greek *kyrios*, "Lord, lord, master." Most modern versions follow that same practice. But in Hebrew, the term is not the title "Lord," but the actual name of God, "Yahweh." Taking the KJV and replacing "Lord" with "Yahweh" yields "Yahweh our God is one Yahweh." I suppose we can make sense out of this, but it is awkward.

The NIV understands the Hebrew (and the Greek) a bit differently: the first phrase is a Pending Nominative as indicated by the comma; then follows the Subject Nominative, Yahweh, and the predicate. Again replacing "the Lord" with "Yahweh" in the NIV yields: "As for Yahweh our God, Yahweh is one." Incidentally, this rendering also agrees with how the LXX translators understood the verse, and therefore the NT, since the Greek has the verb at the end.[1]

So what's the difference? Not a lot; it is a matter of emphasis. The KJV rendering makes the predicate Adj "one" less prominent. The NIV brings out the thrust of the Hebrew (and Greek) more simply and clearly: the Pending Nominative draws attention to the subject in the clause as the covenant God of Israel ("our"). Then the main clause makes the assertion: Yahweh is one, or unique. This is the great truth of the Shema passage.

---

[1] On LXX grammar, see John William Wevers, *Notes on the Greek Text of Deuteronomy* (Atlanta: Scholars, 1995), 114.

WEEK 5

Verbals

CHAPTER 13

Where Is the Action
Overview of Verbals

Objectives

1. Know the parts of speech comprising verbals

2. Know the seven things Hebrew verbs indicate

3. Know two ways that Hebrew verbs can take a DO

4. Understand some general features of Hebrew verbals, including word order

5. Use tools to identify verbs and understand parsing

6. Know how to flowchart main clause functions

Tools Used: Interlinear Bible

Introduction

The heart of any language is the verb. It describes the action related to the actors. In this chapter we will begin with some terminology common to verbs in any language. Then we will turn to general features of Hebrew verbs. There has been much research done in the last several decades on the nature of the Hebrew verbal system, and research is continuing. Some of the traditional models are beginning to be replaced, but traditional language is still common. Therefore you need to learn both traditional descriptions, because you will frequently come across these in your reading, and newer terminology, because it is more precise and it is becoming more current. Finally, we will deal with labeling main clause functions. Let's begin with some terminology.

Essential Concepts

As we introduced in ch. 5, there are two main types of verbal forms, *finite verbs* and *nonfinite verbs*. Some writers use the word *verb* to mean finite verbs as opposed to nonfinite. The term *verbal* is used to refer to both finite and nonfinite verbs.

A *verb* is a word that depicts an action or a state of being. I will call action verbs "dynamic;"[1] examples are *run, see, love*. The most common example of stative verb is *be*, but others are *become* and *remain*. Look at these examples with the verbs or verb phrases italicized:

Figure 13.1: Identifying Stative Verbs

Example	Analysis	Type of Action
The book *is* heavy.	*Be* + Adj	Stative
The man *was running*.	*Be* + Present Participle	Dynamic (Present Progressive)
Dinner *is* eaten.	*Be* + Past Participle	Stative
Dinner *was eaten*.	*Be* + Past Participle	Stative or Dynamic (Past Passive)
He *has eaten*	*Have* + Past Participle	Dynamic (Present Perfect)

Verbs that govern a direct object (DO) are called *transitive verbs*; verbs that do not take a DO are called *intransitive verbs*. Some verbs can do either. Look at the following examples:

S1. Paul ate a sandwich.

S2. Paul ate.

S3. Paul is full.

---

[1] Some grammarians call them "fientive", but I think "dynamic" is more descriptive.

In S1 the verb is *ate* and *sandwich* is what was eaten, the DO. Therefore *ate* is a transitive verb. In S2 there is no DO; and in this sentence, *ate* is intransitive. In S3, another stative verb, the adjective *full* is called a predicate Adj.

A *finite verb* has a grammatical subject. It is *limited* (hence the term *finite*) by that grammatical subject. We will treat Hebrew finite verbs in chapters 14-16. As we learned in chapter 6, a *clause* is an expression having a subject and finite verb (predicate).

A *nonfinite verb* is not limited by a grammatical subject, though it may modify a subject. Nonfinite verbs, therefore, cannot form clauses, but rather form *phrases*. There are two types of nonfinite verbs, infinitives and participles, which we will treat in chapter 17.

Parsing the English Verb

As native speakers, we may not realize it, but English verbs actually tell us many things: (1) person, (2) number, (3) tense, (4) voice, (5) aspect, and (6) mood.

The (1) *person* and (2) *number* of the verb match those of the subject. This is obvious in languages that are highly inflected, i.e., languages that change the "shape" of a verb by adding prefixes, suffixes, or infixes (collectively known as afformatives). English, however, is not a highly inflected language. So, we often use pronouns to indicate whether the grammatical subject is the speaker (first person), the one spoken to (second person), or the one spoken about (third person), and whether or not these are singular or plural.

(3) The word *tense* refers to the time frame of the action with respect to the speaker. It may be past, present, or future. (4) *Voice* is the description of how the action relates to the subject. For an *active voice* verb, the subject is the agent (doer) of the action; for a *passive voice* verb, the grammatical subject is the patient (receiver) of the action. English indicates voice by the presence or absence of the helping verb *to be*. (5) *Aspect* is how the action is portrayed. For example, an action might be simple, as in "Billy played," or progressive, as in "Billy was playing."

(6) *Mood* is generally understood as the relation of the action to reality. The *indicative mood* is the mood of "reality"; that is, events are portrayed as real. The *subjunctive mood* is the mood of "probability"; that is, events are portrayed as having some condition upon which accomplishment depends. Spoken English in America does not use the Subjunctive very much any more, except with "modal" verbs indicating probability, such as *can, may, should, could, ought*, etc. The *imperative*

mood is the mood of "volition"; that is, the fulfillment of the event depends upon the will, or volition, of someone other than the speaker.

Parsing the Hebrew Verb

We have already mentioned that the Hebrew verbal system is comprised of both finite and nonfinite forms. There are three traditional categories of finite forms: the perfect (ch. 14), the imperfect (ch. 15), and the volitional forms (ch. 16). Hebrew finite verbs convey all the information that English verbs convey by using two main features: a system of *afformatives* and a system of *stems*.

To begin, Figure 13.2 is reproduced from ch. 5:

Figure 13.2: Parsing Information for Nominals and Verbals

			← Verbal Qualities →					← Nominal Qualities →			
POS	Word	Lex	Stem	Form	P	G	N	State	Det	Case	Suff
Nn						X	X	X	X	X	
V			X	X	X	X	X				

Besides the root, you may remember that verbs share with nouns the qualities of gender and number (G, N). Unique to verbals is stem and form, and unique to finite verbs is person (P). Hebrew inflects (changes the "shape" of) verbs by using afformatives and stems. In the next chapters, you will get some idea of how that happens. For now, I will simply summarize what information the afformatives and stems provide.

Dynamic and Stative Verbs

One feature of Hebrew verbs (unlike English verbs) is the existence of stative verbs. Hebrew has verbs that indicate state in the Qal stem. These verbs can appear in the Hiphil stem to make them dynamic. For example, גָּדַל in the Qal stem is stative meaning "he was/became great" (note that to form this in English, we must use the verb be/became + the Adj great). In the Hiphil stem the verb הִגְדִּיל means "he made [something] great," and it is no longer stative. Hebrew dynamic verbs may be transitive (taking a DO) or intransitive (not taking a DO). Stative verbs do not take a DO.

Personal Afformatives

Afformatives are prefixes, suffixes, or a combination of both. These afformatives indicate a number of things.

1. **Person** - first, second, third person
2. **Number** - singular, plural
3. **Gender** - masculine, feminine, common.

   The person, gender and number (PGN) agree with that of the grammatical subject. In Hebrew the default gender is masculine. If the subject is "people," a group composed of both men and women, the grammatical gender used to refer to them is the masculine. Sometimes, even when the plural subjects are all women, a masculine personal ending is used, especially in the plural.

4. **"Tense"** - Hebrew traditionally has two "tenses," perfect and imperfect.
5. **Mood** - indicative, subjunctive, imperative, though in a manner different from English. We will use the terms real, corresponding to most of the English indicative mood, and irreal, corresponding to English future tense and subjunctive and imperative moods.

   Stem Formatives. The stems in Hebrew indicate:

6. **Voice** - active, passive, reflexive (in which the grammatical subject acts on itself). The doer of the action is the "agent" and the receiver of the action is "patient."
7. **Intensity** - simple, intensive, causative (but these will require a little further explanation).

Closeup on Hebrew Tenses

The word *tense* normally means "time." The English verbal system is dominated by time. The Hebrew verbal system, though, puts "time" in the background. More prominent is aspect, or a description of the nature of the action. English verbs do indicate time and aspect in a way quite unlike Hebrew. English uses auxiliary verbs; Hebrew uses afformatives and word order. Many commentators and grammarians use the word *tense* in reference to the form or "shape" of the Hebrew word; that is, the verb form with the various afformatives it may take. I use the word *form* to include all verbals, both finite and nonfinite forms.

I will present the Hebrew verb under five verb forms. Unfortunately, there are different names for the Hebrew tenses. Some grammarians use names based on time. Others use names based on aspect, thinking that "Perfect" tense forms represented completed action and "Imperfect" forms represented incompleted action. Due to difficulties with these names, other scholars gave them names based on the shape of the verb. This took two forms. Some named two forms calling them "Prefixed" and "Suffixed" conjugations; others wanted to identify more than two forms and used transliterated forms based on the Hebrew root *qtl* either with or without the vowels.[2] Because different authors use different terminology, you need to know how the different systems compare. Figure 13.3 constitutes a list of the five verb forms we will treat and the various systems of naming.

Figure 13.3:Various Names Used for Hebrew Tense Forms

Form Names	Alternate Form Names	Aspect Names	Time Names
qatal = *qtl*	(Suffixed)	Perfect (Pf)	Past
weqatal = *wqtl*	(Waw-relative + Suffixed)	ו consecutive + Perfect	
yiqtol = *yqtl*	(Prefixed)	Imperfect (Imp)	Future
[*weyiqtol*] [= *wyqtl*]	(Simple Waw + Prefixed)	ו conjunctive + Imperfect	[Future]
wayyiqtol = *wayyqtl*	(Waw-relative + Prefixed)	ו consecutive + Imperfect	Preterite
		ו conversive + Imperfect	
		ו sequential +Imperfect	
qotel	Participle	Progressive	Present

The *weyiqtol* form is in brackets because it has the same range of meanings as *yiqtol* and we will treat them together. I avoid the "Time Names." However, there are advantages to the other systems and I use both interchangeably.

---

[2] The vowels that are included, e.g., *qatal*, also indicate the stem. Since stem is not significant when talking about tense forms, some grammarians chose to leave them out.

So, what about time in Hebrew verbs? Hebrew verbs indicate time relative to the context. Basically, Hebrew verbs with prefixed ו have a time that is relative to a previous verb. Hebrew verbs without prefixed ו have their time determined by adverbial time expressions.

Time in Hebrew is complicated and still not fully understood. In this course it is enough to rely on English translations for time and trust the translators and commentators. Mood and relative time can be combined in chart form.[3]

Figure 13.4: Hebrew Verb Forms, Mood, and Relative Time

	Time Relative to Previous Verb			
	Sequential	**Simultaneous**	**Anterior**	**Background**
qatal (ch. 14)		Real & Irreal	Real	Real
weqatal (ch. 14)	Irreal			
yiqtol (ch. 15)			Irreal	Irreal
wayyiqtol (ch. 15)	Real			
qotel (ch. 17)		Real & Irreal		

The meaning of these time relationships is as follows:

1. **Sequential** - action after the previous modal verb, either chronologically or logically

   But I will establish (V1) my covenant with you, and *you will enter* (V2, וּבָאתָ, *weqatal*) the ark…. (Gen 6:18, NIV - a chronological sequence)

2. **Simultaneous** - action at the same time as the previous verb

   But the LORD came down (V1) to see the city and the tower that the men *were building* (V2, בָּנוּ, *qatal*). (Gen 11:5, NIV)

---

[3] For this treatment I am indebted to Galia Hatav, "Teaching the Biblical Hebrew Verbal System," *Hebrew Higher Education* 12 (2007): 5-52, and her *The Semantics of Aspect and Modality: Evidence from English and Hebrew* (Philadelphia: John Benjamins, 1997), whose work I am adapting and simplifying in this and the next few chapters.

3. **Anterior** - action before the previous verb

God saw (V1) all that he *had made* (V2, עָשָׂה, *qatal*), and it was very good. (Gen 1:31, NIV)

4. **Background** - circumstance existing before the previous verb

The man and his wife were both naked, and they felt (V1) no shame. Now the serpent was (V2, הָיָה, *qatal*) more crafty than any of the wild animals the LORD had made. (Gen 2:25-3:1, NIV)

Close–up on Hebrew Stems

There are seven major verb stems in Hebrew (and a number of minor stems). Some of them, however, are simply the passive forms of the active stems. The most common stem is called the Qal stem. Qal is an actual Hebrew word meaning "light" or "simple," and is used because this stem simply adds personal afformatives to the root without any changes inside the root. The lexical form is the 3ms (third person masculine singular) because it is marked by having no personal afformative; it is "simple."

The other stems are called "derived" stems by modern grammarians, because they are formed by adding some feature to the simple root before attaching the personal afformatives. The name of each of the derived stems is not descriptive, as the word Qal is, but simply an example. Modern grammarians have also created another system of naming using descriptive terms, rather than examples. Since both are used, learning both is helpful.

Figure 13.5: Names and Forms of the Hebrew Stems

Classical Name	Hebrew Pattern	Modern Name	Explanation
Qal	קַל	G *or* Q	"G" is used for a German word meaning "base form"; "Q" is used for Qal. We will use Q.
Niphal	נִפְעַל	N	Stem is characterized by a prefixed נ, or "N."
Piel	פִּעֵל	D	These stems are characterized by a doubled (hence the "D") second root letter. The active stem has an "e-i" theme vowel (note the Tsere)

under the second root; the passive has an "a" theme vowel (note the Patach below).[4]

Pual	פֻּעַל	Dp (passive)	See above.
Hiphil	הִפְעִיל	H	These stems are characterized by a prefixed ה, or "H." Again the active one has an "e-i" theme vowel and the passive has an "a" theme vowel (see below).
Hophal	הָפְעַל	Hp (passive)	See above.
Hithpael	הִתְפַּעֵל	Htd	This stem has a prefixed syllable הִת, "Ht," plus a doubled (d) second letter.

The names of the stems and their basic functions are given in the Figure below. I use as a model the Hebrew root קטל, which means "kill"; the meaning is unfortunate, but this root is useful because it has no "weak" letters that cause deviations from the normal patterns of word formation.

Figure 13.6: Overview of Intensity and Voices of Stems

Voice	Simple	Intensive	Causative
Active	Q – Qal he killed קָטַל	D – Piel he brutally killed קִטֵּל	H – Hiphil he made (someone) kill הִקְטִיל
Passive	N – Niphal he was killed נִקְטַל	Dp – Pual he was brutally killed קֻטַּל	Hp – Hophal he was made to kill הָקְטַל
Reflexive	N – Niphal he killed himself נִקְטַל	HtD – Hithpael he brutally killed himself הִתְקַטֵּל	–

---

[4] Unfortunately, the ע in Hebrew does not take Daghesh. See Fig. 13.6 for a clearer example.

Two Ways Verbs Take a Direct Object (DO)

You learned that Hebrew nouns and prepositions can take pronominal suffixes (PrnSfs). For example, דָּבָר means "word"; and דְּבָרוֹ means "his word." לוֹ is a prepositional phrase meaning "to him." Hebrew verbs can also take a Prn Sf. This is one of two ways that Hebrew can mark the DO. The other way is to introduce a definite DO with the particle אֵת (or אֹת when the DO is a PrnSf). This particle is never translated with an English word.

In the examples below the DO is in grey type.

בָּרָא אֵת הַשָּׁמַיִם	He created	➔	the heavens.
קָטַלְתִּי אֹתוֹ	I killed	➔	him.
קְטַלְתִּיו	I killed	➔	him.

In the first example, the particle אֵת marks הַשָּׁמַיִם as the DO. In קָטַלְתִּי אֹתוֹ, the PrnSf is attached to the other form of the particle אֵת. In קְטַלְתִּיו, the PrnSf is attached directly to the verb. Note three important things:

1. The PrnSf has no effect on the meaning of the verb.

2. The PrnSf attached to a verb functions as the DO.

3. The PrnSf is never reflexive. For example, the form קְטָלוֹ, in which the verb is 3ms and the PrnSf is also 3ms, might be translated "he killed him." The question is, can the PrnSf ("him") ever refer to the grammatical subject ("he") so that it might be understood to mean "he killed himself" with the English reflexive Prn? No, it can't. Hebrew does not have reflexive Prns. Instead it expressed this reflexive idea by using certain verb stems (see Figures 11.1 and 13.6).

Retrieving and Using Information

Getting stem information for Hebrew verbs is now pretty simple. If you were learning full Hebrew, you would learn how to identify the stems from sight. With what you have learned so far, you can use books such as Davidson, *The Analytical Hebrew and Chaldee Lexicon*, or John Joseph Owens, *Analytical Key to the Old Testament*. Of course the computer Bible programs make these books obsolete. The point is that identifying the stem is simple by using these tools.

By using these resources you can sometimes figure out the meaning of the verb in its different stems. But there are actually very few verbs in the OT that appear in all seven stems. For example, קָטַל does not. The meanings I gave are only theoretical to illustrate a point. The actual meaning, as always, must be determined from context. An interesting example of a verb that does appear in all seven stems is יָלַד. Figure 13.7 provides translations of the word in each stem. In the last column I describe the various roles involved.

Figure 13.7: יָלַד in Seven Stems

Stem	Definition	Explanation
Qal	Bear children	The action of the mother (but also used of the father)
Niphal	Be born	The action of the child
Piel	Help at birth	The action of the midwife
Pual	Be born	Child born (with help of midwife ?)
Hiphil	Beget	The action of the father
Hophal	Be born	Child begotten (by a father)
Hithpael	Register	The action of an official recorder of births

Most of these meanings are pretty simple to figure out, such as the Niphal being the passive of the Qal. Some of them, such as the Hithpael, make sense, but are not predictable.

An Important Warning about Stems and Meaning

Figure 13.7 is actually an oversimplification. Notice that the Qal is used of the mother's role, but it is not exclusive to her. The father's role is described by both the Qal and the Hiphil stems. One cannot determine the meaning of a word solely on the basis of identifying the stem. Meaning is determined by usage.

If you were learning full Hebrew, you would learn more about the functions of the stems. Figure 13.7 above gives you only the general functions.

The *SNIVEC* gives you this information in a reliable format. Take for example the entry for G/K 3086 on p. 1409:

Figure 13.8: Verb and Stem Information in SNIVEC

3086 ¹חָרַשׁ *ḥāraš*, v. [27] [➔ 3045, 3046?, 3088, 3093, 3096, 3098, 4739].
[Q] to plow; engrave; plan, plot; [Qp] to be inscribed; [N] to be plowed; [H] to plot
against:- plow (6), plot (3), be plowed (2), plowed (2), plowing (2), craftsman (1),
devises (1), farmer (1), inscribed (1), plan (1), planted (1), plots (1), plotting (1
[+2021 +8288]), plowman (1), plowmen (1), plows (1), tools (1)

The superscript "¹" (with ¹חָרַשׁ) indicates that this is the first in a list of roots
with the same root letters; "v." means it is a verb; the numbers in brackets after the
"➔" are other words derived from this root. Then the definitions are given for
each of the stems in which the verb appears: Q = Qal; Qp = Qal Passive; N =
Niphal; H = Hiphil. The entry concludes with a list of translations and frequencies
for each.

What You Can and Cannot Do.

1. You are *not* qualified to determine the meaning of a word based on the general functions of the stems. Leave this to the experts.

2. You *can* find out what stem a given verb is by using books and computer tools mentioned in this chapter.

3. You *can* now understand what the *SNIVEC* is telling you in the dictionary sections to the Hebrew and Aramaic words (and other study tools).

4. You *can* learn the meaning of a given verb in a given stem using lexicons and word books.

5. You *can* sort your words according to stem when you do word studies on OT verbs and take the stem into account when determining meaning.

"Now, about word order you I will tell!"

If you are a Star Wars fan, perhaps you can hear Yoda's voice speaking the
title to this section. In Yoda-speak, the subject and verb tend to come last. When
we hear it, we laugh, because, though we understand the meaning, the sentence
sounds funny. Normally word order in an English clause is Subject-Verb-Object
(SVO). Normal Hebrew word order is Verb-Subject-Object (VSO). Deviations from
this order are common. What we mean is that whenever a sentence is not VSO, it
may be "marked" for a special purpose.

Hebrew constructions are best classified according to how they begin. You want to pay particular attention to the following constructions ("cj" means "conjunction"):

1. ְו   + verb
2. ְו   + nonverb
3. other cj   + verb
4. other cj   + nonverb
5. no cj   + verb
6. no cj   + nonverb

Because you know the Hebrew alphabet and the cj Waw, you can identify which structure a Hebrew clause has by consulting an interlinear OT. In the coming chapters we will look at these structures with respect to the verbal forms and in the last unit we will look at them with respect to narrative and poetry.

Flowcharting Main/Independent Clauses

In the chapter on clauses you learned how to tell the difference between main/independent clauses and subordinate clauses. In the chapter on conjunctions you learned that the functions for dependent clauses are indicated by the subordinating conjunction. Now you need to know how to label main/independent clauses. Bill Mounce in *Greek for the Rest of Us* calls these "Foundational Expressions." I will build from his list and offer brief explanations.

Labeling Functions

Foundational clauses can be organized around two main categories that correspond roughly to the moods mentioned above. Actions whose reality is assumed by the writer/speaker are called *real*, corresponding to the indicative mood of English. Actions whose reality has to do with necessity or possibility are called *irreal*, corresponding to the English subjunctive and imperative moods. The major difference is that whereas English has a Future tense in the Indicative Mood, in Hebrew expressions in future time are regarded as *irreal*, because they have not yet occurred and are therefore only possible. Some grammarians and commentators use the term *modal* for *irreal*. I prefer *irreal* because it seems broader than *modal*. It is important to understand that *irreal* does not necessarily mean that a statement is *unreal* or untrue, or that it won't happen; it merely means that a particular event has not yet happened.

Figure 13.9: Real Main/Independent Clause Functions

Label	Explanation
Assertion	A statement of simple existence of a fact; usually in present time. **Example (NIV):** "The Lord *is* my strength and my song" (Exod 15:2). "I do not seal my lips, as you *know*, O Lord" (Ps 40:9).
Event/Action	Report of an event as having happened; past time. **Example (NIV):** "In the beginning God *created* the heavens and the earth" (Gen 1:1).
Exclamation	Emphatic Assertion; often an "incomplete" sentence. **Example (NIV):** "*Ah, Sovereign Lord*" (Jer 1:6).
Rhetorical Question	A question intending to make a point, rather than find out information. A rhetorical question therefore assumes a reality. **Example (NIV):** 'And Joshua said, "*Why have you brought this trouble on us?* The Lord will bring trouble on you today"' (Josh 7:25).

Figure 13.10: Irreal Main/Independent Clause Functions

Prediction	A statement in future tense. This includes promises and predictions. **Example (NIV):** "My eyes *will watch* over them for their good, and I will bring them back to this land" (Jer 24:6).
Habitual/Gnomic	An action is viewed as repeated. The time frame may be past, present or future. The term *gnomic* means a general, proverbial truth.

	Example (NIV): "Now Moses *used to take* a tent and pitch it some distance away, calling it the 'tent of meeting'" (Exod 33:7). "For this reason a man *will leave* his father and mother and be united to his wife" (Gen 2:24; cf. the NET, "a man *leaves*").
Command/Request	The speaker is trying to impose his will on another. A command is offered by a superior to an inferior; a request (a.k.a., a prayer) is offered by an inferior to a superior. In English the 2nd person subject is implied. **Example (NIV)**: 'Then the officials said to Baruch, "You and Jeremiah, *go* and *hide*. Don't let anyone know where you are"' (Jer 36:19). "*Show* me your ways, O Lᴏʀᴅ, *teach* me your paths" (Ps 24:4).
Exhortation	Statement by a superior encouraging others to do or be something. Sometimes the speaker is included. Exhortation has the 1st person as the subject. **Example (NIV)**: 'Saul said, "*Let us* go down after the Philistines by night and plunder them till dawn, and let us not leave one of them alive"' (1 Sam 14:36).
Obligation	A "must" statement. Hebrew has also 3rd person imperatives that in English are often translated "may" or "let" with the grammatical subject listed second. **Example (NIV)**: "'Has anyone built a new house and not dedicated it? *Let him go* home'" (Deut 20:5), meaning "he must go" or the *non-question*, "may he go."
Permission	A "may" statement with the subject having permission to do something, but the action is not viewed as having yet ended. **Example (NIV)**: "We *may* eat fruit from the trees in the garden" (Gen 3:2).
Question	A question intending to find out information does not assume anything in existence and is therefore irreal (the

answer may be real).

Example (NIV): 'Then they asked Baruch, "Tell us, *how did you come to write all this? Did Jeremiah dictate it?*"' (Jer 36:17).

Desire   A statement whose reality is in doubt by the speaker, but he is not trying to impose his will on another.

Example (NIV): All the Israelites … said to them, "*If only* we had died in Egypt! Or in this desert!" (Num 14:2).

A Word on Conditional Sentences

Conditional sentences are made up of two clauses, an "if" clause and a "then" clause. The "then" part, called the apodosis, is the main clause and can have any of the above main clause functions. The "if" part, called the protasis, is a subordinate clause (see chapters 6 and 7). These may be possible conditional statements or impossible, known as "contrary to fact." Here is an example of each with the conditional clause indented above the main clause:

Potential Condition: "If anyone kills Cain,
he will suffer vengeance seven times over."
(Gen 4:15)

Contrary to fact condition: "If we had not delayed [but we did],
we could have gone and returned twice."
(Gen 43:10)

One final reminder

In this and the coming chapters, you will be learning many things, but you must not forget that this is not a full Hebrew course. Even a student who completes a two-year course in biblical Hebrew is not knowledgeable enough to engage in exegesis completely independent from the work of professionals. However, you are in a position to make more detailed observations of the text and better understand commentators and translations.

Exercises

1. **Dynamic vs. Stative.** For each clause portion, taken from Isaiah 6, I give the translation. Indicate whether the Hebrew verb is stative or dynamic; the majority will be dynamic. The first one is done as an example.

	Hebrew	NIV Translation	Verb Type
a.	וָאֶרְאֶה	I saw	dynamic
b.	יְכַסֶּה	he covered	
c.	וְקָרָא	and they were calling	
d.	וַיָּנֻעוּ	they shook	
e.	יִמָּלֵא	was filled	
f.	נִדְמֵיתִי	"I am ruined."	
g.	רָעוּ	"... have seen ..."	
h.	וַיָּעָף	"flew"	
I.	לָקַח	he had taken	
j.	אֶשְׁלַח	shall I send	

2. **Noting Word Order at Clause Beginnings.** Using a traditional interlinear Bible or computer program, indicate (1) whether the Hebrew clause begins with a Waw conjunction, other conjunction, or no conjunction by writing "Waw," "cj," or "0" in the Conjunction column, and (2) whether the clause begins with a verb or non-verb by writing "verb" or "non-verb" in the second column. I give two examples, for each of which I have provided an interlinear. For the narrative section of Gen 22, ignore direct speech, which I have put in italic type, and relative clauses, for which I have supplied the answer. Exodus 15 is a poem and is therefore direct speech of the author rather than reported direct speech of someone else by an author.

Gen 23:2	אַרְבַּע	בְּקִרְיַת	שָׂרָה	וַתָּמָת
	Arba	in Kiryath	Sarah	and she died

Ps 23:1	רֹעִי	•	יְהוָה
	my shepherd	(is)	the Lord

Verse	Passage (NIV)	Conjunction	Verb/Nonverb
Gen 23:2	She died at Kiryath Arba.	וֹ	verb
Ps 23:1	The LORD is my shepherd.	0	nonverb
Gen 22:1b	He said to him, "Abraham!"		
Gen 22:1c	"Here I am," he replied.		
Gen 22:2	Then God said, "Take your son ..."		
Gen 22:3a	Early the next morning Abraham got up		
Gen 22:3b	and saddled his donkey.		
Gen 22:3c	He took with him two of his servants and his son Isaac.		
Gen 22:3d	When he had cut enough wood for the burnt offering,		
Gen 22:3e	he set out [note: there are two verbs in Hebrew] for the place		
Gen 22:3f	God had told him about	0	verb
Exod 15:1a	Then Moses and the Israelites sang this song to the LORD		
Exod 15:1b	[NIV leaves untranslated; KJV has "and spake, saying"]		
Exod 15:1c	I will sing to the LORD		

Exod 15:1d	for he is highly exalted.
Exod 15:1e	The horse and its rider he has hurled into the sea.
Exod 15:2a	The LORD is my strength and my song;
Exod 15:2b	he has become my salvation.
Exod 15:2c	He is my God,
Exod 15:2d	and I will praise him,
Exod 15:2e	my father's God,
Exod 15:2f	and I will exalt him.

3. **Flowcharting Main Clauses.** In the text below, I have indented all subordinate clauses. The main clauses are kept far left, even in direct speech. Using the categories from Figures 13.9 and 13.10, write the function in the blank provided. The first one is done as an example. Note that direct discourse is indented 1 inch and marked with bullets.

Function	Vs	Flow Chart: Judg 4:17-21 (NIV)
Event	17	Sisera, however, fled on foot to the tent of Jael,
		the wife of Heber the Kenite,
_____		because there were friendly relations
_____		between Jabin king of Hazor
		and
_____		the clan of Heber the Kenite.
_____	18	Jael went out to meet Sisera
		and
_____		said to him,
_____		• "Come, my lord,

———————————
———————————
———————————

               come right in.

               • Don't be afraid."

So he entered her tent,

    and

———————————

she put a covering over him.

19   •• "I'm thirsty,"

———————————

he said.

———————————

        •• "Please give me some water."

———————————

 She opened a skin of milk,

———————————

gave him a drink,

    and

———————————

covered him up.

20   "Stand in the doorway of the tent,"

———————————

he told her.

———————————

          "If someone comes by and asks you,

———————————

            'Is anyone here?'

———————————

     say 'No.' "

21 But Jael, Heber's wife, picked up a tent peg

———————————

               and

            a hammer

   and

went quietly to him

———————————

       while he lay fast asleep, exhausted.

———————————

She drove the peg through his temple into the ground,

———————————

    and

he died.

———————————

Advanced Information and Curious Facts

One Bible verse well-known to many parents is Prov 22:6, "Train a child in the way he should go, and when he is old he will not depart from it." Putting this in a flowchart yields:

Function	Vs	Flow Chart Prov 22:6 (NIV)		
Command	17	(You)	Train	a child
Sphere				in the way
Description				he should go
Addition			and	
Time				when he is old
?			he	will not depart
Separation				from it

I've labeled all the clauses, except the last one. This is the key. Many people see the future tense, "will not depart," and read this as a promise. This is a grammatical possibility, as you can see from the explanation of the Future label in Figure 13.10. Many parents with straying children cling to this verse as some sort of promise from God that eventually their child will come back to the Lord. When that doesn't happen, the parent may be heading toward a crisis of faith. Are God and his Word trustworthy?

However, this understanding of the proverb may be incorrect in at least a couple of ways. First, this text is specifically speaking about the child trained properly and staying true to the way of the Lord. It says that a person so trained when he is a child will not stray from the truth when he is an adult. It is not promising that a rebellious adult will turn back to the Lord after he has already departed from the right way. Second, "future promise" is not the only possible function that this verb can have. In the next chapters we will learn that this tense (Imperfect) is the tense for irreality. It might have any of the other functions. Most likely the function is gnomic. The gnomic function is proverbial; that is, it is a statement that is generally true. In the explanation, I said that these are often translated with the English present tense. This is one that is not, except in the little used Young's Literal Translation, which reads, "Even when he is old he turneth not from it."

How do you tell what function is best here? As always, context. The most important context for the book of Proverbs is that of genre, or the type of literature. Because details on genre are beyond the scope of this book, after you complete this study, you need to read a book like *How To Read the Bible for All Its Worth* by Fee and Stuart (3rd ed.; Grand Rapids: Zondervan, 2003). They describe the Hebrew term *proverb* as meaning "a *brief, particular* expression of a truth. The briefer a statement is, the less likely it is to be totally precise and universally applicable" (p. 232; italics theirs). To read Proverbs as a collection of universally true promises instead of as a collection of generally true maxims is to misread them in a way different than the author intended. The grammar you have studied this far bears this out. For confirmation of this interpretation based on the conjunction *and*, see the Exegetical Insight by Gordon P. Hugenberger in Pratico and Van Pelt, *Basics of Biblical Hebrew*, 2nd edition, 162-63. Hugenberger makes another important observation on the Hebrew text behind the English "in the way he should go." To get started, look up the verse in an interlinear.

CHAPTER 14

When the Perfect Comes
Perfect Forms

Objectives

1. Understand the concept of "event" and the different ways it can be described

2. Identify the two constructions of the Perfect and its possible meanings

3. Know that verbs can take pronominal suffixes as objects

4. Use tools to identify verb form

Tools Used: Grammatically tagged computer Hebrew interlinear or paper interlinear plus Davidson or Owens

Introduction

In the last chapter you were introduced to the Hebrew verbal system. The first finite verb form is called the Perfect. Remember that Hebrew verb forms indicate aspect rather than time.

In this chapter you will learn (1) the two constructions of the Perfect, (2) how Pf verbs are inflected and how those relate to the subject of the verb, (3) two ways that the direct object (DO) is indicated, (4) how to use tools to find out this information, and most importantly, (5) the main functions of the two constructions.

The Two Perfect Constructions

You will recall from the last chapter that scholars refer to this form by different names. The term Perfect (Pf) is intended to be a description of the perfective aspect, namely, a completed action, typically translated by the English past tense. We will see, however, that the Pf can be used in any time frame. The other terms are "suffixed" and *qatal* or *qtl*.

The two constructions are identified by whether or not the verb has a prefixed Waw. Without Waw the verb form is called *qatal*; with the Waw it's called *weqatal*. Since the *qatal* form often portrays a past event and the *weqatal* form often portrays a future event, earlier grammarians thought the Waw converted the past time to future and therefore called it Waw Conversive. Sometimes the time was not changed; that Waw was then called Waw Conjunctive. Recent studies understand the functions of Waw differently and use the terms *qatal* and *weqatal*.

Inflecting the Perfect Tense

Personal endings on Hebrew verbs indicate person, gender, and number (PGN). Gender may be masculine (m), feminine (f), or common (c). Gender is distinguished only in second and third persons. First person verbs do not distinguish gender. Therefore, we label first person verbs as "common."

Figure 14.1 shows how personal endings in Hebrew attach to the verbal root. The black letters are the personal endings; the gray letters are those of the verbal root. The gray vowels are a function of the stem, not the personal ending. The shading in the English translations corresponds to the shading of the Hebrew. The suffixes indicate PGN, but also mark the verb form as "Perfect." Remember that the translation provided is only one of the several possible translations.

Figure 14.1: Personal Endings for the Pf Tense of the Qal Stem

PGN	Hebrew	Translation
3ms	קָטַל	he killed
3fs	קָטְלָה	she killed
2ms	קָטַ֫לְתָּ	you (ms) killed
2fs	קָטַלְתְּ	you (fs) killed
1cs	קָטַ֫לְתִּי	I killed
3cp	קָטְלוּ	they killed
2mp	קְטַלְתֶּם	you (mp) killed
2fp	קְטַלְתֶּן	you (fp) killed
1cp	קָטַ֫לְנוּ	we killed

Notice:

1. The dictionary form for most verbs is the Qal stem, Pf, 3rd person, masculine gender, singular number. With the abbreviations we are using here, that can be shortened to "Q Pf 3ms."

2. The Hebrew personal endings are a function of the tense form, not the stem. What this means is that these same personal endings are used for all stems. This is good news for you when you learn full Hebrew!

3. The names *qatal* and *weqatal* include any combination of PGN. The personal ending is unimportant for the naming of the tense.

So, how do these personal endings relate to a subject? First, since a verb includes PGN information, a single verb constitutes a complete sentence. For example, to say "he ate" requires only one Hebrew word, אָכַל. In this sentence the identity of the subject is not expressed. To translate it into English the pronoun "he" must be added. Hebrew can also add the pronoun, but it is not required.

Second, when the subject is expressed, it commonly follows the verb; remember that normal word order for a verbal clause is verb-subject-object (VSO). To specify the subject as in "Abram and Sarah went," Hebrew would say הָלְכוּ אַבְרָם וְשָׂרָה, literally, "they went Abram and Sarah." The writer is reporting to the reader that both Abram and Sarah went. Since Abram and Sarah are the subject, the person of the verb is third. The subject of the verb is plural, the number of the verb is plural (there are many exceptions to this, but this is the norm). Since the compound subject is both masculine and feminine and the gender of the Pf 3p ending is common, just like the Prn "they." To translate, English includes the pronoun only when the subject is not expressed. When the subject is expressed, the pronoun must be dropped. So, for הָלְכוּ אַבְרָם וְשָׂרָה, it is incorrect to translate, "they went Abram and Sarah." Since the subject is expressed, it takes the place of the English pronoun: "Abram and Sarah went."

Now you can understand one more feature of the *Lexham Hebrew-English Interlinear Bible*. Here is Gen 1:1.[1]

---

[1] Christo van der Merwe, *The Lexham Hebrew-English Interlinear Bible; Bible. O.T. Hebrew.*, Gen 1:1 (Logos Research Systems, Inc., 2004).

Figure 14.2: Lexham Hebrew-English Interlinear Bible for Gen 1:1

הָאָרֶץ׃	וְאֵת	הַשָּׁמַיִם	אֵת	אֱלֹהִים	בָּרָא	בְּרֵאשִׁית
ה • ארץ	ו • את	ה • שמים	את	אלהים	ברא	ב • ראשית
the • earth	and • [obj]	the • heaven	[obj]	God	create	in • beginning
the • earth	and • [obj]	the • heaven	[obj]	God	(he) created	in • the beginning (of)
XD · NCcSFPH	CC · PA	XD · NCcDMNH	PA	NPDSMN	VqAsSM3	PB · NCcSFC

Notice that in the column for בָּרָא, the second row gives the lexical form, ברא, the lexical meaning, "create," and the inflected meaning "(he) created." The reason the pronoun is there is to alert you to the fact that the PGN is 3ms (which is also indicated in the parsing information in the last row; "SM3" means singular, masculine, 3rd person). The parentheses are there to make clear that the subject, אֱלֹהִים, is expressed and the pronoun *he* ought not to be translated.

Using Tools to Gather Information

Using the tools that you are now familiar with, you are able to complete a parsing chart for verbs. I have given a couple of noun as examples just for comparison. In your work, you will probably not be filling out many of these, but you could. It is a handy way to collect information, especially if you are using books such as Davidson. You will get a chance to practice below.

Figure 14.3: Parsing Information for Nominals and Verbals

			← Verbal Qualities →					← Nominal Qualities →			
POS	Word	Lex	Stem	Form	P	G	N	State	Det	Case	Suff
Nn	דְּבַר	דָּבָר				m	s	cst	[?]	[?]	
Nn	דְּבָרָיו	דָּבָר				m	p	cst	[?]	[?]	3ms
V	קָטַל	קטל	Q	Pf	3	m	s				
V	נִקְטַלְתִּי	קטל	N	Pf	1	c	s				
V	גֵּרַשְׁתִּיו	גרשׁ	D	Pf	1	c	s				3ms
V	וַהֲשִׁבֹתִיךָ	שׁוב	H	ו + Pf	1	c	s				2ms

You'll notice that for the Form I've used "Pf" and "ו + Pf" instead of "*qatal*" and "*weqatal*." The reason is purely practical: "ו + Pf" fits in the chart better.

The Functions of the Perfect Forms

We mentioned above three qualities about action that languages indicate in some way: mood (the relationship of the action to reality), time, and aspect (the portrayal of the progress of the action). In Hebrew, the main functions of verbs are mood and aspect. The tense forms also correspond to the two moods that we saw in ch. 13 (Figures 13.9 and 13.10). In the rest of this chapter I will describe the mood and aspects of each. I will also provide a figure that relates Hebrew and English verb uses using English time frames.

Mood and Aspect of *Qatal* and *Weqatal* [2]

The *qatal* (Perfect) may be either Real or Irreal as indicated in the text by context. It is mostly used, however, for Real functions. The *weqatal* form indicates Irreal functions.

To understand aspect, we need to start with the components of an event. Think of an event as having a beginning, a middle in progress, and an end. Graphically:

Figure 14.4: Phases of an Event

Progression

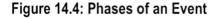
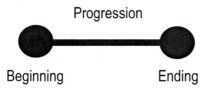

Beginning   Ending

As mentioned in the previous chapter, verbs can describe two broad categories of action: completed or incompleted. Completed action can be subdivided into five distinct aspects; incompleted action can be subdivided into two additional aspects.

---

[2] For this treatment I am indebted to Galia Hatav, "Teaching the Biblical Hebrew Verbal System," *Hebrew Higher Education* 12 (2007): 5-52, and her *The Semantics of Aspect and Modality: Evidence from English and Hebrew* (Philadelphia: John Benjamins, 1997), whose work I am adapting and simplifying.

The aspects are also related to mood. Real mood verbs are limited to perfective aspect. Except for the *qotel* form, which is only incompleted aspect, Irreal mood verbs can have any of the seven aspects. In the next figure, I give the names of these aspects, a description, and a graphic representation, showing the relationship to mood.

Figure 14.5: Seven Aspects of an Event

Mood	Aspect	Description	Representation
Real/Irreal	Constative	Portrays the event as a whole	
Real/Irreal	Instantaneous	Event has no progression; beginning = ending	
Real/Irreal	Ingressive (Inceptive)	Focus on the beginning of the event; progress not really in view	
Real/Irreal	Resultative (Telic)	Focus on the ending of the event; progress not really in view	
Real/Irreal	Perfective	Portrays both a completed action with resulting state	
Irreal	Iterative (Habitual, Customary)	Focus on the progress of a repeated event	
Irreal	Continuous	Focus on the progress of a constant action or state without viewing beginning or ending	

Aspect in the *Qatal* Form

The *qatal* and *weqatal* verbs are flexible forms in terms of how they portray action. What this means is that Hebrew can use these forms to portray any of the seven aspects. The unaffected meaning (i.e., the intrinsic meaning of the form unaffected by word meaning or context) of the *qatal* is Constative. However, that meaning can be affected by word meaning or context to indicate one of the other aspects, either Real or Irreal. The *weqatal* form is sequential to a previous verb and is Irreal. Here are examples of the *qatal* representing each aspect.

1. **Constative.** In the beginning God created (בָּרָא) the heavens and the earth (Gen 1:1, NIV). The seven days are viewed as a totality.

2. **Instantaneous.** "I raise (הֲרִימֹתִי) my hand to the LORD, the Most High God" (Gen 14:22, NET). The event happened at the instant of speaking. Cf. the NIV "I have raised," making it sound as though Abram raised his hand and then described the act.

3. **Ingressive.** In the eighteenth year of the reign of Jeroboam son of Nebat, Abijah became king (מָלַךְ) of Judah (1 Kgs 15:1, NIV). The starting year of the reign makes it clear that this is ingressive.[3]

4. **Resultative.** Just then David's men and Joab returned (בָּא) from a raid and brought with them a great deal of plunder (2 Sam 3:22, NIV). The return, or arrival, was the culmination of their journey.

5. **Perfective.** When Abram heard that his relative (Lot) had been taken captive (נִשְׁבָּה), he called out the 318 trained men (Gen 14:14, NIV). Being taken captive (Pf) was prior to the Abrham's hearing about Lot, and Lot was still in captivity when he heard it. English renders this with a perfect tense, here it is past perfect.

6. **Iterative.** And Tobiah sent (שָׁלַח) letters to intimidate me (Neh 6:19, NIV). It may be that these letters were sent in a series instead of all in one bunch.

7. **Continuous.** But the LORD came down to see the city and the tower that the men were building (בָּנוּ) (Gen 11:5, NIV). Since the building was never completed (v. 8), the ending is not in view.[4]

Relating English Verb Functions to the *Qatal* and *Weqatal*

Qatal and *weqatal* forms can be used in any time frame, past, present, or future. Here are examples of the *weqatal* in various times and aspects.

"For I [the LORD to those with him] have chosen him [Abram], so that he will direct his children and his household after him to keep (וְשָׁמְרוּ, *weqatal*) the way of

---

[3] The *Lexham Interlinear* makes this explicit: "(he) began to reign." Cf. the constative use of the exact form in the very next verse giving the three-year duration of his reign.

[4] The NIV takes the *qatal* as encapsulating the process and renders with the English past progressive. Compare the NET, which prefers an ingressive nuance: "which the people *had started building*."

the Lord by doing what is right and just, so that the Lord will bring about for Abraham what he has promised him" (Gen 18:16, NIV).

This is a future time example. The action is sequential after the verb "he will direct." The idea is that his children should habitually keep the way of the Lord. (Note that the NIV doesn't translate וְשָׁמְרוּ as a finite verb but as an infinitive).

"And Peninnah had children, but Hannah had none. Now this man used to go up (וְעָלָה) year after year from his city to worship …" (1 Sam 1:2b-3, ESV).

This is a past time example. The ESV rightly indicates the habitual nature of the action made explicit by the phrase "year by year." The NIV reads simply "went up" relying on "year by year" to mark the iterative nature of the action.

Figure 14.6: Indicative Structures and Functions

Time	Uses	Examples	*qatal*	*weqatal*
Past	simple past	he <u>ate</u>	x	
	emphatic past	he <u>did eat</u>	x	
	past perfect	he <u>had eaten</u>	x	
	contrary-to-fact condition	(if) he <u>had eaten</u>	x	
	contrary-to-fact assertion	(then) he <u>would have lived</u>		x
	customary past	he <u>used to eat</u>		x
	past progressive (historic present)	he <u>was eating</u>		
	ingressive past	he <u>began eating</u>		x
	historic future (subordinate clauses)	he <u>would (was going to) eat</u>		
Present	simple present (stative)	he <u>eats</u>	x	
	emphatic present	he <u>does eat</u>	x	
	characteristic present (gnomic, habitual)	he <u>eats</u>	x	x

Present	present perfect	he <u>has eaten</u>	x	
	present progressive	he <u>is eating</u>		x
Future	simple future	he <u>shall eat</u>		x
	conditional assertion	(then) he <u>will eat</u>		
	immediate future	he <u>is about to eat</u>		x
	rhetorical/ /dramatic future	he <u>eats</u> (perfected aspect)	x	
	future perfect	he <u>will have eaten</u>	x	
	anterior future	he <u>will have eaten</u>		

Subjunctive and Volitional Structures and Functions

Time	Uses	Examples	*qatal*	*weqatal*
	Condition	(if) he <u>eats</u>/<u>eat</u>/<u>should eat</u>	x	x
	possibility	he <u>might eat</u>		x
	purpose/result	in order that/so that he <u>might eat</u>		x
	capability	he <u>can eat</u>		
	permission	he <u>may eat</u>		
	obligation/ propriety	he <u>ought to eat</u>		x
	command/ prohibition	<u>eat</u>! <u>Do not eat</u>!		x
	Desire/intention	he <u>wants</u>/<u>intends to eat</u>		
	request/wish	<u>please, eat</u>!		

A Plan of Attack

In chapters 13 and 14 we have noticed three qualities of verbs: mood (Real or Irreal), time (i.e., relative time), aspect (the seven aspects from Figure 14.5). What can you do to understand meaning better? First, you can use your tools to identify Hebrew tense forms and look for mood possibilities; second, rely on translations and commentators for time and sequencing of Hebrew verbs; and third, study the context and use Figure 14.5 to identify possible aspects. Here are steps to follow:

1. Determine the verb form. Use a grammatically tagged computer Hebrew OT or interlinear, or else use an interlinear Bible plus Davidson or Owens as needed. For now this is *qatal* or *weqatal*.

2. Determine the Clause and Verb functions. Use Figure 14.6 to identify the verb function. Use Figures 13.9 and 13.10 to identify reality and function of the main clause. This can be repeated for each version compared.

3. Based on your findings, briefly describe the action of the verb in the clause.

As an example of how to use Figure 14.6, look again at Gen 9:9-11 (NIV):

> [9]"I now establish my covenant with you and with your descendants after you [10] and with every living creature that was with you-the birds, the livestock and all the wild animals, all those that came out of the ark with you-every living creature on earth. [11] I establish (וַהֲקִמֹתִי) my covenant with you: Never again will all life be cut off by the waters of a flood; never again will there be a flood to destroy the earth."

(1) A quick look at an Interlinear reveals that the verb "establish" in v. 11 is a *weqatal* form. (2) The NIV renders this as a simple present tense and does not translate the ו cj. Consulting Figure 14.6, you look down the *weqatal* column in the present time section; the possible aspects are constative, stative, habitual, and continuous. (3) Looking at Figure 14.5, the NIV is taking the *weqatal* as instantaneous, completed at the moment of speaking.

You can repeat the last two steps to compare versions. (2) The KJV renders this same phrase with "and I will establish," as future. Studying the *weqatal* column in the future time section for the KJV reveals eight possibilities, but without subordinating cjs, modal auxiliary verbs (could, would, etc.), or a command, the Subjunctive/Volitional forms are not indicated. Neither is this a contingent assertion. So only two possibilities are left: simple future with constative aspect or immediate future with ingressive aspect. (3) Of these two possibilities, the immediate future fits the context best - God is not going to establish his covenant in some distant future. This meaning is about the same as the NIV. The NIV seems to bring out the meaning more clearly.

Exercises

In each of the following exercises the *italicized* verbs are either *qatal* or *weqatal* in Hebrew. (1) Use an interlinear Bible to identify the form, *qatal* or *weqatal*. (2) Based on context, use Figures 13.9 and 13.10 to determine main clause function and Figure 14.6 to identify verb function. (3) Use Figure 14.5 and what you can gather from the context to determine the aspect of the action portrayed.

1. Gen 2:24, "For this reason a man will leave his father and mother and *be united* to his wife, and they will become one flesh" (NIV). Compare the NET, "... and *unites* with his wife ...."

Hebrew Form	Translation	Clause Function	Verb Function	Aspect
qatal weqatal	be united (NIV)			
(circle one)	unites (NET)			

2. Gen 6:18, "But *I will establish* my covenant with you, and *you will enter* the ark" (NIV).

Hebrew Form	Translation	Clause Function	Verb Function	Aspect
qatal weqatal	I will establish			
qatal weqatal	you will enter			

3. Gen 9:13, "*I have set* my rainbow in the clouds" (NIV); cf. the KJV, "I *do set* my bow in the cloud."

Hebrew Form	Translation	Clause Function	Verb Function	Aspect
qatal weqatal	have set (NIV) do set (KJV)			

4. Exod 6:6, "I am the Lord, and *I will bring* you *out* from under the yoke of the Egyptians" (NIV).

Hebrew Form	Translation	Clause Function	Verb Function	Aspect
qatal weqatal	I will bring out (NIV)			

5. Exod 33:8, "And whenever Moses went out to the tent, all the people would rise up ... and each *would stand* at his door and *watch* until Moses had gone inside the tent" (ESV). Compare KJV, "... all the people rose up and *stood* ... and *looked* ...."

Hebrew Form	Translation	Clause Function	Verb Function	Aspect
qatal weqatal	would stand (ESV)			
	stood (KJV)			
qatal weqatal	watch (ESV)			
	looked (KJV)			

6. Judg 4:14, "This is the day that the Lord *has given* Sisera into your hands" (NIV).

Hebrew Form	Translation	Clause Function	Verb Function	Aspect
qatal weqatal	has given (NIV)			

7. Judg 11:31, "whatever *comes* out of the door of my house to meet me when I return in triumph from the Ammonites will be the Lord's, *and I will sacrifice* it as a burnt offering" (NIV).

Hebrew Form	Translation	Clause Function	Verb Function	Aspect
qatal weqatal	and I will sacrifice (NIV)			

CHAPTER 15

There's Nothing Wrong with . . .
Imperfect Forms

Objectives

1. Understand the Hebrew Imperfect
2. Understand three constructions of Imperfects
3. Use tools to identify verbs and understand parsing

Tools Used: Grammatically tagged Computer Hebrew interlinear or paper interlinear plus Davidson or Owens

Introduction

Imperfect (Imp) is the second category of Hebrew finite verbals. As we mentioned in ch. 13, the term *Imperfect* means that the action of the verb is portrayed as incomplete. This is only a generalization. After getting an idea of the shape of this form, we will look at its various functions.

The Imperfect Form and Its Constructions

Names for the Imperfect Tense Form

The three names typically used for this verbal form correspond to the three names for the Pf: (1) *Imperfect*, from the aspect; (2) *prefixed*, because afformatives are attached to the beginning of each verb; and (3) *yiqtol*, because it describes the shape of the Imp (see Figure 13.3).

Once again it is important to identify the presence or absence of the Waw conjunction. So, in addition to *yiqtol*, there is *weyiqtol*. This Waw is called a "Conjunctive Waw" in order to distinguish it from the Waw Consecutive.

Inflecting the Suffixes of the Imperfect Tense

Even though the Imp is often called "prefixed," half of the Imp forms also have suffixes. Figure 15.1 below gives the forms of both the Pf and the Imp for comparison. The black letters are the personal prefixes and suffixes; the gray letters are those of the root; the gray vowels are a function of the stem, not the personal ending. For comparison I give only one possible translation of the forms.

Figure 15.1: A Comparison of Pf and Imp Person Markers

PGN	Perfect	Imperfect	PGN	English
3ms	קָטַל	יִקְטֹל	3ms	he will kill
3fs	קָטְלָה	תִּקְטֹל	3fs	she will kill
2ms	קָטַלְתָּ	תִּקְטֹל	2ms	you will kill
2fs	קָטַלְתְּ	תִּקְטְלִי	2fs	you will kill
1cs	קָטַלְתִּי	אֶקְטֹל	1cs	I will kill
3cp	קָטְלוּ	יִקְטְלוּ	3mp	they will kill
		תִּקְטֹלְנָה	3fs	they will kill
2mp	קְטַלְתֶּם	תִּקְטְלוּ	2mp	you will kill
2fp	קְטַלְתֶּן	תִּקְטֹלְנָה	2fp	you will kill
1cp	קָטַלְנוּ	נִקְטֹל	1cp	we will kill

Notice the following:

1. All of the Imp forms have prefixes; none of the Pf forms do.

2. Notice that while the Pf 3p is common in gender, the Imp distinguishes the 3mp and the 3fp.

3. Notice also that the 3fp and the 2fp are identical. These forms are not common, and there is rarely any confusion. Context is normally clear.

Waw Consecutive and the Imperfect

There is a special form of the Imp. Some grammarians call it "Preterite" (abbreviated Pret) meaning "past time." Others call it *wayyiqtol*. Most call it Waw Consecutive plus the Imperfect (ו cs + Imp) as opposed to Waw conjunctive with the Imperfect (ו cj + Imp).

In the vast majority of instances, this verbal construction refers to a past event, but this is not always the case. Grammarians have identified additional nuances. The most important thing for you to understand about this form is that it is used to describe sequential actions. That is, a series of *wayyiqtol* forms produces a narrative of events in chronological (or logical) order.

Gathering Parsing Information

Parsing works the same way as in the last chapter. In the examples below, I begin with a noun and a Pf form for comparison.

Figure 15.2: Parsing Information for Nominals and Verbals

			← Verbal Qualities →					← Nominal Qualities →			
POS	Word	Lex	Stem	Form	P	G	N	State	Det	Case	Suff
Nn	דְּבָרָיו	דָּבָר				m	p	cst	[?]	[?]	3ms
V	וַהֲשִׁבֹתִיךָ	שׁוב	H	ו + Pf	1	c	s				2ms
V	יִמְשֹׁל	משׁל	Q	Imp	3	m	s				
V	וְיִשְׁכֹּן	שׁכן	Q	ו cj+Imp	3	m	3				
V	וַיְקַדֵּשׁ	קדשׁ	D	ו cs+Imp	3	m	s				
V	וַיַּנְחֵהוּ	נוח	H	ו cs+Imp	3	m	s				3ms

The Functions of the Imperfect Forms

There are three forms covered in this chapter: *yiqtol* (Imp), *weyiqtol* (ו cj+Imp), and *wayyiqtol* (ו cs+Imp = ו cs+Pret). In terms of functions, however, *yiqtol* and *weyiqtol* (with ו cj) function in similar ways. The form *wayyiqtol* is distinct. The result is that, as we talk about functions, we only need to discuss *yiqtol* and *wayyiqtol*.

Before we get to functions, however, there are two special forms that require our attention.

The Forms וַיְהִי and וְהָיָה

The construction וַיְהִי is very common in the Hebrew Bible (784 times). Parsed this is a Q וcs + Imp 3ms from the root הָיָה. The construction וְהָיָה is a Q ו+Pf 3ms from the same root (402 times).

These forms are used in two ways, (1) as a main clause or (2) as a temporal clause. As a main clause, it has the meaning "become." It is more commonly used as a marker for an adverbial time phrase. The KJV usually renders וַיְהִי, "and it came to pass" and וְהָיָה as the future tense, "and it shall come to pass." A couple of examples with וַיְהִי will illustrate sufficiently.

Gen 19:26b	מֶלַח	נְצִיב	וַתְּהִי
	salt	a pillar of	and she became

NIV   And she became a pillar of salt.

The first word is וַתְּהִי. The subject, of course, is the wife of Lot. Clearly the meaning of the sentence is that she *became* a pillar of salt, not that she was one. In this case, וַתְּהִי should be treated as any other ו cs+Imp form.

Josh 1:1	יְהוָה	וַיֹּאמֶר	יְהוָה	עֶבֶד	מֹשֶׁה	מוֹת	אַחֲרֵי	וַיְהִי
	the Lord	and (he) said	the Lord	the ser-vant of	Moses	the death of	after	and it was

NIV   After the death of Moses the servant of the Lᴏʀᴅ, the Lord said …

KJV   *Now* after the death of Moses the servant of the Lᴏʀᴅ, *it came to pass* that the Lord spake …

Notice here that וַיְהִי does not mean "become" and that it is followed by a time phrase. There is nothing wrong with the KJV translation; people simply don't talk like that anymore. The NIV is more idiomatic by leaving וַיְהִי untranslated. In fact the NIV more precisely brings out the adverbial function of this clause. The main clause is "the Lᴏʀᴅ said." We will come back to this form in ch. 20 on prose.

Mood and Aspect of *Yiqtol* and *Wayyiqtol*

The mood of the *yiqtol* is irreal. *Wayyiqtol* has about the same range of meaning as *qatal*, i.e., it usually portrays real action. It can portray irreal action, but that is a function of context rather than verb form.

The aspect of the *yiqtol* (and *weyiqtol*) form is primarily iterative or continuous. It portrays aspect similarly to the *qatal*, the chief difference being that *yiqtol* portrays Irreal mood. The *wayyiqtol* is sequential like *weqatal*, but portraying action in the Real mood.

Figure 15.3 expands on the forms from Figure 14.6 by adding our two new forms. Remember that this figure is an approximation; you must not use it to argue with scholars about a particular use. We will complete the figure in ch. 17.

Figure 15.3: Indicative Structures and Functions

Time	Uses	Examples	*qatal*	*weqatal*	*yiqtol*	*wayyiqtol*
Past	simple past	he <u>ate</u>	x			x
	emphatic past	he <u>did eat</u>	x			x
	past perfect	he <u>had eaten</u>	x			x
	contrary-to-fact condition	(if) he <u>had eaten</u>	x			
	contrary-to-fact assertion	(then) he <u>would have eaten</u>		x	x	
	customary past	he <u>used to eat</u>		x	x	
	past progressive (historic present)	he <u>was eating</u>			x	
	ingressive past	he <u>began eating</u>		x		
	historic future (in subordinate clauses)	he <u>would</u> (<u>was going to</u>) <u>eat</u>			x	

Time	Uses	Examples	qatal	weqatal	yiqtol	wayyiqtol
Present	simple present (stative)	he <u>eats</u>	x			x
	emphatic present	he <u>does eat</u>	x			
	characteristic present (gnomic, habitual)	he <u>eats</u>	x	x	x	x
	present perfect	he <u>has eaten</u>	x			x
	present progressive	he <u>is eating</u>		x		
Future	simple future	he <u>shall eat</u>		x	x	
	conditional assertion	(then) he <u>will eat</u>			x	
	immediate future	he <u>is about to eat</u>		x		
	rhetorical/ dramatic future	he <u>eats</u> (perfected aspect)	x			x
	future perfect	he <u>will have eaten</u>	x			
	anterior future	he <u>will have eaten</u>			x	

Subjunctive and Volitional Structures and Functions

Time	Uses	Examples	qatal	weqatal	yiqtol	wayyiqtol
Future	condition (protasis) (protasis)	if <u>he eats</u>, <u>eat</u>, <u>should eat</u>	x	x	x	
	possibility	he <u>might eat</u>		x	x	
	purpose/result	in order that/so that he <u>might eat</u>		x		
	capability	he <u>can eat</u>			x	
	permission	he <u>may eat</u>			x	

Time	Uses	Examples	qatal	weqatal	yiqtol	wayyiqtol
Future	obligation/ propriety	he <u>ought to eat</u>		X	X	
					X	
	command/ prohibition	<u>eat</u>!/<u>Do not eat</u>!		X	X	
					X	
	Desire/intention	he <u>wants</u>/<u>intends to eat</u>			X	
	request/wish	<u>please, eat</u>!			X	

You can use the information in this figure as you did in the last chapter. Take for example Gen 3:16b. The NIV translates it like the other versions, "Your desire will be for your husband, and *he will rule* over you." For the second half, the NET reads similarly, "… but *he will dominate* you." What kind of "rule" is envisioned? The NET Bible, note 49, says,

> The translation assumes the imperfect verb form has an objective/indicative sense here. Another option is to understand it as having a modal, desiderative nuance, "but he *will want to dominate* [italic added] you." In this case, the Lord simply announces the struggle without indicating who will emerge victorious.

A quick glance at an interlinear shows that the verb under consideration is *yiqtol*. Glancing at the chart you can see that in their note, they are suggesting that the *yiqtol* be understood as expressing desire. How do scholars decide which use? Context. We will come back to this verse in ch. 18 on word studies.

Exercises

For each of the following verbs indicated, (1) using either a computer Bible or an interlinear + Davidson or Owens, identify the form: *qatal, weqatal, yiqtol/ weyiqtol*, or *wayyiqtol*. If you do not have these tools, I have listed the verb forms at the end of the exercises. If you do have the tools, use them first, then verify with my answers. (2) Use Figures 13.9 and 13.10 and context to determine the clause function and use Figure 15.3 to identify verb function. (3) Use Figure 14.5 and what you can gather from the context to determine the aspect of the action portrayed.

1. Gen 2:24, "For this reason a man *will leave* his father and mother and be united to his wife, and they will become one flesh" (NIV). Compare the NET, "That is why a man *leaves* ...."

Hebrew Form	Translation	Clause Function	Verb Function	Aspect
qatal weqatal	will leave (NIV)			
yiqtol wayyiqtol	leaves (NET)			
(circle one)				

2. Exod 20:25, "If *you make* an altar of stones for me, do not build it with dressed stones, for *you will defile* it *if you use* a tool on it." (NIV)

Hebrew Form	Translation	Clause Function	Verb Function	Aspect
qatal weqatal	you make (NIV)			
yiqtol wayyiqtol				
qatal weqatal	you will defile (NIV)			
yiqtol wayyiqtol				
qatal weqatal	if you use (NIV)			
yiqtol wayyiqtol				

3. Deut 4:31, "For the Lord your God is a merciful God; he will not abandon or destroy you or *forget* the covenant with your forefathers, which he confirmed to them by an oath" (NIV). Compare the NET, "... for *he cannot forget* the covenant ...."

Hebrew Form	Translation	Clause Function	Verb Function	Aspect
qatal weqatal	forget (NIV)			
yiqtol wayyiqtol	cannot forget (NET)			

4. Prov 7:21, "With persuasive words *she led* him astray; *she seduced* him with her smooth talk" (NIV). Compare the ESV, "With much seductive speech *she persuades* him; with her smooth talk *she compels* him."

Hebrew Form	Translation	Clause Function	Verb Function	Aspect
qatal weqatal	she led (NIV)			
yiqtol wayyiqtol	she persuades (ESV)			
qatal weqatal	she seduced (NIV)			
yiqtol wayyiqtol	she compels (ESV)			

5. Num 19:7, "After that, the priest *must wash* his clothes and bathe himself with water. Then *he may enter* the camp, but he will be ceremonially unclean till evening" (NIV). Compare the ESV, "Then the priest *shall wash* ...."

Hebrew Form	Translation	Clause Function	Verb Function	Aspect
qatal weqatal	must wash (NIV)			
yiqtol wayyiqtol	shall wash (ESV)			
qatal weqatal	he may enter (NIV)			
yiqtol wayyiqtol				

6. Exod 8:27 [Hebrew 8:23], "*We must take* a three-day journey into the desert ..." (NIV). Compare the KJV, "*We will go* three days' journey into the wilderness ...."

Hebrew Form	Translation	Clause Function	Verb Function	Aspect
qatal weqatal	we must take (NIV)			
yiqtol wayyiqtol	we will go (KJV)			

*Important to note here is the KJV use of "will." In 1611, the auxiliary verb "will" when used with the first person indicated more than just future time, but also desire or intentionality. This distinction is rarely maintained in modern, informal English.

7. Num 5:4b, *"They did just as the* LORD *had instructed* Moses" (NIV).

Hebrew Form	Translation	Clause Function	Verb Function	Aspect
qatal weqatal	they did			
yiqtol wayyiqtol				
qatal weqatal	had instructed			
yiqtol wayyiqtol				

Note the relative order of the two events. Is there a devotional message that you can apply to yourself and present to others based on this observation from slow, careful reading?

Verb forms for exercises:

1.	will leave	יַעֲזֹב	yiqtol
2.	you make	תַּעֲשֶׂה	yiqtol
	you will defile	הֲנִפְתָּ	qatal
	(if) you use	וַתְּחַלְלֶהָ	wayyiqtol
3.	forget	יִשְׁכַּח	yiqtol
4.	she led	הַטַּתּוּ	qatal
	she seduced	תַּדִּיחֶנּוּ	yiqtol
5.	must wash	וְכִבֶּס	weqatal
	he may enter	יָבוֹא	yiqtol
6.	we must take	נֵלֵךְ	yiqtol
7.	they did	עָשׂוּ	qatal
	had instructed	דִּבֶּר	qatal

CHAPTER 16

Where There's a Will, There Are . . .
Volitional Forms

Objectives

1. Understand that Hebrew has three volitional verbs

2. Understand that Hebrew places volitional forms in sequence to form subordinate clauses

3. Understand the functions of volitional verbs

4. Identify and understand the two types of Hebrew prohibitions

5. Flowchart volitional and subordinate clauses

Tools Used: Interlinear Bible

Introduction

You have already been introduced to the meaning of volitional verbs (ch. 13). Volition has to do with the will. Because these actions depend on the will of another, the fulfillment of these actions is in doubt and they are future by nature. In English, these actions are put in the subjunctive and imperative moods. In Hebrew, these actions fall under the irreal mood. We have already seen that some non-volitional forms are used to represent irreal action. In this chapter we will learn the rest of the irreal functions that are performed by volitional verbs, the last category of finite verbs.

We will begin with the names and "shapes" of volitional verbs and their functions. Next you need to understand the way Hebrew strings together various verb forms using the Waw conjunction to indicate meaning. Scholars call this "consecution of tenses." We will conclude with parsing information and flowcharting verbal sequences.

Volitional Forms

There are three types of volitional verbs, the Cohortative (Coh), Imperative (Imv), and Jussive (Juss). The one most familiar to you, of course, is the Imperative. This is the verb form, whose chief function is to indicate a command in the second person. The simplest way to explain the Coh and Juss is that they serve similar purposes for the first and third persons, respectively.

Figure 16.1: Hebrew and English Methods of Expressing Volitional Moods

Person	Hebrew Forms	English Forms
1st	Coh	I will go, let me go
	weqatal	I will go, let me go
2nd	Imv (pos.)	Go!
	Imp + אַל/לֹא (neg.)	Do not go!
3rd	Juss	Let him go, he must go
	yiqtol	Let him go, he must go

As for the forms themselves, the Imv has the most distinctive form. They look like the Imp forms with the prefixes removed. For example, תִּקְטֹל is the Q Imp 2ms for "you will kill"; the Imv 2ms is simply קְטֹל. (By the way, it is not really necessary to write the "2" for the person of the Imv, since the Imv is only the 2nd person. It's okay to do it, though.) The only variation is that the 2ms may add ה to the end of the verbal form. Here are the basic forms for the Q Imv. You may notice some changes in vowel pointing. If you want to know why, you will need to learn full Hebrew.

Figure 16.2: Comparison of Qal Imperfect and Imperative Forms

PGN	Imp	Imv	Long Form
2ms	תִּקְטֹל	קְטֹל	קָטְלָה
2fs	תִּקְטְלִי	קִטְלִי	
2mp	תִּקְטְלוּ	קִטְלוּ	
2fp	תִּקְטֹלְנָה	קְטֹלְנָה	

The Coh and Juss frequently look just like the Imp form. The only difference is that ה may be added to the Cohortative verb. Compare the following:

Figure 16.3: Comparing the Imperfect with the Long Cohortative Form

Parsing	Hebrew	English
Q Imp 1cs	אֶקְטֹל	"I will write"
Q Coh 1cs	אֶקְטְלָה	"let me write"

So how does Hebrew indicate when a form without the emphatic ה should be understood as volitional? They put it at the beginning of the clause. In Gen 33:12, Esau says,

Gen 33:12	נִסְעָה
	let us
	journey

NIV   Let us be on our way

In the priestly blessing of Num 6:24,

Num 6:24	וְיִשְׁמְרֶךָ	יְהוָה	יְבָרֶכְךָ
	and may he	the	may he
	keep you	Lord	bless you

NLT   May the Lord bless you and protect you

Volitional forms may appear with or without the Conjunctive Waw, as in "and may he keep you" in Num 6:24 above. It may be preceded by the negative, as in Gen 18:30 below. After the author narrates, "And he said," we read the direct speech of Abraham:

Gen 18:30	לַאדֹנָי	יִחַר	אַל־נָא
	to the	may it	not
	Lord	be hot	

NIV   May the Lord not be angry...

The word אַל means "not"; the particle נָא is perhaps a marker of emotion or emphasis. The verb חָרָה means "to be hot." This is an idiom; the full expression is, "may the nose be hot."[1] The point is that the לְ pp before Adonai is possessive.

Just like the other finite verb forms, the volitional forms may add PrnSfs to the end. In Isa 6:8, when the Lord asks, "Whom shall I send? And who will go for us?" Isaiah answers, "Here am I. Send me!" The form for "Send me!" is one word in Hebrew: שְׁלָחֵנִי. The נִי– suffix means "me."

Volitional Functions

The function of volitional forms requires little explanation. We will start with the Imv, because it is the most familiar. Then we will cover Juss and Coh. Finally, there is a special note on 2nd person prohibitions, which are not made with the Imv. Function is determined by context.

Main Imperative Functions

1. **Command** - a directive from a superior to an inferior (note: this does not include prohibitions! See below.)

   Gen 12:1: The LORD had said to Abram, "*Leave* (לֶךְ) your country, your people and your father's household" (NIV).

2. **Request** - a directive by an inferior to a superior (a.k.a. prayer)

   Ps 26:1: "*Vindicate me* (טֵנִי), O LORD, for I have led ..." (NIV).

3. **Advice** - a directive in which no superiority is in view (though one may still be the superior to the other, in offering advice that distinction is not pressed)

   Exod 18:19: [Jethro says to Moses, when he is overwhelmed by judging the people's disputes] "*Listen* (שְׁמַע) now to me and I will give you some advice ..." (NIV).

4. **Interjection** - a directive used to draw the listener's attention

   Deut 30:15: "*See* (רְאֵה), I set before you today life and prosperity" (NIV).

---

[1] This expression was their way of using a body part that physically takes place in an emotional response to refer to the emotion. It may seem strange at first, but we do the same thing in English with expressions like "That makes my blood boil!"

Main Jussive Functions

1. **Command** - a directive from a superior concerning an inferior (note: this may take a negative; compare the Imv and see below).

   Gen 1:3: 'And God said, "*Let there be* (יְהִי) light," and there was light'(NIV).

   Exod 19:24: "Go down and bring Aaron up with you. But the priests and the people *must not force* (אַל־יֶהֶרְסוּ) their way through" (NIV).

   In both of these cases the speaker, God, is not directly addressing the parties that are being commanded. In Gen 1:3, the command concerns the light, but light does not yet exist to hear the command. The hearers are not specifically identified. In Exod 19:24 the Lord's (negative) command concerns the priests and the people, but the Lord is speaking to Moses.

2. **Request** - a directive by an inferior to a superior (a.k.a. prayer or benediction), including both positive and negative requests.

   Ps 12:3a: "*May* the Lord *cut off* (יַכְרֵת) all the flattering lips" (NIV).

   1 Kgs 8:57b: "*may he* [the Lord] *never leave us* (אַל־יַעַזְבֵנוּ) or forsake us" (NIV).

3. **Permission** - a request by an inferior to a superior.

   2 Sam 19:37 [Hebrew 38]: "*Let* your servant *return* (יָשָׁב־נָא) .... *Let* him *cross over* (יַעֲבֹר) with my lord the king " (NIV).

   English does not have this construction. The English expression "let me ..." is actually a 2nd person Imv. This function is the result of the fact that for the sake of politeness, speakers often referred to themselves in the 3rd person. In 2 Sam 19:37, the "servant" is the speaker, Barzillai.

Main Cohortative Functions

1. **Request** - a directive used when the fulfillment of the action depends on the power of another.

   Gen 18:30: "May the Lord not be angry, but *let me speak* (וַאֲדַבְּרָה)" (NIV).

2. **Resolve** - a directive used when the speaker has the ability to fulfill the action.

   Gen 18:21: "I [the Lord] *will go down* (אֵרֲדָה־נָּא) and see if what they have done is as bad as the outcry that has reached me" (NIV).

3. **Exhortation** - used only with the 1st person plural, an encouragement for two or more to participate in an action.

   Gen 24:57: "*Let's call* (נִקְרָא) the girl and ask her about it" (NIV).

Prohibitions

Unlike English, Hebrew does not form a prohibition (negative command), such as "Do not steal," by placing a negative particle before an Imv form. Instead a negative adverb is placed immediately before a verb in the 2nd person Imp (*yiqtol*) form. When we discussed adverbs, I said that negative particles were adverbial and that Hebrew had two forms, אַל and לֹא. There has been a lengthy discussion over whether they mean anything different or not, and if so, what is that difference. Here is the current consensus:

1. **General Prohibition** (לֹא + Imp) - prohibition of an action in general.

   Exod 2:15: "*You shall not steal* (לֹא תִגְנֹב)" (NIV).

2. **Specific Prohibition** (אַל + Imp) - prohibition of a specific action immediately in view.

   Gen 19:8: '[Lot said,] "But *don't do* (אַל תַּעֲשׂוּ) anything to these men, for they have come under the protection under my roof"' (NIV).

These are summarized in Figure 16.4.

Figure 16.4: Summary of Volitional Functions and Forms

Function	Imv	Juss	Coh	לֹא + Imp	אַל + Imp
Command	x	x			
Prohibition				General	Specific
Request	x	x	x		

Function	Imv	Juss	Coh	לֹא + Imp	אַל + Imp
Advice	x				
Interjection	x				
Permission		x			
Resolve			x		
Exhortation			x		

Parsing

You already know how to get the information from printed and electronic tools. Figure 16.5 shows how these forms compare using the parsing chart.

Figure 16.5: Parsing Information for Nominals and Verbals

			← Verbal Qualities →					← Nominal Qualities →			
POS	Word	Lex	Stem	Form	P	G	N	State	Det	Case	Suff
Nn	דְּבָרָיו	דָּבָר				m	p	cst	[?]	[?]	3ms
V	וַהֲשִׁבֹתִיךָ	שׁוב	H	ו + Pf	1	c	s				2ms
V	וַיַּנְחֵהוּ	נוח	H	ו cs+Imp	3	m	s				3ms
V	אֵלְכָה	הלך	Q	Coh	1	c	s				Emph
V	בַּקְּשׁוּנִי	בקשׁ	D	Imv	2	m	p				1cs
V	וְהַעֲלֵהוּ	עלה	H	ו + Imv	2	m	s				3ms
V	וַאֲדַבְּרָה	דבר	D	ו + Coh	1	c	s				
V	יִחַר	חרה	Q	Juss	3	m	s				

Sequencing of Volitional Forms

In ch. 7 on the Waw conjunction, you read that Hebrew is paratactic; that is, it prefers to coordinate clauses instead of subordinate clauses, and the ו is considered to be a coordinating conjunction. However, you also read that Hebrew had certain constructions by which it can convey subordinate relationships using the Waw conjunction. Now you are ready to understand this.

What we are looking at here is a series of two or more clauses joined by Waw in which the first clause is volitional (Coh, Imv, or Juss). If the series is more than two clauses long, then you must treat each pair in turn. It is beyond the study of pre-Hebrew for you to learn about the constructions in detail. You will need to rely on translations. However, a couple of examples may be helpful, so that you can understand why translations differ.

When a volitional form has a prefixed ו (V2) to join it to a preceding clause (V1), it may function either as an independent clause or as a subordinate clause. The identity of the function is determined by context. Here are just two examples:

> **Independent - Sequential** = V2 has the same volitional force as V1, V2 simply happens afterward.

> Gen 1:22: 'God blessed them and said, "Be fruitful and increase (ו + Imv) in number and fill (ו + Imv) the water in the seas, and let the birds increase on the earth."' (NIV)

> **Dependent - Purpose** = V2 give the intentioned outcome of the action of V1.

> Gen 18:21: "I will go down (Coh) to see (ו + Coh) whether they have done altogether according to the outcry that has come to me" (ESV).

Flowcharting

There are two new things to learn: how to flowchart commands and how to flowchart subordinate clauses formed from ו + Volitional Form. In modern English Imperatives, the subject, the Prn "you," is left out. If you wish, you can insert "[you]" to fill the subject slot so you can align verbs. When a ו + Volitional Form is subordinate, it should be indented just as explicit subordinate clauses. No exercises are needed, but here are a couple of examples to illustrate.

Function	Vs	Text: Gen 27:7 (NIV)
Command	7	Bring (Imv) me some game
Addition		and
Command		prepare (ו + Imv) me some tasty food
Purpose		to eat (ו + Coh),
Result		so that I may give you my blessing (ו + Coh)
Place		in the presence of the Lᴏʀᴅ

Function	Vs	Text: 1 Chr 16:31 (NIV)
Command	31	'Let the heavens rejoice,
Command		let the earth be glad;
Command		let them say among the nations,
Content		•• "The Lᴏʀᴅ reigns!'"

Advanced Information and Curious Facts

Amy Grant produced a popular Christian song a number of years ago entitled "El Shaddai." Most people know that El Shaddai is traditionally translated "God Almighty." One of the lines continues with the Hebrew phrase, "Erkamka na Adonai." This phrase comes from Ps 18:1 (Hebrew 18:2). The verb is אֶרְחָמְךָ. The ךָ– is the 2ms object suffix. The "na" syllable in the verse is the Hebrew particle נָא mentioned above. The Hebrew Bible does not include it; the song writer cleverly added it for a needed syllable. The NIV translates this form, "I love you." However, because it is first in the clause, the verb form is a Coh. This form strengthens the emotion of the verb in a way that simply cannot be brought out easily in an English translation. But it needs to be brought out in teaching and preaching. "I will love the Lᴏʀᴅ"; no mere future tense, but with an intense act of the will. May we all vow desperately to love our Lᴏʀᴅ!

CHAPTER 17

To Infinitives and Beyond!
Infinitives & Participles

Objectives

1. Understand how English can translate various non-finite verbs in Hebrew
2. Understand parsing of Participles and Infinitives in Hebrew

Introduction

Finite verbs, you remember, are limited (hence the term *finite*) because they have the quality of person. In other words, they have a grammatical subject built into the verb form; those are the afformatives you saw on the Perfect, Imperfect, and volitional forms. This chapter deals with the non-finite verbal forms, which are forms not limited by person. The non-finite forms are sort of a hybrid of a verb and a noun, but they are properly treated with verbs because they have a stem. Also, participles may function like verbs so that they are used to convey aspect. Infinitives sometimes function in the place of finite verbs. When they function as non-finite verbs, they form phrases, not clauses. When they function as verbs, they form clauses.

In Hebrew there are two types of non-finite verbal forms, infinitives and participles. In the chapter title I listed Infinitives first, just to be clever; we will treat the participle first, because it is the most familiar, and then infinitives.

A word of caution: before you finish this chapter you may have a sense of being overwhelmed. Don't be intimidated. I am going to give you plenty of examples so that you can understand the principles involved. You don't need to know all the details. Focus on the functions of each form so that you can understand what commentators are talking about.

Participles

A participle (Ptc) is a verbal adjective. This means that it has qualities of both verbs and Adjs.

Like a verb, a Ptc

1. implies some action, though the focus is on the participant, whereas in a finite verb the focus is on the action.

2. has a verbal stem.

3. has voice, active or passive. The Qal stem has two forms, the active (PtcA) and passive (PtcP). The other stems only have one, and the voice is determined by the stem.

4. may take a DO and be modified by adverbial expressions.

5. the negative is indicated with אֵין.

Like an Adjective, a Ptc

1. has the qualities of gender, number, and state.

2. may be determined or undetermined.

3. may have case functions.

4. may have a PrnSf.

Figure 17.1 summarizes the information contained in Participle forms. You will notice that I have marked the boxes under the purely nominal qualities (State, Determination, and Case) with an X in brackets: [X]. This is to indicate that these qualities are present when the Ptc is acting as an adjective. They are not present when the Ptc is acting as a verb.

Figure 17.1: Parsing Information for Nominals and Verbals

			← Verbal Qualities →					← Nominal Qualities →			
POS	Word	Lex	Stem	Form	P	G	N	State	Det	Case	Suff
V			x	x	x	x	x				
Nn						x	x	x	x	x	
Adj						x	x	x	x	x	
Ptc			x	x		x	x	[x]	[x]	[x]	

Forms of the Participle

Because participles do not have the quality of person, they do not have personal afformatives. They do have the characteristics of their stem. For the Qal, the "simple" pattern, active participles (PtcA) are pronounced with a long $\bar{o}$ (Holem) or $\hat{o}$ (Holem Waw) after the first root letter. Passive participles (PtcP) are pronounced with $\hat{u}$ (Shureq) after the second root letter. Some grammarians call the Ptc, whether active or passive, the "*qotel*" form, corresponding to the names *qatal* for the Pf and *yiqtol* for the Imp. I will use both terms.

Because Ptcs function like Adjs, they do take adjectival endings. Figure 17.2 gives the forms for the Qal PtcA and PtcP. The roots are in gray type and the gender and number endings are in black type. Characteristic vowels of the Qal Ptc are also in black.

Figure 17.2: Forms for the Qal Participle

Gender	Active Absolute	Active Construct	Passive Absolute	Passive Construct
ms	קֹטֵל	קֹטֵל	קָטוּל	קְטוּל
fs	קֹטֶלֶת	קֹטֶלֶת	קְטוּלָה	קְטוּלַת
	קֹטְלָה	קֹטְלַת		
mp	קֹטְלִים	קֹטְלֵי	קְטוּלִים	קְטוּלֵי
fp	קֹטְלוֹת	קֹטְלוֹת	קְטוּלוֹת	קְטוּלוֹת

Of course the Ptcs in the other stems have their own "shapes." Most notably, all of them but the Niphal have a prefixed Mem (מ); the Niphal has a prefixed Nun (נ).

Adjectival Uses of the Participle

A Ptc may function either like an Adj or a verb. The Ptc in the predicate position (review the ch. 12 on Adjs) and the "verbal" Ptc have the same construction. The difference is that a predicate Adj describes the state of the subject and is always in a noun clause; the passive Ptc is especially suited for this. The verbal Ptc describes an action in which the subject is engaged; the active Ptc is suited for this. When a Ptc is used adjectivally, it can function in any of the three ways an Adj can function: attributively, predicatively, or substantivally. Their function is determined by grammatical structure in just the same way the function of an Adj is determined. Figure 17.3 is reproduced from Figure 12.2, except that I have substituted the Ptc מֹשֵׁל, "ruling," for the Adj "good."

Figure 17.3: Positions and Agreement of Adjectives

Construction	Noun	Definite Noun	Article with Adj	Example	Pattern
Attributive	Y	Y	Y	הַמֶּלֶךְ הַמֹּשֵׁל מֶלֶךְ הַמֹּשֵׁל the ruling king	T-N-T-Ptc N-T-Ptc
Predicate	Y	Y	N	מֹשֵׁל הַמֶּלֶךְ הַמֶּלֶךְ מֹשֵׁל the king (is) ruling	Ptc-T-N T-N-Ptc
Ambiguous (Attributive or Predicate)	Y	N	N	מֶלֶךְ מֹשֵׁל מֹשֵׁל מֶלֶךְ a ruling king *or* a king (is) ruling	N-Ptc Ptc-N

Construction	Noun	Definite Noun	Article with Adj	Example	Pattern
Isolated *(Substantival)*	N	–	Y/N	מֹשֵׁל הַמֹּשֵׁל a ruler (man) the ruler (man)	T-Ptc Ptc

In the examples below, I used *The ESV English-Hebrew Reverse Interlinear Old Testament.*[1] Remember that the reverse interlinear scrambles the Hebrew into English word order; the *Reverse Interlinear* uses subscript numbers to indicate the Hebrew word order. I will decode their abbreviations then transfer that information to the parsing charts we have been using.

Attributive Adjectival Ptc

Both active and passive Ptcs may be used attributively. Just as with Adjs, the Attributive Ptc will agree with the noun it modifies in gender, number, and determination, and it will follow the substantive. Furthermore, since it is attributive, it must also agree in case. Here are a couple of examples.

1.   PtcA; Exodus 24:17a

Now   the   appearance   of   the   glory   of   the   Lord   was   like   a   devouring   fire

וֽ‎‍₁ → מַרְאֵה₂ → → כְּבוֹד₃ → → יהוה₄ · כְּ₅ ₆ → ₇ אֹכֶלֶת₆ אֵשׁ₆

ו   מראה   כבוד   יהוה   ךְ   אכל   שׁ אש

CC   NCcSMC   NCcSMC NPDSMN   PK   VqAtSF-NNCcSFN

Word 6 = fire   NCcSFN   Nn, Common, s f Abs [no Art]
Word 7 = devouring   VqAtSF-N   Vb, Q active, pure noun Ptc, s f Abs [no Art]

POS	Word	Lex	← Verbal Qualities →					← Nominal Qualities →			
			Stem	Form	P	G	N	State	Det	Case	Suff
Nn	אֵשׁ	אשׁ				f	s	abs	U	Gen	
Ptc	אֹכֶלֶת	אכל	Q	PtcA		f	s	abs	U	Gen	

Note the agreement of the Ptc with its noun in G, N, State, and Case (remember, I view objects of prepositions as in the Gen case, whose function is determined by the preposition). Note also its position right after the noun, as indicated by the number: 7 comes right after 6, of course!

2. PtcP; Gen 49:21

Naphtali	is	a	doe	let	loose
נַפְתָּלִי₁	•	•	אַיָּלָה₂	→	שְׁלֻחָה₃
נפלתי			אילה		שלח
NPHSMN			NCcSFN		VQPtSF-N

POS	Word	Lex	← Verbal Qualities →					← Nominal Qualities →			
			Stem	Form	P	G	N	State	Det	Case	Suff
Nn	נפתי נַפְתָּלִי					f	s	abs	U	Nom	
Ptc	שׁלח שְׁלֻחָה	שלח	Q	PtcP		f	s	abs	U	Nom	

Again, note the agreement of the Ptc with its noun in G, N, and State. Note also its position, word 3, right after the noun, word 2.

Predicate Adjectival Ptc (in noun [verbless] clauses)

Predicate Ptcs are typically passive, indicating a state. Just like Adjs, they agree with the noun they modify in gender and number, but they are *always* indefinite. The absence of the article here is as a function marker, namely, to mark the predicate position. It has virtually no semantic significance. See ch. 12 on the article. Most often they are located before their noun, giving predicate-subject (P-S) word order. Since they are part of a noun (verbless) clause, however, the subject may come first (S-P). The case will always be Nom.

1. P-S order: this answers the question, "What is the subject?"; Gen 3:17

cursed	is	the	ground	because	of	you

אֲרוּרָה 25 • הָ 26 אֲדָמָה 27 בַּעֲבוּר 28 ← הָ 29

ארר   ה   אדמה   בעבור   אתה

VQPtSF-N   XD   NCcSFNH   PS   RBSM2

	← Verbal Qualities →			← Nominal Qualities →				

POS	Word	Lex	Stem	Form	P	G	N	State	Det	Case	Suff
Nn	אדמה הָאֲדָמָה					f	s	abs	D	Nom	
Ptc	ארר אֲרוּרָה	ארר	Q	PtcP		f	s	abs	U	Nom	

Notice that the Ptc agrees in G, N and State, but disagrees in Det. Also, the Ptc, word 25, precedes the noun, word 27. What is it that is cursed? The ground.

2. S-P order: this answers the question, "Who is characterized this way?"; 1 Sam 21:8 [Hebrew 21:9]

because	the	king's	business	required	haste

כִּי 29 הַ 32 מֶּלֶךְ 33 דְּבַר 31 נָחוּץ 30 הָיָה 34 ←

כי   ה   מלך   דבר   נחץ   היה

CK   XD   NCcSMNH   NCcSMC   VqAsSM3, VQPtSM-N

	← Verbal Qualities →			← Nominal Qualities →				

POS	Word	Lex	Stem	Form	P	G	N	State	Det	Case	Suff
Nn	דְּבַר דָּבָר	דָּבָר				m	s	cst	D	Nom	
Ptc	נָחוּץ נחץ	נחץ	Q	PtcP		m	s	abs	U	Nom	

The predicate Ptc is "haste," word 34; it might also be translated "urged, urgent." Its noun is "business of," word 31. Notice that the Ptc agrees in G, N and Case, but disagrees in State and Det. Also, its predicate Ptc follows the noun. What is it that is urgent? The business (of the king). In this example the verb *to be* (הָיָה) is present to specify the time frame as past.

Substantival Ptc

Even though a Ptc forms a phrase instead of a clause, English commonly must translate the substantival Ptc as a relative clause, "the one who/he who X-es," unless English has an acceptable way of saying, "the X-er." For example, הַשֹּׁמֵר might be translated either "the one who/he who keeps" or "the keeper."

Both active and passive Ptcs may function like a noun. They can fill any noun slot, Nom, Gen, or Acc, with any of the case functions. In other words, they should be treated just like nouns. Therefore I don't need to give you examples for all the noun uses. Here is one illustration, from Exod 22:6 [Hebrew 22:5], in which the substantival Ptc is functioning as a subject Nom.

he	who	started	•	the	fire	shall	make	full	restitution
→	→	₁₉הַמַּבְעִר ₂₀אֵת ₁₈הַ	₂₁הַ	₂₂בְּעֵרָה	→	→	→	₁₆יְשַׁלֵּם₁₇ שַׁלֵּם
		בער ה את	ה	בער				שלם שלם
		XD, VhApSM-NH PA XD	NCcSFNH					VpAa, VpAMSM3

	← Verbal Qualities →				← Nominal Qualities →		
POS	Word	Lex	Stem	Form	P	G	N	State	Det	Case	Suff
Ptc	הַמַּבְעִר	בער	H	PtcA		m	s	abs	D		

The complete Ptc phrase is translated "he who started the fire." Notice that English changed the construction into a relative clause. Another way to translate this would be "the fire starter," but that is awkward. Within the Ptc phrase, the Ptc takes a DO, *fire*, just like a verb. The entire phrase functions as a noun in the Nom case. There is no antecedent to the Ptc; it is simply functioning as the subject of the verb phrase "shall make full restitution." You might flowchart as follows:

Function	**Vs**	**Flow Chart** Exod 22:6 [Hebrew 22:5]		
Assertion	6 [5]	He...	shall make	→ full restitution
Description		who	started	→ the fire

Verbal Uses of a Participle and Noun Clauses

Now we come to the verbal uses of the Ptc. Noun clauses fall into this same category, because they function with the same range as the verbal Ptc. Structurally the verbal Ptc is identical to the predicate Ptc. A verbal Ptc may be either active or passive, but clear cases are much more commonly active. The difference is in meaning; the predicate Ptc functions like an Adj, while the verbal Ptc functions like a finite verb. When making flowcharts, treat these as finite verbs.

The verbal Ptc indicates continuous or progressive aspect and is irreal in mood (it is debatable if all Futures are constative as I have marked them or if the Ptc in future time still indicates progressive action). The time frame may be past, present, or future, and the time is determined by context. If there is need to specify time, the speaker or writer includes a form of to be (הָיָה). Here are some examples of the verbal Ptc used in different time frames:

1. **Past Time**

    "When Moses' father-in-law saw all that he was doing (עֹשֶׂה); Q PtcA ms) for the people." (Exod 18:14, ESV)

    The Ptc is part of a RC modifying the word "all." The main verb is "saw," a *wayyiqtol* form, which is past time. The Ptc piggybacks on the past time of the main verb indicating progressive action. The ESV rightly brings this out with the English progressive, "was doing."

2. **Present Time**

    "How have I wronged your father, that he is trying to take (מְבַקֵּשׁ, D Ptc ms) my life?" (1 Sam 20:1d, NIV)

    The Ptc is describing an action in progress currently with respect to the speaker.

3. **Future Time**

    Then the Lᴏʀᴅ said to him, "Know for certain that your descendants will be strangers in a country not their own, and they will be enslaved and mistreated four hundred years. But I will punish (דָּן; Q PtcA ms) the nation they serve as slaves ...." (Gen 15:14, NIV)

    The previous underlined clauses clearly set up a future time frame. Usually the time is imminent, but this case is 400 years in the future.

Now we can complete the chart of non-volitional functions from Figure 15.3:

Figure 17.4: Non-volitional Structures and Functions

Time	Uses	Examples	*qatal*	*weqatal*	*yiqtol*	*wayyiqtol*	*qotel*
Past	simple past	he <u>ate</u>	x			x	
	emphatic past	he <u>did eat</u>	x			x	
	past perfect	he <u>had eaten</u>	x			x	
	contrary-to-fact condition	(if) he <u>had eaten</u>	x				
	contrary-to-fact assertion	(then) he <u>would have eaten</u>		x	x		
	customary past	he <u>used to eat</u>		x	x		
	past progressive (historic present)	he <u>was eating</u>			x		x
	ingressive past	he <u>began eating</u>		x			
	historic future (subordinate clauses)	he <u>would</u> (<u>was going to</u>) <u>eat</u>			x		
Present	simple present (stative)	he <u>eats</u>	x			x	
	emphatic present	he <u>does eat</u>	x				
	characteristic present (gnomic, habitual)	he <u>eats</u>	x	x	x	x	
	present perfect	he <u>has eaten</u>	x			x	
	present progressive	he <u>is eating</u>		x			x
Future	simple future	he <u>shall eat</u>		x	x		x
	conditional assertion	(then) he <u>will eat</u>			x		

Time	Uses	Examples	qatal	weqatal	yiqtol	wayyiqtol	qotel
Future	immediate future	he <u>is about to eat</u>		x			x
	rhetorical/ dramatic future	he <u>eats</u> (perfected aspect used for future action)	x			x	
	future perfect	he <u>will have eaten</u>	x				
	anterior future	he <u>will have eaten</u> .		x			

Subjunctive and Volitional Structures and Functions

Time	Uses	Examples	qatal	weqatal	yiqtol	wayyiqtol	qotel
Future	condition (protasis) (protasis)	if he <u>eats</u>, <u>eat</u>, <u>should eat</u>	x	x	x		x
	possibility	he <u>might eat</u>		x	x		
	purpose/result	in order that/so that he <u>might eat</u>		x			
	capability	he <u>can eat</u>			x		
	permission	he <u>may eat</u>			x		
	obligation/ propriety	he <u>ought to eat</u>		x	x		
					x		
	command/ prohibition	<u>eat</u>!/<u>Do not eat</u>!		x	x		
					x		
	Desire/intention	he <u>wants</u>/<u>intends to eat</u>			x		
	request/wish	<u>please, eat</u>!			x		

Infinitives

An Inf is a verbal noun, meaning that it has both verbal and nominal qualities. They are not inflected for person, gender, or number. For forms, see Advanced Information and Curious Facts at the end of this chapter.

Like a verb, an Infinitive

1. implies some action.

2. has a verbal stem, though the focus is on the process rather than on the participant.

3. may also take a DO and be modified by other adverbial phrases.

4. may take a negative, but the negative particle is בִּלְתִּי or לְבִלְתִּי.

Like a noun, an Infinitive

5. functions as a noun in any case.

6. can be the object of a preposition or be the head noun in a construct chain.

Figure 17.5 summarizes the parsing information for Infs with comparisons to other forms. Not only do they have no personal ending like verbs, they don't have gender and number as nominals do. Just as with the Ptc, the Inf has noun qualities when it is acting like a noun, so State, Det, and Case are marked with an X in brackets.

Figure 17.5: Parsing Information for Nominals and Verbals

			← Verbal Qualities →					← Nominal Qualities →			
POS	Word	Lex	Stem	Form	P	G	N	State	Det	Case	Suff
V			X	X	X	X	X				
Nn						X	X	X	X	X	
Ptc			X	X		X	X	[x]	[x]	[x]	
Inf			X	X				[x]	[x]	[x]	

Overall, the uses of Hebrew Infs are pretty simple. The trick with them is that there are two separate types of Infs. We'll treat the Infinitive Construct (InfC) first, because it is similar to English. The second type is the Infinitive Absolute (InfA). English has no formal equivalent to the Hebrew InfA, so translations must use other parts of speech.

Uses of the Infinitive Construct

The Infinitive Construct as a noun.

The InfC can function in any role that a noun plays. This means that it can appear in any case. Furthermore, it may function as the head noun in a construct chain! It may take a PrnSf, and that PrnSf is often either the subjective Gen or the objective Gen, as context dictates. An InfC may also be the object of a preposition. Because noun functions have already been covered, just a few examples will suffice.

1. *Nom*

   Prov 21:3: *"To do* (עֲשֹׂה) what is right and just is more acceptable to the Lord than sacrifice" (NIV)

   The entire Inf phrase is "to do what is right and just." This entire phrase serves as the subject of the noun clause. Incidentally, *acceptable* in Hebrew is a Ptc used predicatively.

2. *Gen*

   Eccl 6:9: "Better what the eye sees *than the roving* (מֵהֲלָךְ) of the appetite" (NIV).

   The InfC is the Gen object of the pp מִן. The entire Inf phrase is "the roving of the appetite." Notice here that the InfC is in a construct chain with "the appetite." The Gen function is subjective; i.e., the appetite is doing the roving. Note also that the מִן is used comparatively.

3. *Acc* - including the *complementary* use

   Gen 24:45: "Before I had finished *praying* (לְדַבֵּר) in my heart, ..." (NIV).

   The DO of *had finished* is the Inf phrase "praying in my heart"; the PP "in my heart" modifies the InfC. Note also that the InfC has the pp לְ.

The Infinitive Construct as an adverb

The InfC commonly functions adverbially when it is the object of a preposition, mainly the inseparable prepositions. Figure 17.7 summarizes the functions and constructions. In the boxes I have placed "key words" that might be used to translate the construction.

Figure 17.6: Prepositions and Adverbial Infinitive Functions

Function	ל	בּ	כּ	Other
Time		when	when, as	
Means		by		
Manner	by	by		
Cause				because, *since*
Concession	(as) though			although
Purpose	to, in order that			
Result	so that			

1. **Time**

   Prov 31:23: "Her husband is known in the gates *when he sits* (בְּשִׁבְתּוֹ) among the elders of the land" (ESV).

   Compare the NIV, *"where he sits."* A reader might infer from the NIV rendering that this is used adjectivally to describe the gate. This InfC + pp בּ is adverbial, and the ESV makes this more clear. Note also that the 3ms PrnSf is a subjective Gen.

2. **Means**

   Isa 27:8: "By warfare and *exile* (בְּשַׁלְחָהּ) you contend with her" (NIV).

   The InfC follows the pp בּ indicating the instrument or means of the action of the main verb. If you can substitute "using" for the preposition, the function is means.

3. **Manner**

   Prov 30:32: "If you have played the fool *and exalted yourself* (בְּהִתְנַשֵּׂא)" (NIV).

   Compare the ESV, *"exalting yourself."* The Inf phrase is giving the manner in which "playing the fool" is done. By translating with *and* the NIV opens up the possible interpretation that two separate actions are involved, as though it meant, "If you have played the fool, or if you have exalted yourself." This is clearly not the intent. The ESV brings out the adverbial nature of the Inf phrase, but does not choose which adverbial function is best.

4. Cause

Isa 37:29: "Because *you raged* (הִתְרַגֶּזְךָ) against me and because your insolence has reached my ears, I will put my hook in your nose ..." (NIV).

The InfC is the object of the pp יַעַן ("because"). The InfC has a PrnSf that is a subjective Gen.

5. Concession

1 Sam 20:20: "I will shoot three arrows to the side of it, *as though* I *were shooting* (לְשַׁלַּח) at a target" (NIV).

The action of the shooting is a pretense. Note the לְ pp.

6. Purpose

Prov 23:4: "Do not wear yourself out *to get rich* (לְהַעֲשִׁיר)" (NIV).

There may be times when it is worthwhile to weary yourself, but to do so for the purpose of getting rich is not wise.

7. Result

2 Chr 36:19: "... they burned all the palaces and *destroyed* everything of value there" (NIV).

The result of all the burning was that everything of value was destroyed.

Uses of the Infinitive Absolute

The infinitive absolute (InfA) is a verbal noun, just like the InfC. Unlike the InfC, the InfA is never in construct with a following noun (hence the term "absolute"). The InfA has three classes of functions. In addition to functioning like (1) a noun or (2) an adverb just like the InfC, the InfA may also function as (3) as a finite verb, substituting for any of the five verb forms we've studied, except the Participle.

Here are just a few examples.

1. **As a Noun**- in any case

   Isa 22:13: "But see, there is … *slaughtering* (הָרֹג) of cattle" (NIV).

   The InfA phrase is "slaying cattle." The entire phrase is functioning as a Nom case noun. Notice that the InfA takes a DO; the NIV adds the word *of* for sake of English style, but this is not a construct chain.

2. **As a Finite Verb**

   a. Substitute for the וֹ *cs + Imp (wayyiqtol)*

   Judg 7:19: "They blew their trumpets and *shattered* (וְנָפוֹץ) the jars that were in their hands" (NIV).

   The InfA follows a *wayyiqtol* form and has the same function.

   b. Substitute for the *Pf (qatal)*

   Jer 14:5: "Yea the hind also calved in the field and *forsook* (וְעָזוֹב) it" (KJV).

   The InfA follows a *qatal* form and has the same function. The KJV does not catch the correct use of the *qatal* "calved" (it should be gnomic translated with an English simple present tense). Most modern translations render these as one clause. Compare the NIV, "Even the doe in the field *deserts* her newborn fawn."

   c. Substitute for the *Imp (yiqtol)*

   Jer 32:44: "Men shall buy fields for money and deeds *shall be signed* (וְכָתוֹב) and *sealed* (וְחָתוֹם) and *witnessed* (וְהָעֵד)" (NIV).

   Three InfA follow a *yiqtol* form all with the same function in relation to the main verb, "shall buy."

3. **Adverbial - Emphasis**

   a. *Emphasis of the certainty of its main verb* - InfA preceding main verb of same root

2 Kgs 14:10: "You have *indeed* struck down (הַכֵּה הִכִּיתָ)Edom" (NIV).

The InfA precedes the finite verb of the same root (נכה). The NIV renders the InfA with an adverb.

b. *Emphasis of the intensity of its main verb* - InfA following main verb of same root

Num 11:15: "If this is how you are going to treat me, put me to death *right now* (הָרְגֵנִי הָרֹג)" (NIV).

The InfA follows its finite verb of the same root. The NIV translates with the adverb *right now* to bring out the intensity of the action.

4. **Adverbial – Complementary**

Judg 14:9: "He scraped it out into his hands and went on, *eating* as he went (וְאָכֹל)" (ESV).

The ESV understands this semi-independent use of the InfA as simultaneous action.

Summary and Flowcharting

This chapter has covered a lot of ground, but congratulations! You have finished all the grammar! If you are feeling overwhelmed at this point, remember, you don't have to know all the details - you are not learning full Hebrew. All you need to understand is the main functions of Ptcs and Infs in order to understand references in commentaries.

First, let me summarize the functions of the non-finite forms:

Figure 17.7: Summary of Main Functions of Non-Finite Verbals

Major Function	Part of Speech	Description
Substantival	*Participle*	As a noun in any case with a focus on the participant; may govern a Gen
	Infinitive Construct	As a noun in any case with a focus on the action; may govern a Gen; may govern a DO

Substantival	Infinitive Absolute	As a noun in any case with a focus on the action; may not govern a Gen; may govern a DO
Adjectival	Participle	Attributively, Predicatively
	Infinitive Construct	none
	Infinitive Absolute	none
Verbal	Participle	Real or irreal action simultaneous to the verb in the previous clause
	Infinitive Construct	none
Major Function	**Part of Speech**	**Description**
Verbal (cont)	Infinitive Absolute	ꞮCS + Imp (*wayyiqtol*); Pf (*qatal*); Imp (*yiqtol*); ꞮCJ + Imp (*weyiqtol*); Imv
Adverbial	Participle	none
	Infinitive Construct	Time, Means, Manner, Cause, Concession, Purpose, Result
	Infinitive Absolute	Emphasis of certainty; Emphasis of intensity; Complementary of simultaneous action

Second, as for flowcharting, simply chart the Ptc or Inf according to its function in the text. If it is acting like a finite verb, chart it that way; as a noun, then like a noun. If it is has an adverbial function, the English translation will usually change the Inf construction to a subordinate clause introduced by a subordinating conjunction and you make the flowchart as you learned in ch. 7.

Exercises

In each item below an expression in italic type is labeled as Ptc, InfC, or InfA. Using Figure 17.9, see if you can determine the function, substantival, adjectival, or verbal, by simply placing an X in the correct column. If it is adverbial, write the more precise function. The first three are done as examples.

Item	Sbsl	Adjl	Vrbl	Advl	Passage
1.	X				But *those who hope* (Ptc) in the LORD will renew their strength. (Isa 40:31a, NIV)
2.	X^2				It is the glory of God *to conceal* (InfC) a matter. (Prov 25:2, NIV)
3.				Purpose	But Jonah rose *to flee* (InfC) to Tarshish from the presence of the LORD. (Jon 1:3, ESV)
4.					Better *to meet* (InfC) a bear robbed of her cubs than a fool in his folly. (Prov 17:12, NIV)
5.					*Let* a man *meet* (InfC) a she-bear robbed of her cubs rather than a fool in his folly. (Prov 17:12, ESV)
6.					They all plotted together *to come* (InfC) and fight against Jerusalem. (Neh 4:8 [Hebrew 4:2], NIV)
7.					"You will not *surely* (InfA) die," said the serpent to the woman. (Gen 3:4, NIV)
8.					"I am not able *to carry* (InfC) all this people alone." (Num 11:14, ESV)
9.					*With praise* and *thanksgiving* (both are InfC) they sang to the LORD. (Ezra 3:11, NIV)
10.					"Do not weep for the dead king or mourn his loss; rather, weep *bitterly* (InfA) for him who is exiled." (Jer 22:10, NIV)
11.					My help comes from the LORD, *the Maker* (Ptc) of heaven and earth. (Ps 121:2, NIV)

---

[2] The InfC is the predicate nominative and is identical to the subject "it."

Advanced Information and Curious Facts

What is a Tanak?

A Hebrew term you may hear or read is Tanak. In fact, there is a book entitled, *Tanakh*. This should never be confused with *Torah*. *Torah* is a word meaning "law, instruction." The Torah *par excellence* is the Mosaic writings, Genesis through Deuteronomy, the Pentateuch. *Tanak*, on the other hand, is an acronym. The three consonants, T, N, K stand for three Hebrew words:

Torah	➔	**Law**
Nebi'im	➔	**Prophets**
Kethubim	➔	**Writings**

In other words, Tanak refers to the three parts of the Jewish canon, the Christian OT. I bring this up, because the last term, *Kethubim*, is from the root כתב, "to write": כְּתוּבִים. You may recognize the Shureq as the sign of the Qal PtcP. This is one more example of a Ptc being used as a noun. Literally it means "things written." More idiomatically, we say "Writings." Oh, and that book, *Tanakh*? It's full title is *Tanakh: The Holy Scriptures - The New JPS Translation according to the Hebrew Text*. This *Tanakh* is a translation of the Hebrew Bible done by Jewish scholars. You might find it interesting to read.

Is Gen 1:1 a main clause or subordinate?

We have studied Gen 1:1 several times. The first word in Hebrew is a prepositional phrase, בְּרֵאשִׁית, "in (the) beginning." The Hebrew pointing has no article. Yet a definite beginning seems to be in view. The *Lexham Hebrew-English Interlinear Bible*, along with some commentators, parses רֵאשִׁית in the cst state rather than the absolute state, and suggest the translation "in the beginning of." But if this is correct, what is the tail noun for רֵאשִׁית? Some suggest the pointing of the Q Pf 3ms verb בָּרָא, "he created," be changed to the בְּרֹא, which would be followed by a subjective Gen and two direct objects. The result would be a long construct chain made definite by the tail noun, *God*. A formal translation would be, "In the beginning of God's creating the heavens and the earth." In fact, the *Tanakh Translation* renders, "When God began to create the heavens and the earth."[3]

---

[3] Reprinted from *Tanakh: The New JPS Translation According to the Traditional Hebrew Text*

In an unpointed text, ברא could be either the Pf or the InfC. Obviously the Masoretes preserved a tradition that the verb should be finite and רֵאשִׁית should be in the absolute state. The note to this verse in *The Jewish Study Bible* explains that Rashi, a famous 11th century Jewish commentator, suggested reading this as a temporal clause. They explain further that other ancient creation stories begin similarly, including Gen 2:4.[4]

The difference between these is significant. In the traditional interpretation, Gen 1:1 is the first act of creation; matter is brought into existence. In the other view, God created, narrated in vv. 2 or 3 and following, from previously existing unstructured matter, described in v. 1. Here is Wenham's analysis:

> First and fundamental is the observation that the absence of the article in בראשית does not imply that it is in the construct state. Temporal phrases often lack the article (e.g., Isa 46:10; 40:21; 41:4, 26; Gen 3:22; 6:3, 4; Mic 5:1; Hab 1:12). Nor can it be shown that רֵאשִׁית may not have an absolute sense. It may well have an absolute sense in Isa 46:10, and the analogous expression מראשׁ in Prov 8:23 certainly refers to the beginning of all creation. The context of בראשית standing at the start of the account of world history makes an absolute sense highly appropriate here. The parallel with Gen 2:4b disappears, if, as argued below, the next section of Genesis begins with 2:4a, not 4b. As for the alleged parallels with Mesopotamian sources, most of those who acknowledge such dependence point out that better parallels with extrabiblical material may be found in Gen 1:2-3 than in 1:1. The first verse is the work of the editor of the chapter; his indebtedness to earlier tradition first becomes apparent in v 2.[5]

By learning the things in this course, you are able to follow the lines of reasoning in this comment very well. This should give you confidence to understand the issues involved.

(New York: The Jewish Publication Society, 1985) with the permission of the publisher. For a discussion of the various views, see Gordon J. Wenham, *Genesis 1-15*, Word Biblical Commentary (Dallas: Word, 2002) 11-13.

[4] *The Jewish Study Bible* (Oxford: Oxford Univ. Press, 2004) 13.

[5] Wenham, *Genesis 1-15*, WBC, 12.

WEEK 6

A Method to Our Madness

CHAPTER 18

What Do You Mean?
Hebrew Word Studies

Objectives

1. Understand how to perform word studies properly
2. Avoid common pitfalls in using biblical tools.

Tools Used:

- *The Interlinear Bible: Hebrew-Greek-English* by Jay P. Green, ed. (*IBHGE*)
- At least three English translations (in addition to NIV, NASB)
- *The Strongest NIV Exhaustive Concordance* (*SNIVEC*)
- *The Hebrew-English Concordance to the OT with the NIV* (*HECOT*)
- *Mounce's Complete Expository Dictionary of Old & New Testament Words* (*MCED*)

Introduction

One Sunday you have a special speaker in church. The speaker uses the verse on his organization's logo as the central passage in his sermon: "Where there *is* no vision, the people perish" (Prov 29:18; KJV). He makes use of this passage to spur your congregation to plan for church growth: if you have no goals and no plan, you will not grow. You agree with his point, but when you follow along in your NIV, you read, "Where there is no revelation, the people cast off restraint." What catches your eye is that *revelation* in the NIV implies something different to you than the point the preacher was making. The issue is that you need to know the meaning of this word translated "vision" in the KJV.

Out of all the things covered in this book, the topic of word studies is probably the one people will use most often. Word studies are fun. They are interesting. Preachers usually have people's attention when they explain (briefly!!) the background to a word's meaning. However, there are pitfalls to be avoided. In this chapter, you will learn a procedure for doing your own word studies. Many authors write about proper practice, and they all follow the same basic procedures. I will mention in footnotes some of those writers to whom I am most indebted. The last part of the chapter identifies common pitfalls to avoid.

Performing Proper Word Studies

One way to think about the idea of context in Bible study is as a target with a bull's eye, as in Figure 18.1. At the center is the word in the passage we are studying, the immediate context. Next closest is the context of that book and other books by that author. Then other books in the same genre (e.g., poetry, prophecy, law, history). Farther removed is all the OT. Beyond that there is some ancient Hebrew literature outside the Bible. Ancient translations of Scripture are even farther removed from our immediate context, but still very important, such as the LXX. Finally, cognate languages (see ch. 2).

Figure 18.1: Contexts

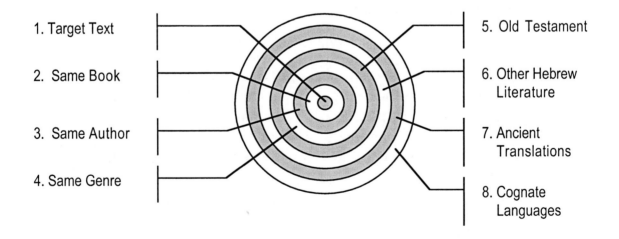

1. Target Text

2. Same Book

3. Same Author

4. Same Genre

5. Old Testament

6. Other Hebrew Literature

7. Ancient Translations

8. Cognate Languages

As you move out from the center you increase the number of possible contexts for your word. The more examples you have towards the center, the less you need to extend your search outward.

Of course the best research includes all levels of context. As a pre-Hebrew student, you can do very little with levels 6-8. You will have to rely on the experts for that research. The good news is that you can do quite a lot with levels 1-5. In keeping with the overall purpose of this book, the aim of this chapter is to empower you to study a word on your own before you turn to the experts. Why? Because (1) those books may not cover your passage specifically and therefore do not help in your particular case, and when they do cover your word (2) you will be better able to recognize careful research in commentaries and word study books you may read.

Step 1: Identifying the Word

1. *Choose a word in your passage to study.* You don't have time to study every word, so your choice needs to be significant and you need to choose a word with enough occurrences to arrive at a valid range of meanings. Duvall and Hays recommend that you study words that are...[1]

   - crucial to the passage

   - repeated

   - figures of speech

   - unclear, puzzling, or difficult (clue: if versions differ over translation, it is probably a difficult word)

2. *Identify the Hebrew word you are investigating.* Determine the G/K and the Strong's numbers for your word. You learned how to use the *SNIVEC* in ch. 7. You may also start with the *IBHEG* to find the Strong's number or use the conversion table in the *SNIVEC*

3. *Frame the question.* You want to answer the question, "What does the word *X* mean in this target text?"

---

[1]   J. Scott Duvall and J. Daniel Hays, *Grasping God's Word* (2nd ed.; Grand Rapids: Zondervan, 2005) 136.

Prov 29:18: Example – Step 1

I have selected the word *vision* in Prov 29:18. I want to study this word because it appears to be crucial to the passage. In particular, I want to find out if the speaker I heard understood the word properly. He understood it to mean "plan." But the NIV translation "revelation" suggests that the word might be interpreted as revelation from God. Which is it? Are there other possibilities? Complete a chart comparing how various translations render the word.

Looking up the word "revelation" in *NIVEC*, I see that it is G/K number 2606 (חָזוֹן). By using the conversion table (p. 1630), I learn that the Strong's number is 2377. I write these down on my word study guide.

I frame the question on the Word Study Guide.

Step 2: Determine the Range of Meaning

4. *Find all the occurrences of your word.* If you are using the *SNIVEC*, look up the G/K Number in the Dictionary section and write down the frequency of the word. Look up the concordance entry for each translation of your word (it may help to jot them down) by using the appropriate dictionary in the back of the *SNIVEC*. In each concordance entry find and record all the passages that have your G/K number. A much more efficient tool is the *HECOT*; you simply look up the word by the G/K number and all the entries are collected for you, no matter how the NIV translated the word. Computer Bibles are even faster.

5. *Look up each occurrence (except your passage) and write a brief definition based on context.* You may list multiple passages under one definition, but list all occurrences. Try to answer such questions as:

    • Is there a contrast or a comparison that seems to define the word?

    • Does the subject matter or topic dictate a word's meaning?

    • Does the author's usage of the same word elsewhere in a similar context help you decide?

    • Does the author's argument in the book suggest a meaning?

    • Does the historical-cultural situation tilt the evidence in a certain direction?

Prov 29:18: Example – Step 2

It is very important here to make a distinction between a "gloss" and a "definition." A gloss is the nearest equivalent of the original word in a translation. A definition is a description of what the word means. The *SNIVEC* dictionary section gives you glosses. In our example the *MCED* gives you definitions. What you need to do is write brief definitions and list every passage, except the target text under those definitions.

Step 3: Meaning of the Word in the Target Text

6. *Draw preliminary conclusions.* Based on your understanding of the word in your context, choose the definition from your analysis in the previous step that best fits your target text. If you think it means something else in your context, add that as a separate category.

7. *Verify with experts.* Look up the word in *MCED* or any other resources. Summarize your conclusions.

Prov 29:18: Example – Step 3

Based on the context of my target text, I choose one of the definitions made that fits best and draw some preliminary conclusions. Then I compare with word study books. Finally I draw a final conclusion and answer the question I posed at the beginning.

Sample Word Study Guide (WSG)

Step 1: Identifying the Word

1. **Question to answer:** Does the word *vision* mean "a plan for the future," or does it mean something different.

WSG 1: Comparison of Versions

Literal	Dynamic Equivalent	Free	Paraphrase
NASB95: vision	**NIV**: revelation	**NLT**: divine guidance	**MSG**: see what
KJV: vision	**NET**: prophetic vision	**NCV**:	God is doing
ESV: prophetic vision	**NAB**:	**TEV**:	**LB**:

NRSV: **JB:**   **GNB:**
RSV: **NEB:**

2. GK# 2606; Strong's # 2377

3. Frame the question: What does the word translated "vision" in the KJV version mean in Prov 29:18?

Step 2: Range of Meaning

4. Find all the Occurrences of the Word

   • Number of occurrences 35

   • Distribution of occurrences:

WSG 2: Distribution of Occurrences of the Word (optional)

Category	Passages
In the same book	None
Other books	
by same author	None
OT Law	None
OT History	1 Sam 3:1; 1 Chr 17:15; 2 Chr 32:32
OT Poetry	Lam 2:2
OT Prophets	Hos 12:10; Obad 1:1; Mic 3:6; Nah 1:1; Hab 2:2, 3; Isa 1:1; 29:7; Jer 14:14; 23:16; Ezek 7:13, 26; 12:22, 23, 24, 27; 13:16; Dan 1:17; 8:1, 2, 2, 13, 15, 17, 26; 9:21, 24; 10:14; 11:14

5. Definitions

   a. Miraculous divine revelation from God;

      (1a) Specific messages genuinely from God
          Passages: 1 Sam 3:1; Lam 2:2; 1 Chr 17:15; Ezek 7:13, 26; 12:23, 27; Dan 8:1, 2, 13, 15, 17, 26; 9:21; 10:14; Hab 2:2, 3

      (1b) Specific messages genuinely from God recorded in written form
          Passages: Obad 1; Nah 1:1

      (2) General reference of messages to biblical writing prophet
          Passages: 2 Chr 32:32; Ps 89:19; Isa 1:1; Dan 9:24; 11:14(?); Hos 12:10; Micah 3:6

(3) Dream intended to be interpreted by prophet of God
Passages: Dan 1:17

(4) False vision; genuineness claimed by people lying about it
Passages: Jer 14:14; 23:16: Ezek 12:22, 24; 13:16; 11:14(?)

b. Normal dream of the night, a symbol of unreality
Passages: Isa 29:7

c. Planning based on human forethought
Passages: NONE

Step 3: Meaning of the Word in the Target Text

6. Preliminary conclusions on the meaning in your passage.

In all but one case, the word G/K 2606 is used of miraculous, divine revelation from God, including those of false prophets who make the same claim. In one case, Isa 29:7, the meaning seems to be a normal dream without any miraculous element implied. In Prov 28:19, the second half of the verse contrasts "vision" with the law, presumably the law of Moses. Since this is clearly miraculous revelation, the meaning in Prov 28:19 is likely miraculous, prophetic revelation from God.

7. Verify with experts (notes from word-books).

This word is not treated in the main word study section of *MCED*. There is a Hebrew–English Dictionary section that gives brief definitions (note: not merely glosses!). The conclusion there agrees with mine, adding something that I didn't notice: "with a possible focus on the visual aspects of the message" (p. 932).

Conclusions

- Meaning of target word in target passage: miraculous revelation from God

- Effect of the meaning of target word on the meaning of target passage: Since there were no references where the word meant planning for the future, that meaning can be eliminated, and the speaker did not properly use the passage.

Trouble Shooting Word Studies

Verbs

Remember when you are studying verbs, that different stems have different meanings. You may need to separate your list of passages by verbal stem. You also learned that prepositions may alter the meaning of a verb; so you may need to identify those passages that are followed by certain prepositions. Computer programs will help to identify the form, and some actually sort them automatically. Mostly, though, you will have to rely on experts. As a pre-Hebrew student, you need to be aware of your limitations. Note that for verbs in *HECOT*, a code by each NIV verse indicates the verbal stem. Learn to use the code (printed at the bottom of each page).

Rare and Common Words

Both rare and common words are worthy of your study. You can usually get a good sampling if you have 20-50 occurrences. The problem with choosing a word that is rare is that you don't have enough examples for a good sampling. The more rare the word, the more important it is to include the outer rings of the "Context Target." This also means, however, that you will be more dependent on the "Work of Others" (Figure 18.1). That's okay though.

Words that are common give you too large of a number to be manageable. If a word occurs, say 500 times, you usually don't have time to study every context. What you can do, though, is focus on the occurrences in your genre or time period. Even when you do this, though, you will need to rely more on the work of others, because you aren't looking at every context. Sometimes, if your question is worded appropriately, you can go through enough verses to find a context that answers your question clearly. Also, don't be afraid to say, "I don't know the answer."

A Short Cut

Sometimes you are in a time pinch. One option is to skip looking up the contexts and just classify the glosses in the Dictionary section of the *SNIVEC*. Obviously this process is inferior because you may misunderstand the meaning of the gloss. A second option is to go straight to the word study books *after* you have identified the G/K number. This process is also inferior, because you don't make the study your own. If you only have one word study book, you are relying even more heavily than if you could check other word books, but it is better than nothing. Finally, looking up the other passages can give you some great illustration.

One more thing: please never use an English dictionary to define a biblical word!

Avoiding Word Study Pitfalls

Duvall and Hays do a nice job of describing eight pitfalls to avoid.[2] I have summarized and arranged these below with examples.

Fallacy	Description
English-Only	Studying an English word rather than an original language word.
	Example: This is the error made in the Prov 29:18 example above.
Root	The notion that the meaning of a word is determined by the parts (roots) that make it up.
	Example: Some say the root used for the word for *priest* (כהן) is one who builds a bridge, and therefore a priest is a bridge-builder between God and man. Even if this etymology were correct (scholarship suggests that it isn't), this would not help us to understand what a biblical priest is.
Time-Frame	Neglecting the change of a word's meaning over time, especially after the time of the Bible.
	Example: A *prophet* now means someone who predicts the future. But in the OT, prophets were spokesmen for God, and the predictive element takes a comparatively minor role.
Overload	Most words have a range of meanings. But to state that every time a word occurs that it means all of those things is wrong.
	Example: This can be a problem with those who use the Amplified Bible, which gives multiple translations of key words. E.g., in Gen 1:2: "The Spirit of God was moving (hovering, brooding) over the face of the waters."

---

[2] *Grasping God's Word* (2nd ed.) 133-5.

Word Count	Neglects the fact that a given word may have more than one meaning and the meaning is determined by the meaning that occurs most often.
	Example: It is a mistake to say, "Since שָׂנֵא commonly means 'to hate,' Jacob hated Leah (Gen 29:30; KJV), and the NIV rendering, 'not loved' is wrong."
Word-Concept	Notion that if one understands a word meaning one understands the whole concept.
	Example: Studying חָזוֹן, the word in Prov 29:18, even properly, does not mean you understand everything the Bible says about the concept of the prophecy.
Selective Evidence	Looking only at passages that support your point.
	Example: To say that בָּרָא, "to create," in Gen 1:1 means to create *out of nothing* neglects passages that is used in the sense of creating out of something. So in Gen 5:1 we read that God created (בָּרָא) man, which refers to the event in which "God formed (יָצַר) the man *from the dust* of the ground" (NIV, italics added).[3]

Exercises

Here are some words to practice on. If you are working on a paper for another assignment, your teacher may let you choose a word for that assignment. Follow the procedure given in this chapter. Appendix 4 includes a blank "Word Study Guide" that you can use as a model. An electronic version is found at www.teknia.com.

1. Gen 1:26: "Then God said, "Let us make man in our image, in our *likeness*" (NIV).

   Question to answer: Does *likeness* mean that we are like God in full deity?

---

[3] This example comes from John H. Walton, *Chronological and Background Charts of the Old Testament* (rev. ed.; Grand Rapids: Zondervan, 1994) 95.

2. Gen 2:7: "And the Lord God formed man *of* the dust of the ground, and breathed into his nostrils the breath of life; and man became a living *soul*" (KJV).

    Question to answer: Does *soul* refer to that invisible, inner consciousness in man that distinguishes humans from animals?

3. Gen 2:18: "I will make a *helper* suitable for him" (NIV).

    Question to answer: Does *helper* imply that Eve was a notch below Adam in status?

4. Exod 31:16: "Therefore the people of Israel shall keep the Sabbath, observing the Sabbath throughout their generations, as a covenant *forever*" (ESV).

    Question to answer: Does *forever* mean Christians should observe Sabbath laws today?

5. Deut 6:4: "Hear, O Israel: The LORD our God, the LORD is *one*" (NIV).

    Question to answer: Does *one* mean that God is literally homogeneous and indistinguishable within himself, namely that God is not a Trinity?

6. Job 1:1: "There was a man in the land of Uz, whose name was Job; and that man was *perfect* and upright, and one that feared God, and eschewed evil" (KJV).

    Question to answer: Was Job absolutely perfectly without sin?

7. Isa 1:18: '"Come now, *let us reason* together," says the LORD' (NIV).

    Question to answer: Is this a pleasant conversation between two friends?

8. Gen 31:49: "And Mizpah; for he said, The Lord *watch* between me and thee, when we are absent one from another" (KJV).

    Question to answer: Is this watch a prayer for God's care for the other person?

9. Ps 16:10: "For thou wilt not leave my soul in *hell*; neither wilt thou suffer thy Holy One to see corruption" (KJV).

    Question to answer: Does this OT passage teach that Jesus went to actual hell (cf. Acts 2:31)?

10. Select a word from Josh 1 to study. Go through all the steps for the full word study, including clearly stating the question you want to answer.

Advanced Information and Curious Facts

Here is a sequel to Gen 3:16. The immediate context is the first half of the verse, "your desire will be for your husband" (NIV). The NET note 48 on this reads,

> **tn** *Heb* "and toward your husband [will be] your desire." The nominal sentence does not have a verb; a future verb must be supplied, because the focus of the oracle is on the future struggle. The precise meaning of the noun תְּשׁוּקָה (*téshuqah* [sic], "desire") is debated. Many interpreters conclude that it refers to sexual desire here, because the subject of the passage is the relationship between a wife and her husband, and because the word is used in a romantic sense in Song 7:11 HT[4] (7:10 ET). However, this interpretation makes little sense in Gen 3:16. First, it does not fit well with the assertion "he will dominate you." Second, it implies that sexual desire was not part of the original creation, even though the man and the woman were told to multiply. And third, it ignores the usage of the word in Gen 4:7, where it refers to sin's desire to control and dominate Cain. (Even in Song of Songs it carries the basic idea of "control," for it describes the young man's desire to "have his way sexually" with the young woman.) In Gen 3:16 the Lord announces a struggle, a conflict between the man and the woman. She will desire to control him, but he will dominate her

---

[4] HT means *Hebrew text*; ET means *English text*.

instead. This interpretation also fits the tone of the passage, which is a judgment oracle. See further Susan T. Foh, "What is the Woman's Desire?" *WTJ*[5] 37 (1975): 376-83.

Take a minute to reflect on how well you would have understood this note before you started this course. If you can read these comments and understand them, then you are achieving the goals for this study. Celebrate!

---

[5] *WTJ* means *Westminster Theological Journal.*

CHAPTER 19

Tools of the Trade
Books in Paper and Electronic Form

Objectives

1. Learn how to use a commentary
2. Learn about tools to supplement this book
3. Develop a buying strategy

Introduction

Once after coming back from a used bookstore with a few treasures (*bargains*, really, is what they were), one of my wife's well-meaning relatives asked her, "Does he really need all those books?"

What kind of a carpenter doesn't own a hammer? If you want to be a Bible student, you need to view books as tools just as important as a hammer is to a carpenter. These days, of course, carpenters don't use hammers nearly as much as they use air guns. In the same way, the tools for the trade of Bible study are much better, as you have seen in this course. Don't be afraid to invest a little. For the price of a compressor and air gun, you can have quite a nice collection of tools that will enhance your personal Bible study and your ability to minister to others.

Using Commentaries

If you have never used a commentary, you will be amazed. Your first thought might be, "Well, they've done all the work for me. I don't have to!" This is living on borrowed opinions – or dying on them. Commentaries are wonderful tools, when used properly. Like anything else, there are good ones and bad. Here are a few guidelines on choosing and using them.

There are different types of commentaries: exegetical, homiletical, and devotional. *Exegetical* commentaries seek to explain the meaning of the Bible text. The better ones not only explain the commentator's understanding of the text, but give alternative views and reasons for or against various interpretations. *Homiletical* commentaries also explain the meaning of the text, but in less detail. Their primary aim is to guide preachers in sermon preparation. This may include sermon illustrations and outlines. *Devotional* commentaries are relatively weak in the explanation of the meaning of the text, spending most space on applying the Bible text to life. Because many authors for these books are often not Bible scholars, their exegesis is usually less carefully done. To study a passage, you should use the exegetical commentaries primarily.

Commentaries may also be categorized by level of detail; that is, what knowledge the author assumes the reader will have. A *level one* commentator assumes the typical reader does not know biblical languages. When original language terms are used, they are always in transliteration. The more reliable commentators do know the original language and will still treat the difficult passages in some detail. A *level two* commentator expects that some readers may know biblical languages and usually places words and grammatical discussions on the original languages in footnotes. A *level three* commentator assumes that readers know biblical languages and interact with the original languages in the text, often without translation or transliteration. (They might also assume that the reader knows German, French and Latin!) Do not be afraid to use these. Usually English-only readers can benefit from this level of work. You as a pre-Hebrew student will be able to benefit even more.

Here are some common sense guidelines

1. *Complete your own study of your passage before turning to the commentaries.* While you are making your own observations, write down any questions you may have, including both ones you have answered (use commentaries for verification) and ones you were not able to figure out (use commentaries for information).

2. *Select at least three commentaries for your passage.* People have been writing commentaries on the Bible for over 2,000 years. Making a selection can be difficult.

a. *Tend to use the more modern commentaries.* Don't necessarily avoid the older ones (those done within the last 150 years or so); many of them are still valuable. Modern commentators use them as well and can save you time since they have worked through that material.

b. *Tend to use exegetical commentaries, including levels two and three.*

c. *Get suggestions from published bibliographies and from fellow Christians who read good commentaries.* I give two sources for bibliographies below.

d. *Get to know publishers and authors.* This is a slow process, but valuable. In particular you want to know the theological starting points of the commentator. You may disagree with those starting points, but you can still learn things from them.

3. *Take notes from your reading of commentaries.*

a. *Always record the author and title of each commentary* you use as well as the page number for each note you take. Not only do you want to avoid plagiarism, you want to be able to find that reference again if needed.

b. *Record notes in verse-by-verse order, not commentary order.* You may even want to go phrase-by-phrase. Notes are *summaries* of what the commentator says. Be selective. Write only those things you think are valuable to your understanding of the passage.

c. *Take notes that answer the questions you have.* Some commentaries seem to be shallow and only deal with the simple matters. Good commentators help you answer the questions you have and may even help you raise more questions. All such questions may be good for asking students or using as sermon or lesson points.

d. *Evaluate commentators' reasons for interpretations* to help you decide which interpretation you think is best, where they disagree. You cannot merely take a majority vote.

e. *Note where your interpretations agree or differ.* Have an attitude of respect for the experts, but remember that they are not infallible.

Many commentaries do not discuss the grammar of every word. When they do, it is because the grammar is important for understanding the passage. They can't afford the space to discuss routine matters, and they assume that those who know the biblical languages can understand such matters, and those who do not understand the biblical languages could not follow along. This is why what you have learned in this study can help you to understand the commentaries better. You are able to make some of your own observations.

Tools

Below is a categorized list of a few tools for OT study. I have tried to be brief by choosing to focus on resources dealing with the topics we have covered in this book. I do not give a list of commentaries. Instead I list a couple of bibliographic resources that you can consult.

Computer Bibles

Because Bible programs vary so much in content, cost, and design, and because they are continually being upgraded, I am not going to comment on any of them. You should go to their websites to compare costs and features that will fulfill your needs both now and in the future. Some online programs are free. In your evaluation, you need identify what electronic books are included. The less expensive programs contain mainly (or only) works that are public domain. These are usually too old to help you very much, and certainly not for serious study. Here are some of the more recognized resources listed alphabetically with their web addresses.

Accordance. At www.accordancebible.com. (Mac)

Biblesoft PC Study Bible. At biblesoft.com. (PC)

Bibleworks. At www.bibleworks.com. (PC)

Gramcord. At www.gramcord.org. (PC)

Logos Bible Software. At www.logos.com. (PC, Mac)

Pradis. At www.zondervan.com. (PC)

Wordsearch. At www.wordsearchbible.com. (PC)

Bibliographies

Duvall, J. Scott, and J. Daniel Hays. *Grasping God's Word*. 2nd ed. Grand Rapids: Zondervan, 2005. This is actually a book to teach how to interpret the Bible. The bibliography on pp. 426-50 is classified according to type of work and includes commentaries on every book of the Bible. The list is reliable.

Klein, William, Craig L. Blomberg, and Robert L. Hubbard. *Introduction to Biblical Interpretation*. Rev. ed. Nashville: Nelson, 2004. This is another book on interpretation in much more detail. It has an extensive bibliography on pp. 506-43. The entries are annotated; i.e., the authors give brief insights into the nature of each work.

Longman, Tremper, III. *Old Testament Commentary Survey*. 4th ed. Grand Rapids: Baker, 2007. This book is completely devoted to bibliography of works for OT studies. It goes beyond commentaries, covering all types of works for studying the OT. Entries are briefly annotated. In addition, Longman indicates the level of reader the work is appropriate for (Layperson, Minister, Scholar) and grades it for quality on a 1-5 scale.

Basic Introductions to the Old Testament Studies

Arnold, Bill T., and Bryan E. Beyer. *Encountering the Old Testament: A Christian Survey*. Grand Rapids: Baker, 1998. Survey of the OT in book-by-book format.

Dillard, Raymond B., and Tremper Longman, III. *An Introduction to the Old Testament*. 2nd ed. Grand Rapids: Zondervan, 2007. In-depth treatment of special introduction (authorship, date, outline, etc.) for each book of the OT.

Hill, Andrew E., and John Walton H. *The Old Testament Today*. Grand Rapids: Zondervan, 2004. Survey of the OT in book-by-book format.

Patzia, Arthur G., and Anthony J. Patrotta. *Pocket Dictionary of Biblical Studies*. Downers Grove, Ill.: InterVarsity, 2002. Dictionary of technical terms used in biblical and theological studies.

Schultz, Samuel. *The Old Testament Speaks*. 4th ed. San Francisco: Harper & Row, 1990. Surveys the OT chronologically.

Soulen, Richard N., and R. Kendall Soulen. *Handbook of Biblical Criticism*. 3rd ed. revised and expanded. Louisville: Westminster John Knox, 2001. Dictionary of technical terms used in biblical and theological studies.

Walton, John H. *Chronological and Background Charts of the Old Testament*. Rev. ed., Grand Rapids: Zondervan, 1994. Helpful collection of charts on many topics of OT studies.

Old Testament Literature

Chisholm, Robert B. *Interpreting the Historical Books: An Exegetical Handbook*. Grand Rapids: Kregel, 2006. Treatment of how to study narrative literature of the OT.

Fee, Gordon D., and Douglas Stuart. *How To Read the Bible for All Its Worth*. 3rd ed. Grand Rapids: Zondervan, 2003. Treatment of how to study all types of literature in both testaments.

Lucas, Ernest C. *A Guide to the Psalms & Wisdom Literature*. Exploring the Old Testament, vol. 3. Downers Grove, Ill.: InterVarsity, 2003. Treatment of how to study poetic literature of the OT.

Waltke, Bruce K., and Cathi J. Fredricks. *Genesis: A Commentary*. Grand Rapids: Zondervan, 2001. I'm including this commentary, because it is a model of how to deal with OT narrative texts.

Interlinear Bibles and Specialty Bibles

Abegg, Martin A., Jr., Peter Flint, and Eugene Ulrich. *The Dead Sea Scrolls Bible*. San Francisco: Harper, 1999. English translation of the biblical manuscripts of the Hebrew Bible. Translations are arranged in OT order and variations in fonts allow you to see quickly where the DSS Bible manuscripts differ from the MT.

The Apostolic Bible. Apostolic Press, 2004. Modern translation of the LXX into English under the auspices of the Greek Orthodox Church. It is available in e-text at septuagint-interlinear-greek-bible.com/downbook.htm, in free and printable online in Adobe format. A hard copy edition is available. The translation is based on the 1709 edition of the LXX published by Lambert Bos, which ultimately derives its text from Codex Vaticanus. Words are coded to Strong's numbering system.

The Apostolic Bible Polyglot. Apostolic Press, 2004. The Greek and English text of the LXX plus the English translation is available on CD or online at http://septuagint-interlinear-greek-bible.com/. It can be downloaded for a fee.

Brenton, L. C. *The Septuagint with Apocrypha: Greek and English.* Rpt.; Peabody, Mass.: Hendrickson, 1986. A 19th century English translation of the Septuagint (not the Hebrew!) in parallel columns with the Greek text. Available in print and online. The translation was done by one person using the Greek texts available in the 19th century.

Green, Jay P., ed. *The Interlinear Bible: Hebrew-Greek-English.* 1 vol. ed.; Peabody, Mass.: Hendrickson, 2005. Traditional interlinear using the same text base as the KJV. Includes Strong's numbers above most words.

Kohlenberger, John R., III. *The Interlinear NIV Hebrew-English Old Testament.* Grand Rapids: Zondervan, 1993. Traditional interlinear using the BHS as its text base.

McDaniel, Chip, and C. John Collins. *The ESV English-Hebrew Reverse Interlinear Old Testament.* Logos Research Systems, Inc., 2006. The ESV with the Hebrew MT arranged beneath. This includes parsing information.

The New English Translation of the Septuagint. Oxford: Oxford Press, 2007. Modern English translation of the Septuagint done by committee using the latest research available. This is also available online. For information, see http://ccat.sas.upenn.edu/nets.

Tov, Emanuel, and Computer Assisted Tools for Septuagint Studies. *The Parallel Aligned Hebrew-Aramaic and Greek Texts of Jewish Scripture.* Bellingham, WA: Logos Research Systems, Inc., 2003. The MT text with the LXX arranged beneath.

van der Merwe, Christo. *The Lexham Hebrew-English Interlinear Bible; Bible. O.T. Hebrew.* Logos Research Systems, Inc., 2004. Interlinear with the Hebrew first and the English arranged beneath each word. This includes parsing information.

Concordances

Kohlenberger, J. R., and E. Goodrick. *The Strongest NIV Exhaustive Concordance of the Bible.* Rev. ed. Grand Rapids: Zondervan, 2004. Based on the NIV. This series by Zondervan also has produced exhaustive concordances for KJV and NASB.

Kohlenberger, J. R., and E. Goodrick. *The Hebrew-English Concordance to the Old Testament.* Grand Rapids: Zondervan, 1998. Concordance arranged by Hebrew word based on the G/K numbers rather than English translation.

The Lexical Concordance to the Apostolic Bible. Apostolic Press, 2004. CD–ROM. Concordance to *The Apostolic Bible Polyglot* of the LXX. It is available on CD or online at septuagint-interlinear-greek-bible.com/. It can be downloaded for a fee.

Wigram, George V. *The New Englishman's Hebrew Concordance.* Rev. by Jay P. Green. Peabody, MA: Hendrickson, 1984. Concordance arranged by Hebrew word based on the Strong's numbers rather than English translation.

Parsing Tools (not counting computer software)

Davidson, Benjamin. *Analytical Hebrew and Chaldee Lexicon.* Rpt.; Peabody, Mass.: Hendrickson, 1981.

Owens, John Joseph. *Analytical Key to the Old Testament.* 4 vols. Grand Rapids: Baker, 1995.

Word Study Books and Tools

Many of these books are considered to be advanced. In the past, the user had to know Hebrew to use them, because entries are not coded to numbers. But you are now able to identify roots and lexical forms. Furthermore, a good computer

Bible can make it possible for you to go directly to the right entry in an electronic version of a technical work.

Botterweck, G. J., and H. Ringgren, eds. *Theological Dictionary of the Old Testament.* Eng. Trans. 15 vols. Grand Rapids: Eerdmans, 1974-2006. Technical and up-to-date treatment of theologically significant OT Hebrew words.. A more reliable treatment of words than is the Greek counterpart to the NT. Abbreviated *TDOT.*

Brown, F., S. R. Driver, and C. A. Briggs. *The New Hebrew -English Lexicon of the Old Testament.* Peabody. MA: Hendrickson, 1979. Technical and often outdated treatment of all OT Hebrew words. Still valuable. Coded to the Strong's numbering system. Also covers Aramaic. Abbreviated BDB.

Clines, David A., ed. *Dictionary of Classical Hebrew.* 5 [of projected 8] vols. Sheffield: Sheffield Academic, 1993-. Technical treatment of all OT Hebrew words. Includes Hebrew literature beyond the OT. Abbreviated *DCH.*

Harris, R. L., et al., eds. *Theological Wordbook of the Old Testament.* 2 vols. Chicago: Moody, 1980. Less technical treatment of theologically significant OT Hebrew words. It uses its own numbering system, but is cross-referenced to Strong's numbering system. Abbreviated *TWOT.*

Jenni, Ernst, and Claus Westermann, eds. *Theological Lexicon of the Old Testament.* (Mark E. Biddle, trans.) Peabody. MA: Hendrickson, 1997. Very thorough work treating theologically significant OT Hebrew words. One feature that makes it even more valuable is that at the beginning of every entry article, in addition to the Strong's number are cross-references to where the word is treated in BDB, *HALOT, TDOT, TWOT,* and *NIDOTTE.* Abbreviated *TLOT.*

Koehler, Ludwig, Walter Baumgartner, M. E. J. Richardson, and Johann Jakob Stamm. 5 vols. *The Hebrew and Aramaic Lexicon of the Old Testament.* Leiden; New York: E.J. Brill, 1994-1996. Technical work treating all OT words, including Aramaic. The electronic edition was published in 1999. Abbreviated *HALOT.*

Mounce, William D, ed. *Mounce's Complete Expository Dictionary of Old and New Testament Words*. Grand Rapids: Zondervan, 2006. Popular level treatment of theologically significant words from both testaments. It is reliable and up-to-date. Many words are treated with articles; other words are treated with only brief definitions. This supersedes the old *Vine's Complete Expository Dictionary of Old and New Testament Words*.

Swanson, James. *Dictionary of Biblical Languages With Semantic Domains: Hebrew (Old Testament)*. electronic ed. Oak Harbor: Logos Research Systems, Inc., 1997. Thorough treatment of all the words of the OT, including Aramaic. Words are arranged, however, according to meaning ("semantic domain"). Therefore a given Hebrew word will be found in multiple locations. The electronic version makes it very easy to use.

Van Gemeren, W., et al., eds. *New International Dictionary of Old Testament Theology*. 5 vols. Grand Rapids: Zondervan, 1996. Very thorough treatment of theologically significant Hebrew words of OT. Abbreviated *NIDOTTE*. Keyed to G/K numbering system.

A Buying Strategy

There are so many great study tools out there! Where should you start? Duvall and Hays in *Grasping God's Word*, p. 425, offer a sensible strategy for filling your tool chest. Remember that many works are available in electronic format. You should consider a Bible program that allows you to buy more books to add on later.

Phase 1: Cover all your bases

If you have the following types of books, a Bible school teacher will be able to cover almost all needs. For specific recommendations, see the bibliographies mentioned above. I have listed various types of tools beginning with what I think is the greatest priority.

1. Concordance

2. Commentary on the whole Bible (preferably at least a two-volume work)

3. Bible dictionary

4. Bible wordbook

5. Bible handbook

6. Dictionary of theology

7. Atlas

Phase 2: Plan for growth

When you preach or teach on a new book of the Bible, buy something on that book. Begin by buying at least one reliable commentary on each book of the Bible as you study. You may get more for your money if you buy commentary sets. Because they are often done by different authors, the quality of volumes within sets may vary. Occasionally buy additional reference books, after you look them over to see how useful they will be for you. The more serious student that you are, the greater the need you will have to keep detailed works handy. Building a church library is an excellent idea, but someone will need to take charge of that as a ministry, so that the library can be both usable and used.

Exercises

1. *Evaluate your personal library.* How many "Phase 1" books do you currently own? What books would you like to have to fill in some of the missing gaps? Do you have a Bible computer program?

2. *Plan for future growth.* What Bible books do you plan on studying? What books would you like to add to your library? Make a gift list for Christmas or birthday.

Advanced Information and Curious Facts

I want to show you that reading the English translations of the Septuagint (LXX) and of the Dead Sea Scrolls from the bibliographies can pay off. In Heb 1:6, the author quotes from the OT: "Let all God's angels worship him" (NIV). The job of the interpreter is to study first what the OT meant in its original context, then see how the NT author used it, noting any significant twists. For this quotation, the identity of where it comes from is the first issue. Some say it comes from the end of

Ps 97:7, which reads, "worship him, all you gods!" (NIV). However, the wording is not exactly the same as Hebrews. The first difference is that the subject of the verb as quoted in Heb 1:6 is 3rd plural, whereas in Ps 97:7, it is a 2mp imperative. The second difference is that the plural noun in Heb 1:6 is *angels*, while that in Ps 97:7 is *gods*. This problem is not insurmountable, since the word *gods* (אֱלֹהִים) can be used to mean "angels." In fact, using Brenton's translation, we can see that the LXX translates this into the Greek word "angels." Still, it would be nice to find a better alternative.

The NIV footnote gives the cross reference Deut 32:43 and adds, "see Dead Sea Scrolls and Septuagint." If you look up this passage in the *DSSB*,[1] mentioned in the bibliography above, you can read a translation of a Hebrew Bible from the Qumran community. Figure 19.1 compares the first part of Deut 32:43 in the KJV, NIV plus footnote, Brenton's LXX, and the *DSSB*. In the center I've placed the quotation according to Heb 1:6 with the key words in italic type.

Figure 19.1: Comparison of Heb 1:6 and Deut 32:43

Deut 32:43 (KJV)

Rejoice, O ye nations, with his people;
for he will avenge …

Deut 32:43 (NIV with Footnote)

Rejoice, O nations, with his people,
And let all the angels worship him
for he will avenge …

Heb 1:6 (NIV)

Let all God's angels worship him

Deut 32:43 (LXX)

Rejoice, ye heavens, with him,
and let all the angels of God worship him
rejoice ye Gentiles

Deut 32:43 (DSSB)

Rejoice, O *heavens, together with him;*
and bow down to him all you gods,
for he will avenge …

---

[1] Abegg, Flint and Ulrich, *The Dead Sea Scrolls Bible*, 193.

The KJV of Deut 32:43 and the main text of the NIV do not contain the italicized phrase, because the Hebrew text that the translators used (the Masoretic Text) did not have it. This phrase is included in the footnote to the NIV, because it is found in the LXX, which the author of Hebrews seems to be quoting. The LXX reading was not something the translators just plopped in willy-nilly; it is supported by a Hebrew manuscript of Deuteronomy among the DSS. The exact words as recorded by the author of Hebrews are found here, though the quotation is abbreviated.

There is more to research for this passage, but at least we can be reasonably confident that the original context is Deut 32. Now we are ready to interpret. This chapter is a song that Moses recited before the assembly of Israel about the Lord's judgment on the wicked. In the LXX, the song concludes at verse 43 with a call for the heavens to rejoice and for the angels of God to worship "him." Our author identifies the speaker as the Father and *him* as the Son, the object of worship. In doing this, our author is also attributing to the Son the great deeds of the Lord mentioned in Deut 32. The point is clear: since the angels worship the Son, he is clearly superior to them, because of his great deeds.

CHAPTER 20

If It's Not Poetry, It's . . .
Hebrew Prose

Objectives

1. Understand conjunctive and disjunctive clauses as devices in Hebrew narrative
2. Using adjusted flowcharting

Tools Used: paper or electronic Interlinear Bible

Introduction

You have already learned that in verbless clauses either the subject or the predicate noun may be placed first in the clause, or "fronted." If the subject is fronted (S-P), the clause answers the question, "Whom does the predicate describe?" If the predicate is fronted (P-S), the clause answers the question, "How would you describe the subject?"

You have also learned that normal word order in a Hebrew verbal clause is VSO (verb – subject – object). Many grammarians refer to this normal order as "unmarked"; i.e., there is nothing unusual in the construction of the sentence and the verb takes its place as the primary focal point. What you want to pay attention to are deviations from the norm. "Fronting" may be done to (1) set a time frame, (2) emphasize the fronted element, or (3) form a disjunctive clause.

In this chapter, you will learn about how clauses work in Hebrew narrative. Narrative literature in the OT constitutes the story parts. Narrative is found most commonly in the historical books, of course, but it is also found in all sections of the OT. Describing the interpretation of this kind of literature is beyond the scope of this book.[1] What you can do is grasp the big picture of narrative literature and then see how what you've learned in these previous weeks can give you insights that are normally lost in translation.

There are three principles to keep in mind when studying Hebrew narrative. First, all narrative has three basic elements: setting, characterization, and plot. Second, the player behind the scenes is the narrator. He is the one describing the setting and characters and relating the story. We want to observe what the narrator is trying to make visible to our mind's eye. Third, one task of the interpreter is to find the section breaks between and within stories – to pay attention to the story line and to what the author points out. Hebrew can do this with conjunctive and disjunctive clauses. This aspect of Hebrew narrative is frequently lost in English translation. But since you are now equipped to use a traditional interlinear, that information will no longer be lost on you! In this chapter you will learn to identify conjunctive and disjunctive clauses and use this information in flowcharting.

Conjunctive and Disjunctive Clauses

When the conjunction Waw connects one clause to another, it may introduce a conjunctive clause or a disjunctive clause. Simply put, a *conjunctive clause* is a clause that begins with Waw + Finite Verb. We treated these in the chapters on the verb. A *disjunctive clause* is one that begins with Waw + Nonverb. Conjunctive clauses may be either independent/main or dependent.

Terminology overlaps a little here, so it is important to keep things straight. A Waw is considered to be a *coordinating* conjunction. The function of the clause it introduces, however, may be either a main/independent clause or a subordinate clause. Waw may introduce a *conjunctive clause* or a *disjunctive clause*.

One of the characteristics of narrative in the OT is the abundance of direct speech. Reading narrative is sort of like watching a play. The main difference is that a play is meant to be acted and watched while a narrative includes a narrator who provides important information. The conjunctive and disjunctive clauses in narrative literature are the words of the narrator, not the recorded speech. First you will learn the functions of conjunctive and disjunctive clauses. Then you will learn how to work with them. The last section illustrates how to incorporate these features into a flowchart.

---

[1] For further reading, see the books listed in ch. 19 under the heading Old Testament Literature. Fee and Stuart cover OT narrative in ch. 5. Chisholm's work is more advanced.

Conjunctive Clauses

The standard construction for a conjunctive clause in Hebrew narrative is the *wayyiqtol* verb form. This structure is considered unmarked. A series of *wayyiqtol* clauses builds a sequence or series of activities. A negative clause in such a sequence is usually expressed by וְלֹא + Pf. Occasionally the negative will be expressed by וְלֹא + Imp, with one of two senses: (1) customary past (e.g., "he *used to* not go into town") or (2) past progressive (e.g., "he *was* not go*ing* into town").

You learned in ch. 15 that וַיְהִי is a common verb form in the Hebrew Bible and that it may function in one of two ways: either to mark a temporal clause or as a main clause. The construction וַיְהִי + a temporal clause often introduces a new narrative or scene; וַיְהִי + a subject is used as a main verb and translated, "And [subject] was/became."

In a series, *wayyiqtol* can have any of the following semantic notions:[2]

Figure 20.1: Eight Basic Functions of Wayyiqtol Clauses

Function	Description
Introductory	Begins a scene or narrative by providing background information for an upcoming story
Initiatory	Begins a story
Sequential/ Consequential	Describes events in temporal or logical sequence [most common use]
Flashback	Interrupts a story to refer to prior action that now becomes relevant
Focusing	Draws attention to an individual in the event just described, gives a more detailed account of the event or aspect thereof, or provides specific example
Resumptive/ (Con)sequential	follows a supplementary, focusing, or flashback statement.

---

[2] This chart is a summary taken from Robert B. Chisholm, Jr., *A Workbook for Intermediate Hebrew* (Grand Rapids: Kregel, 2006), 263.

Function	Description
Resumptive/ Reiterative	repeats or paraphrases a previous statement
Complementary	Completes preceding statement by describing an action that naturally or typically accompanies what precedes
Summarizing/ Concluding	Summarizes or marks the conclusion of a narrative

Disjunctive Clauses

A disjunctive clause may be either a verbal clause or a noun clause. The key factor is how the clause begins. In short, it begins with Waw + a nonverb. A nonverb includes any nonfinite verb such as a noun, pronoun, participle, or particle, except the negatives לֹא and אַל.

A disjunctive clause functions to break up a sequence of events. Using Bible study tools, you should be able to identify disjunctive clauses. Once you find one, what do you do? You may use Figure 20.2 to determine how versions have rendered a given disjunctive clause.[3] These differences may show up in words, punctuation, or chapter and verse divisions.

Figure 20.2: Functions of Disjunctive Clauses[4]

Function	Description
Initial	Marks beginning of new section **Key Words**: now
Concluding	Marks the end of a section

---

[3] This chart is a reformatting of information in Robert B. Chisholm, Jr., *A Workbook for Intermediate Hebrew*, 264, in Allen P. Ross, *Introducing Biblical Hebrew* (Grand Rapids: Baker, 2001), 156-7, and in Gary Pratico and Miles V. Van Pelt, *Basics of Biblical Hebrew Grammar* (2nd ed.; Grand Rapids: Zondervan, 2007), §23.10.

[4] This chart is a reformatting of information in Robert B. Chisholm, Jr., *A Workbook for Intermediate Hebrew*, 264, in Allen P. Ross, *Introducing Biblical Hebrew* (Grand Rapids: Baker, 2001), 156-7, and in Gary Pratico and Miles V. Van Pelt, *Basics of Biblical Hebrew Grammar* (2nd ed.; Grand Rapids: Zondervan, 2007), §23.10.

Function	Description
Adverbial	Also called "circumstantial," this clause provides information about the action of a main clause (Simultaneous Time, Manner, Concession, Cause, Description) **Key Words**: *while, when, by, although, because*
Parenthetic	Information parenthetic to main clause (meet needs of reader) **Key Words**: *now*
Contrastive	Contrasts with main clause **Key Words**: *but*
Focusing	Draws reader's attention as a witness to the events (particularly when introduced by וְהִנֵּה). **Key Words**: *Look*

A Strategy

1. Flowchart your passage from your English version, adding a fourth column entitled "Hebrew Clause Structure."

2. Use a traditional interlinear Bible to discover all the clauses, both verbal and nominal, in your passage. Match each with your English translation. *Ignore all quotations.*

3. Label the beginning of each clause according to conjunction and the following word.

4. Use the following flowchart to identify the function of the clause.

Figure 20.3: Flowchart to Determine Narrative Clause Function

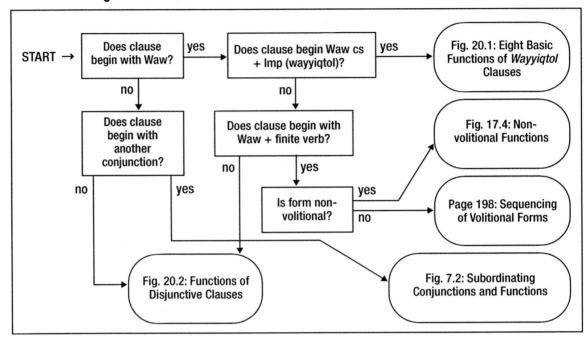

Here is an example of how a completed flowchart might look. I have placed all the recorded speech in bold. We are ignoring clause structure for these. Ø means no cj; NV means "nonverb."

Flowcharting Hebrew Clause Structure

Function	Vs	Flow Chart: Ezekiel 37:1-14	Clause Structure – Function
Event	1	The hand of the LORD was upon me,	Ø + Pf Initial
addition		and	
Event		he brought me out by the Spirit of the LORD	ꝩcs + Imp Initiatory
addition		and	
Event		set me in the middle of a valley;	ꝩcs + Imp Sequential
Assertion		it was full of bones.	ו + NV Parenthetic
Event	2	He led me back and forth among them,	ו + Pf Past Progressive
		and	
Event		I saw a great many bones on the floor of the valley,	ו + NV הִנֵּה Focusing

Assertion	bones that were very dry.	ו + NV Focusing
Event	3 He asked me,	וcs + Imp Sequential
Question	•• "Son of man, can these bones live?"	
Event	I said,	וcs + Imp Sequential
Assertion	•• "O Sovereign LORD, you alone know."	
Event	4 Then he said to me,	וcs + Imp Sequential
Command	• "Prophesy to these bones and say to them,	
Content	• 'Dry bones,	
Command	hear the word of the LORD!	
Assertion	5 This is what the Sovereign LORD says to these bones:	
Immediate Fut	I will make breath enter you,	
Addition	and	
Result	you will come to life.	
Simple Future	6 I will attach tendons to you	
Addition	and	
Simple Future	make flesh come upon you	
Addition	and	
Simple Future	cover you with skin;	
Simple Future	I will put breath in you,	
Addition	and	
Result	you will come to life.	
	Then	
Result	you will know	
Content	• • that I am the LORD.' "	
Event	7 So I prophesied	ו + Pf Inceptive past
Description	as I was commanded.	RC Past perfect
Addition	And	
Time	as I was prophesying,	

Event	there was a noise,	wcs + Imp Sequential
Description	a rattling sound,	wcs + Imp Focusing
	and	
Event	the bones came together, bone to bone.	וְ + NV הִנֵּה Sequential

Event	8 I looked,	וְ + Pf Inceptive past
	and	
Assertion	tendons and flesh appeared on them	וְ + NV הִנֵּה Focusing
	and	
Assertion	skin covered them,	wcs + Imp Sequential
Contrast	but	
Assertion	there was no breath in them.	וְ + NV Contrastive

Sequence	9 Then	
Event	he said to me,	wcs + Imp Sequential
Command	• **"Prophesy to the breath;**	
Command	**prophesy, son of man,**	
	and	
Command	**say to it,**	
Content	• **'This is what the Sovereign** Lord **says:**	
Command	**Come from the four winds, O breath,**	
Addition	**and**	
Command	**breathe into these slain,**	
Purpose	• • **that they may live.'"**	

Event	10 So I prophesied	וְ + Pf Inceptive past
Description	as he commanded me,	RC Past perfect
Addition	and	
Event	breath entered them;	wcs + Imp Sequential
Event	they came to life	wcs + Imp Sequential
Addition	and	
Event	stood up on their feet	wcs + Imp Sequential
Assertion	—a vast army.	Ø + NV Focusing

Sequence	11	Then	
Event		he said to me:	wcs + Imp Sequential
Assertion		• "Son of man, these bones are the whole house of Israel.	
Assertion		They say,	
Content: Assertion		• 'Our bones are dried up	
Addition		and	
Addition		our hope is gone;	
Assertion		• we are cut off.'	

Command	12	Therefore prophesy
		and
Command		say to them:
Content		• 'This is what the Sovereign LORD says:
Address		O my people,
Immediate Future		I am going to open your graves
		and
Immediate Future		bring you up from them;
Immediate Future		I will bring you back to the land of Israel.

	13	Then
Result		you, my people, will know
Content		That I am the LORD,
Time		when I open your graves
addition		and
Time		bring you up from them.

Simple Future	14	I will put my Spirit in you
Addition		and
Result		you will live,
Addition		and
Simple Future		I will settle you in your own land.
Sequence		Then
Result		you will know
Content		that I the LORD have spoken,

Addition			and
Content			I have done it,
Exclamation	•	•	declares the LORD.'"

Event		15	The word of the LORD came to me:	wcs + Imp Introductory

What good is this? What can you do with it? Here are a few things to note:

1. I included v. 15 because it has a form that marks a new unit. You can actually tell this from the English. There are cases, though, in which the English doesn't make this clear. At least now you know what to look for and what commentators may discuss.

2. The nonbold areas represent the narrator. There are several places in which the structure is disjunctive though it is not represented as disjunctive in the English translations. For example, v. 8 has four clauses. The first one is ו + Pf. The English is a simple past. But using the figures helps us to understand that the narrator is trying to increase the vividness with a progressive aspect. The second is ו + הִנֵּה (nonverb). Here the author is trying to focus the reader's attention. This important activity includes the third clause, which is sequential to the second. The fourth clause is also disjunctive. The presence of the negative makes it clear that contrast is in view.

3. You should be willing to disagree with any of the labels that I have selected. That's part of the fun of interpreting using these tools and techniques.

Exercises

1. Is Gen 3:1 a good section break? What difference does it make? Read a good commentary and take notes on this matter.

2. Look at Josh 1:1–18 in an interlinear. Where do you think the Hebrew author marks section breaks? Choose one of the sections to produce a flowchart similar to the example given in this chapter.

Advanced Information and Curious Facts

Paraphrasing. Many people confuse paraphrasing with summarizing. A summary is briefer than the original and focuses on highlights. By the term *paraphrase*, on the other hand, I mean a statement longer than the original. The aim is to make explicit that which is less obvious in the original. It represents the fruit of study.

Often in sermons and lessons on narrative, you will paraphrase in order to be more vivid. Paying attention to the clause structure can guide preaching and teaching of narrative literature and aid you in producing a better paraphrase. For example, in Ezek 37:8 there are four clauses. A preacher or teacher may make a major point out of the "I saw," because it is the first. However, this would be an incorrect emphasis. The *weqatal* clause in v. 8, "I saw," is perhaps ingressive. By means of the following הִנֵּה clause, the narrator is drawing attention to the appearance of tendons, flesh, and skin on the bones. Then the fourth clause in v. 8 draws an important contrast. A careful teacher might paraphrase v. 8 to bring out the vividness that the Hebrew author does: "As Ezekiel was prophesying, and these bones were coming together, he suddenly begins seeing tendons and muscle start to appear on the bones and then skin covering them. Even after all of this amazing restoration, however, there is still no breath in the body; they are not yet alive. Something more is needed." The contrast heightens the suspense in the story for the reader to discover the "something needed."

CHAPTER 21

It May Not Rhyme, But It's Still . . . Hebrew Poetry

Objectives

1. Understand the nature of Hebrew poetry
2. Using adjusted phrasing

Tools Used: Interlinear Bible

Introduction

> When poetry I think about,
>> It sometimes turns me inside out.
> Word order often strange,
>> The lines of odd arrange.
> But worst of all to me it seems
>> Is when the poet writes his themes
> In a fashion without rhyme -
>> To be sure it's quite appalling![1]

When I and those like me, who are unlearned in sophisticated literature, think of poetry, we think that there simply must be rhyme. How else would you recognize a poem? Of course, many poems rhyme, but that is not the essence of poetry, even in English. Hebrew poetry has far less rhyming than English. Because Hebrew has more inflections than English, rhyming would be a simple matter; there would be little challenge to it. Understanding Hebrew poetry can enhance our understanding and appreciation of the poetic sections of the OT.

---

[1] This poem is offered with my apologies to all true poets out there.

In this chapter you will not learn all you need to know about interpreting Hebrew poetry, but in keeping with our theme, you will learn how to use tools, in particular an interlinear Bible, to study one of the main features of Hebrew poetry. First you will learn what Hebrew poetry is. Then I will give you a three-step strategy for studying poetry. Finally, I will take you through some examples from Proverbs and Psalms to fine-tune your flowcharting technique.

What is Hebrew Poetry and How Do You Identify It?

About one-third of the OT is written in poetry. Poems occur in the Pentateuch (e.g., Exod 15:1-18) and in the historical books (e.g., 2 Sam 1:19-27) as well as in the poetic books. Poetry is a major feature of the prophets (Joel 1:2-20). But just what is poetry, and how can you recognize it when you see it? Poetry is the type of literature which uses a concentration literary devices to embellish the author's message in a way that is memorable.[2]

Identifying Hebrew poetry is a task you must leave to others. Thankfully, modern versions, such as the NIV, delineate poetry into stanzas. You can use such a translation to recognize poetic passage. At times there may be some disagreement, so comparing versions is also a good idea.

Even though Hebrew poetry is often delineated in English, much is lost in translation. Only an advanced knowledge of Hebrew can enable a reader to comprehend the full beauty of Hebrew poetry. However, as a pre-Hebrew student, you are now skilled in the use of an interlinear such that you can appreciate more of what is there. James E. Smith has conveniently summarized five major features of Hebrew poetry:[3]

1. *Alliteration*: the repetition of similar sounds at the beginning of words, or in stressed (accented) positions within a verse.

2. *Paronomasia*: play on the sound and meaning of words.

3. *Acrostic Structure*: consecutive verses (or half verses or stanzas) beginning with successive letters of the alphabet.

---

[2] Ernst R. Wendland, *Analyzing the Psalms* (2nd ed.; Winona Lake, Ind.: Eisenbrauns, 2002), 62.

[3] James E. Smith, *The Wisdom Literature and the Psalms* (Joplin, Mo.: College Press, 1996), 17-8.

4. *Terseness*: much said in few words. In particular, it is common in poetry that function words, such as the article and conjunctions, are left out; the writer expects the reader to figure out the meaning.

5. *Imagery:* use of an image to both convey information and evoke emotion.

Of these five features, the last one is least likely to be lost in English, though even here more functional translations tend to alter or simplify the Hebrew imagery. The skills developed in this book will allow you to follow discussions by others. In fact, you may observe some things for yourself (for example, look at your interlinear and explain why Lamentations 1 has 22 verses).

Another important feature of Hebrew poetry is parallelism. Parallelism is the joining together of related ideas to form a complete thought. Repeated elements may be related phonologically (sound), lexically (meaning), or syntactically (word order). Noticing sound in pronunciation requires more sensitivity than we have developed, though some reading this book may be able to pick up on this. You can, however, observe lexical and syntactic qualities. The parallel elements may be adjacent lines, what Wendland calls "connected (or near) parallelism," or they may be unconnected lines in the same passage, "disconnected (or distant) parallelism." Disconnected parallelism is something you can observe without using the tools and techniques taught in this book, and I will leave this topic for other studies in how to interpret the Bible. We want to look at connected parallelism.

A Strategy for Reading Hebrew Poetry

Students of Hebrew poetry are indebted to Robert Lowth, who in the middle of the 1700s observed that there are three basic types of parallelism: synonymous, antithetic, and synthetic. In recent years, scholars have added categories. Longman gives a list and explanation of Lowth's three categories and five more recent additions.[4] The treatment below reduces the eight to seven and divides them into two groups, one based on structure and one based on meaning. These will form the last two parts of a three-step process for studying Hebrew poetry: line count, structure, and meaning. Line count is simply identifying how many lines go together to form a unit. Structure is the arrangement of words and encompasses the four

---

[4] Tremper Longman, III, *How To Read the Psalms* (Downers Grove, Ill.: InterVarsity, 1988), 99-104.

categories. Meaning involves Lowth's three categories with some fine-tuning. As we go through these three steps, remember that the goal is to figure out how one line (line B) relates to the previous line (line A).

Step 1: Line Count

The first task is to determine the number of parallel lines. The Latin term *colon* (pl. *cola*) means "line." The number of lines in a thought unit is determined by the lexical (meaning) content of the lines. As you read, look for thoughts that are closely connected in some way. The number of lines normally forming a thought unit ranges from one to four. This can often be done with a modern translation, and I will begin with examples taken from the NIV. However, we will see below that an interlinear Bible works much better.

Just as narrative has an "unmarked" form, so does poetry. The unmarked form is the bicolon, or two-liner, with an "a" line + "b" line. For example, look at Prov 8:1-2 (NIV):

1a   *Does not wisdom call out?*

1b   *Does not understanding raise her voice?*

2a   On the heights along the way,

2b   where the paths meet, she takes her stand;

In this example I want to focus in on verse 1. I have numbered each line by its biblical verse number (1, 2) and line (with lower case letters a, b). Notice that v. 2 clearly moves on to a new pair. In other words, v. 1 has two lines and is therefore a bicolon. Pretty simple, eh?

When the poet wants to draw special attention to a line, he varies from the bicolon. The variations from the bicolon usually serve to indicate some special discourse function, perhaps to give additional emphasis or reveal beginning or ending of stanzas. Ps 1:1 is an example of a tricolon, three-liner (NIV):

1a   Blessed is the man

1b   *who does not walk in the counsel of the wicked*

1c   *or stand in the way of sinners*

1d   *or sit in the seat of mockers.*

Clearly 1b-1d are related to each other in such a way that they are distinct from 1a.

Two very long lines can be broken up into a tetracolon, a four-liner, as in Ps 5.7:

7a	*But I, by your great mercy,*
7b	*will come into your house;*
7c	*in reverence will I bow down*
7d	*toward your holy temple.*

Notice that 7a and 7b form a unit and 7c and 7d form another.

The line number considered to be strongly marked is the monocolon, a single line with no parallel. Ps 11:1 serves well here:

1a	*In the Lord I take refuge.*
1b	How then can you say to me:
1c	"Flee like a bird to your mountain.

The NIV correctly indents in such a way that 1b and 1c go together. 1a stands as a monocolon.

Step 2: Identify the Structure

The second task is to identify structure. The structure is largely determined by the syntax (word order). Each line has identifiable grammatical elements: nouns, verbs, prepositional phrases, etc. We want to note the arrangement both within a line and between lines.

1. **Simple parallelism:** the elements of Line b are in the same order as the elements of Line a. This structure is unmarked.

Line	Proverbs 10:1 (NIV)			
1a	A wise son	brings	joy	to his father
1b	but a foolish son		grief	to his mother.

In charting poetry, keep all the elements of each clause on the same line, rather than indenting clauses above or beneath the S–V–IO–DO line as you did in narrative. In this verse, the parallel elements in each line are obviously in the same order.

2. **Chiastic parallelism**: the elements of Line b appear in reverse order from those of Line a. The chiastic parallelism is marked; the center element(s) is normally the focal point.

Line	Ps 76:1 (NIV)		
1a	A: In Judah		B: God is known
1b	B´: his name is great		A´: in Israel

For this example, I have labeled the elements "A" and "A¹" (read as "a prime"). If you draw a line connecting a to a¹ and b to b¹, the shape forms is similar to the Greek letter χ, *chi*, from which we get the term chiasm. These lines form this chiastic pattern. The focal point is the two "B" elements. The problem is that most often English translations do not maintain Hebrew chiastic structure. There is no way you can accurately analyze structure with English translations alone; you must check an interlinear. For example, Ps 76:2 [Hebrew 76:3] reads, "His tent is in Salem, his dwelling place in Zion" (NIV), apparently simple parallelism. An interlinear shows otherwise:

סֻכּוֹ	בְּשָׁלֵם	וַיְהִי	2a
[B]	[A]		
his tent	in Salem		

בְצִיּוֹן	וּמְעוֹנָתוֹ		2b
[A¹]	[B¹]		
in Zion	and his dwelling place		

Clearly v. 2 is chiastic, just like v. 1. The focal point is on the dwelling place and tent of the Lord. In conjunction with v. 1 above, focusing on the fame of God, we can understand that the terms "tent" and "dwelling place" are not intended to draw our attention to physical structures, but to the very presence of God himself. This subtlety is brought out in the identification of the chiastic structure of the elements of the two lines.

3. **Repetitive parallelism:** Line b repeats all or part of Line a, but adds to it. This is a subset of simple parallelism.

Line	Ps 29:3-5 (NIV)		
3a	The voice of the LORD	is	over the waters;
3b	the God of glory	thunders,	
3c	the LORD	thunders	over the mighty waters.
4a	The voice of the LORD	is powerful;	
4b	the voice of the LORD	is majestic.	
5a	The voice of the LORD	breaks the cedars;	
5b	the LORD	breaks in pieces the cedars	of Lebanon.

    These verses give two examples: v. 3 is a tricolon; vv. 4-5 form a tetracolon. The repetition is obvious. Notice in Lines 3c and 5b the additional element.

4. **Pivot parallelism:** The final element in Line 5a below is not repeated in Line 5b, but must be included in the thought of Line 5b. This structure is the opposite of Repetitive and a subset of Chiastic. Because it is located at the center, the pivoting element is the focus of the parallel.

Line	Ps 119:105 (NIV rearranged)		
105a	a-lamp	to-my-feet(is)	Your-word
105b	and-a-light	for-my-path.	

    The NIV reads, "Your word is a lamp to my feet and a light for my path." In the chart I have taken NIV words and used hyphens to connect English words that are one word in Hebrew, and I have rearranged the words to follow their Hebrew order (you can discover this using an interlinear). The last element in 105a is not repeated in 105b, but it functions in both clauses. Since it comes in the middle, it acts as a hinge between the two clauses and constitutes the focal point.

Step 3: Determining Logical Meaning between Lines

This step involves applying line labels describing logical relationships between lines (cola). The norm in poetry is the absence of conjunctions marking relationships between lines; the writer expects the reader to figure this out. Lowth's three categories of parallelism serve well as the major classes of meaning. Within these, especially the third class, we can make more specific identifications between lines.

1. **Synonymous**: Line b says the same thing as Line a, but in different words.

Line	Ps 3:1 (NIV)		
1a	O Lᴏʀᴅ,	how many	are my foes!
1b		How many	rise up against me!

Structurally line 1a is a noun clause and line 1b is a verb clause. Nevertheless, the line meanings are synonymous.

2. **Antithetic**: Line b makes the same point as Line a, but in contrasting terms, such as antonyms or the negative adverbs. A key word is *but*, which is usually marked by the conjunction Waw in Hebrew.

Line	Prov 10:3 (NET)		
3a	The Lᴏʀᴅ	satisfies	the appetite	of the righteous
3b	*but* he	thwarts	the craving	of the wicked.

The parallelism is brought out nicely by the NET. To do this, they changed the verb in 3a from "does not let … go hungry" (NIV). The NIV, however, did not translate the Hebrew word rendered "appetite" in the NET.

3. **Synthetic**: Line b completes the thought of line a.

Line	Ps 116:18-19 (NIV)	
18a	I will fulfill	my vows	to the Lᴏʀᴅ
18b	in the presence	of all his people	
19a	in the courts	of the house of the Lord	
19b	in your midst		O Jerusalem.

Line 18b completes the thought of 18a; notice that 18b is only two phrases. Lines 18b-19b form a tricolon, all of which relate synthetically to 18b. The additions may be features of time, cause, or completion.

Figure 21.1 helps to clarify these logical relationships. Ernst Wendland has provided a detailed list of logical relationships between lines.[5] Figure 21.1 is adapted from his list, including his explanations. His examples come from the book Psalms, but they apply to all Hebrew poetry. Remember: line a is always the reference point or "base"; we want to describe how subsequent lines relate to this base line. However, the logical relationships may occur in either order, e.g., cause-effect or effect-cause.

Figure 21.1: Meaning in Hebrew Poetic Parallelism

Class	Line a	Line b	Explanation
Synonymous	Base	Restatement	**b** is very similar in meaning to **a** (61:1)
	General	Specific	**b** is a more specific than **a** (60:12)
Contrastive	Base	Contrast	**b** makes same point as **a** by contrast (145:20)
Synthetic			
Temporal	Base	Sequential	**b** occurs after **a** (105:23)
	Base	Simultaneous	**b** occurs during **a** (105:26)
	Base	Circumstantial	**b** is subordinated to main event **a** (31:22b)
Synthetic			
Causal	Reason	Result	**b** happens because **a** happens (116:2)
	Ground	Conclusion	**b** is the conclusion based on evidence of **a** (48:8)
	Reason	Request	**b** is a request based on **a** (82:8)
	Means	Request	**b** is a request that an action be done by means of **a** (79:11b)

---

[5] Ernst R. Wendland, *Analyzing the Psalms* (2nd ed.; Winona Lake, Ind.: Eisenbrauns, 2002), 67-99.

Class	Line a	Line b	Explanation
	Means	Result	**b** happens by means of **a** (17:4)
	Base	Purpose	**b** is the purpose for which **a** was done (78:71)
	Request	Purpose	**b** is the purpose for the requested action in **a** (24:7)
Real Condition	Result		**b** will happen if **a** happens (7:12)
Unreal Condition	Result		**b** would have happened if **a** had happened, but **a** did not happen (66:18)
Concession	Result		**b** happens unexpectedly in spite of **a** (118:18)
Complementary	Base	Attribution	**b** describes **a** (53:4)
	Base	Location	**b** gives location for **a** (116:18-19)
	Base	Manner	**b** is the manner in which **a** was done (55:20, 21)
	Base	Response	**b** is a reply to what was said in **a** (118:2-4)
	Base	Content	**b** gives content of **a** (30:6)
	Base	Comparison	**b** is compared to **a** in likeness or degree (118:9)
	Base	Addition	**b** adds content to **a** (68:31)
	Base	Alternative	**b** is an alternative to **a** (1:1)

After you consider the logic of the adjacent lines, you apply these categories to larger blocks until the entire poem is treated.

Putting It Together

Let's look at some examples. Figure 21.2 is a figure similar to the one I used in an adult Bible school class at a small country church (I didn't give them the "Logic" column). I collected several proverbs from the lesson that had similar forms and treated them together with the NIV text. I had the class members complete some of the blanks. The columns below are more detailed than the examples above. Feel free to vary your technique as you see fit.

Figure 21.2: Prov 28:4, 5, 7, 10 (NIV)

VS	Subject (What they do...)	(...to what)	Verb	Object	Logic
5a	Evil men		do not understand	justice	Base
5b	But those who seek	the LORD	understand	it (justice) fully	Contrast
7a	He who keeps	the law	is	discerning	Base
7b	But a companion of gluttons		disgraces	his father	Contrast
10a	he who leads along an evil path	the upright	will fall	into his own trap	Base
10b	the blameless		will receive	good inheritance	Contrast

Now some observations may be based on what items are parallel. These are good questions to ask your students.

1. In v. 5: How are "evil men" to be understood in view of the parallelism?

   They are those who do not seek the Lord

2. In v. 7: What is the relationship between keeping the law and being a companion with gluttons?

   The contrast is between who or what one spends time with and what one allows to influence him.

3. In v. 7: What disgraces one's father?

   Being a fool who pursues only his own desires.

4. v. 10: Define what it means to be blameless.

   To live righteously and lead others in the same *good* path.

Here is another example taken from Ps 13 (*The Interlinear Bible*), excluding the title. I will give a brief analysis and then make a few observations. The verse numbers follow the Hebrew.

Figure 21.3: Sample Analysis of Ps 13

Verse	Elements				
2a	Until=when, O-Jehovah	will-You-forget-me		forever?	
2b	Until=when,	will-You-hide	your-face	from-me?	
3a	Until=when	shall-I-set	counsel	in-my-soul?	
3b			(having-)sorrow	in-my-heart	daily?
3c	Until=when	shall-be-lifted-up my-enemy		over-me?	
4a		Look!			
4b		Answer me, O-Jehovah,	my God!		
4c		Make-gleam	my-eyes,		
4d	Lest=	I-sleep		in-death;	
5a	Lest=	say	my-enemy,		
5b		I-have-beaten-him;			
5c		My-foes	rejoice		
5d	when	I-	am-shaken.		
6a	But-I		in-your-mercy	have-trusted;	
6b		Shall-rejoice	my-heart	in-your-salvation.	
6c		I-will-sing	to-Jehovah,		
6d	for	He-has-rewarded	me.		

Step 1: Line Count. The way I analyzed the text, v. 2 is a bicolon, v. 3 is a tricolon, and v. 4 is a tetracolon. Verse 5 is viewed as a tetracolon or as two bicola; I chose the latter. I took v. 6 as a tetracolon in which 6a-c and 6d relate to the 6a-c group. I have lined up parallel items as best I can; sometimes it's not as tidy as we might like, but that's okay.

Step 2: Identify Structure. Structurally, 2ab is simple parallelism. In 3abc, 3a and 3c are simple parallelism; 3b might be analyzed as a monocolon, but the tricolon involves a chiasmus. Lines 4a-d are simple; so are 5a-d. Lines 6a-b form a chiasm.

Step 3: Determine Logic. The first level of examination considers the adjacent lines. Then relate adjacent groups until the entire psalm is covered. To do this, first determine whether the lines are synonymous, antithetic, or synthetic. Then use Figure 23.1 to get the specific relationship. You may analyze lines differently, but here are my suggestions:

Cola	First Level Logic	Additional Level Logic		
2a-b	Synonymous: base-amplification	**2ab-3abc:** Synonymous: base-amplification	**2a/3c-4a/5d:** Synthetic: Cause: reason-request[6]	**2a/5d-6a/d:** Constrastive: base-contrast[7]
3a-b	Synthetic: Completion: base-description			
3ab-c[8]	Synonymous: general-specific			
4a-b	Synonymous: base-amplification	**4ad-5ad:** Synthetic: Cause: request-purpose		
4ab-c	Synonymous: general-specific			

---

[6] I viewed 2a-3c as a description of the psalmist's fear over his circumstances. That fear causes him to turn to the Lord in prayer, 4a-5d.

[7] The key word here is at the beginning of v. 6, "but." Verses 2-3 express the psalmist's fear, vv. 4-5, the resulting prayer, and v. 6 the psalmist's faith in God to deliver in spite of circumstances.

[8] I understand 3a and b to be more closely related as a unit. 3c, then, relates to the pair, 3ab.

4abc-d   Synthetic: Cause:

          request-purpose

5a-b   Synthetic: Completion:

          base-content

5c-d   Synthetic: Time:

          base-circumstance

6a-b   Synonymous:

          general-specific[9]

6ab-c   Synonymous:

          general-specific

6abc-d   Synthetic: Cause:

          result-reason

Exercises

1. The NIV marks Ps 55:1-3 as one stanza. Produce a flowchart for these verses.

2. Ps 5:10 reads (NIV):

   10a   Declare them guilty, O God!

   10b   Let their intrigues be their downfall.

   10c   Banish them for their many sins,

   10d   for they have rebelled against you.

   The NIV has these lines arranged as two bicola, even punctuating with a period after 10b. Follow the procedures from this chapter to determine if you agree with this punctuation.

3. Take Ps 1 through the entire process explained in this chapter. Particularly, note the line counts. Do they give a clue as to how to outline the psalm? How does this help you appreciate the artfulness of Hebrew poetry?

4. Take a group of eight verses from Ps 119 through the entire process explained in this chapter.

---

[9] I understood lines a and b to have similar meaning; i.e., I took the promise to rejoice as a more specific description of the current trust he has.

A Final Word

If you have finished all 21 chapters, congratulations! Your skills in using tools and techniques to study the OT should have grown significantly. You are much farther along the road to greater independence in understanding the OT.

No matter how much you feel you did or did not understand, there is always more to learn. Don't let this fact be discouraging; let it spur you on to continue growing. The genius of Scripture is demonstrated in the fact that the basic message of the Gospel is simple enough that even the unlearned person can understand it; but the depth of the message is so profound that no one this side of heaven will ever comprehend it fully. You are studying the words of the infinite God of the universe.

Using these tools and techniques does not make Bible study easier or faster, but it does make it better and more rewarding. I hope you will never again be satisfied with regular Bible study. I hope you will appreciate more the preparation that goes into good sermons and commentaries. I hope you will encourage others to join with you in studying God's Word. May we all grow in our understanding of and submission to this Word.

APPENDIX 1

The Hebrew Aleph Beth Song

Lee M. Fields

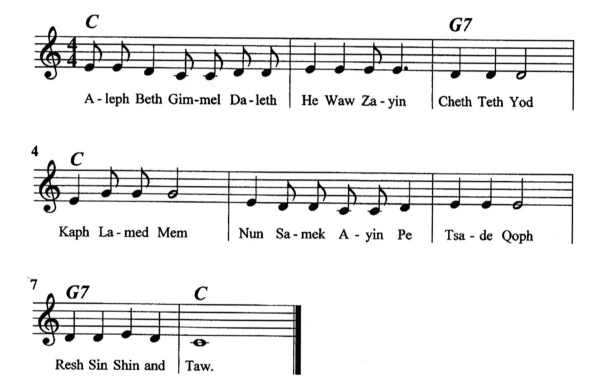

Praise Ye the Lord, the Almighty

Joachim Neander; Catherine Winkworth, trans.

Hal - le - lu - jah Sha - dai - Me - lek ha - O - la - m!

Hal - le - lu - jah naph-shi ki hu shlo - mek wiy-sha - the - k!

Qir - bu nah kol ha-sho - m'im el bey - tho; Bith - hil - lath

sim-chah hith - cha - bru - ni. A - men.

Praise Ye the Lord, the Almighty

I've translated the English lyrics of this hymn into Hebrew. Catherine Winkworth's words were:

Praise ye the Lord, the Almighty, the King of creation!

O my soul praise him for he is thy health and salvation!

All ye who hear unto his temple draw near;

Join me in glad adoration!

Below I give the Hebrew in Hebrew letters and a back-translation of my Hebrew into English.

הָעוֹלָם	מֶלֶךְ	שַׁדַּי	הַלְלוּיָה
the universe!	the king of	the Almighty	Praise ye the Lord

וִישׁוּעָתֶךָ	שְׁלוֹמֶךָ	הוּא	כִּי	נַפְשִׁי	הַלְלוּיָה
and your Salvation	your health	He (is)	for	O my Soul	Praise ye the Lord

בֵּיתוֹ	אֶל־	הַשֹּׁמְעִים	כָּל־	קָרְבוּ־נָא
His temple	to	who hear	all	Draw ye near

אָמֵן	הִתְחַבְּרוּנִי	שִׂמְחָה	בִּתְהִלַּת
Amen!	join me!	gladness	In adoration of

Notes:

1. The first three lines begin with Imperatives; the fourth ends with one. The poetry would be better if the Imperative began the fourth line also, but I thought the syllables fit the music better this way.

2. I used הָעוֹלָם for "creation, universe." Hebrew does have a word for creation, בְּרִיאָה, but it is not found in the OT. הָעוֹלָם is found in the sense of "creation" in the OT; its usual meaning is "eternity, age." However, in rabbinic literature, both of these words are found. In the rabbinic prayers, מֶלֶךְ הָעוֹלָם is a common designation for God.

3. In the second line, all the pronouns are feminine, because the person uses "soul" to address himself and נֶפֶשׁ is a feminine noun.

4. In the last line, the Gen case "gladness" is attributive meaning "in glad adoration."

Appendix 2

Word Study Guide

Step 1: Identifying the Word

1. Question to answer:

WSG Figure 1: Comparison of Versions

Literal	Dynamic Equivalent	Free	Paraphrase
NASB95:	NIV:	NLT:	MSG:
KJV:	NET:	NCV:	LB:
ESV:	NAB:	TEV:	
NRSV:	JB:	GNB:	
RSV:	NEB:		

2. GK# _____   Strong's # _____

3. Frame the question: What does the word translated _____ in the

   _____ version mean in the passage _____?

Step 2: Range of Meaning

1. Find all the Occurrences of the Word

   - Number of occurrences _____

   - Distribution of occurrences:

     WSG 2: Distribution of Occurrences of the Word (optional)

Category	Passages
In the same book	
Other books by same author	
OT Law	
OT History	
OT Poetry	
OT Prophets	

2. Definitions – Remember to list verb meanings grouped by stem (Q, N, D, Dp, H, Hp, HtD)

   WSG 3: Definitions

Definitions	Passages

Step 3: Meaning of the Word in the Target Text

1. Preliminary conclusions on the meaning in your passage.

2. Verify with experts (notes from word books).

3. Conclusions

    a. Meaning of target word in target passage:

    b. Effect of the meaning of target word on the meaning of target passage (How does the meaning answer the question you began to answer?):

Appendix 3

Action Figures

Throughout the text of *Hebrew for the Rest of Us* I have prepared many figures. Most of these figures illustrate the principles under discussion. A few of the figures, however, are designed for use when applying the various techniques and tools you have learned. Below is a list of figures that you will work from most often. You may wish to photocopy them. A ready-made set is available in a convenient format from www.teknia.com. I have also included page numbers for two topics that are related to other figures, but they are located in the body of the text rather than in figures.

Figure	Figure Title	Page Number
7.1	Coordinating Conjunctions and Functions	77
7.2	Subordinating Conjunctions and Functions	78
7.3	Function Explanations for Conjunctions	79-80
8.3	English Prepositions and Functions	90-91
(Text)	Nominative, Accusative, and Vocative Case Functions	116-119
11.6	Genitive Functions of the Construct State	121-122
13.6	Overview of Intensity and Voice of Stems	155
13.9	Real/Main Clause Functions	160
13.10	Irreal/Main Clause Functions	160-162
13.4	Hebrew Verb Forms, Mood, and Relative Time	153

17.4   Non-volitional Structures and Functions   209-210

16.4   Summary of Volitional Functions and Forms   196-197

(Text)   Sequencing of Volitional Forms   198

17.7   Summary of Main Functions of Non-finite Verbals   216-217

20.1   Eight Basic Functions of Wayyiqtol Clauses   249-250

20.2   Functions of Disjunctive Clauses   250-251

20.3   Flowchart to Determine Narrative Clause Function   252

21.1   Meaning in Hebrew Poetic Parallelism   266-267

We want to hear from you. Please send your comments about this book to us in care of zreview@zondervan.com. Thank you.

CPSIA information can be obtained at www.ICGtesting.com
Printed in the USA
LVOW080639290812

296385LV00003B/2/P